Microsoft Office XP
explained

Books Available

By both authors:
BP341   MS-DOS explained
BP346   Programming in Visual Basic for Windows
BP388   Why not personalise your PC
BP400   Windows 95 explained
BP406   MS Word 95 explained
BP407   Excel 95 explained
BP408   Access 95 one step at a time
BP409   MS Office 95 one step at a time
BP420   E-mail on the Internet*
BP426   MS-Office 97 explained
BP428   MS-Word 97 explained
BP429   MS-Excel 97 explained
BP430   MS-Access 97 one step at a time
BP433   Your own Web site on the Internet
BP448   Lotus SmartSuite 97 explained
BP456   Windows 98 explained*
BP464   E-mail and news with Outlook Express*
BP465   Lotus SmartSuite Millennium explained
BP471   Microsoft Office 2000 explained
BP472   Microsoft Word 2000 explained
BP473   Microsoft Excel 2000 explained
BP474   Microsoft Access 2000 explained
BP478   Microsoft Works 2000 explained
BP486   Using Linux the easy way*
BP488   Internet Explorer 5 explained*
BP487   Quicken 2000 UK explained*
BP491   Windows 2000 explained*
BP493   Windows Me explained*
BP498   Using Visual Basic
BP505   Microsoft Works Suite 2001 explained
BP509   Microsoft Office XP explained
BP510   Microsoft Word 2002 explained
BP511   Microsoft Excel 2002 explained
BP512   Microsoft Access 2002 explained
BP513   Internet Explorer 6 explained

By Noel Kantaris:
BP258   Learning to Program in C
BP259   A Concise Introduction to UNIX*
BP284   Programming in QuickBASIC
BP325   A Concise User's Guide to Windows 3.1

Microsoft Office XP explained

by

N. Kantaris
and
P.R.M. Oliver

Bernard Babani (publishing) Ltd
The Grampians
Shepherds Bush Road
London W6 7NF
England
www.babanibooks.com

Please Note

© 2001 BERNARD BABANI (publishing) LTD

First Published - August 2001
Reprinted - February 2002
Reprinted - September 2002

British Library Cataloguing in Publication Data:

A catalogue record for this book is available from the British Library

ISBN 0 85934 509 2

Cover Design by Gregor Arthur
Printed and Bound in Great Britain by Cox & Wyman Ltd, Reading

About this Book

Microsoft Office XP explained has been written to help users to get to grips with the integrated components of this package, namely, the e-mail and desktop manager *Outlook*, the word processor *Word*, the spreadsheet *Excel*, the presentation graphics *PowerPoint*, the database *Access*, and the *Microsoft Publisher*. The latter is bundled with one of the four *Microsoft Office XP* sets - the *Professional Special Edition* set. All these components were specifically designed for the *Windows 98, 2000, Me, NT* and *XP* environments.

Microsoft Office XP is an exciting new (version 2002) Office suite that will help you with the new millennium challenges and opportunities to business. It offers new tools that use Web technology to provide enhanced workgroup productivity and the ability to access and analyse important business data more efficiently. *Microsoft Office XP* also provides new levels of intelligence and integration, making it much easier to use than before.

The individual applications which make up *Microsoft Office XP* are designed to work together and have the same look and feel, which makes it easy to learn. For example, the majority of menus, toolbar buttons, and dialogue boxes are the same in each application, which gives them a consistent user interface.

The package incorporates several new features, as well as improvements on previous Office capabilities. These include:

Ask a Question box - When you want help you can type a question in this new box, located on the menu bar, and get a list of Help choices.

Task Panes - Some of the most common tasks in Office applications are now organised in panes that display alongside your working document. You can, for instance, quickly create new documents or open files using the Task Pane that appears when you start an application, or continue working while you search for a file using the **Search** Task Pane, or pick from a gallery of items to paste in the Office **Clipboard** Task Pane.

Smart Tags - New in-place buttons let you immediately adjust how information is pasted or how automatic changes are made by an Office application.

Updated Clip Organiser (formerly the Clip Gallery) - Has hundreds of new clip art files and an easy Task Pane interface.

Improved handling of pictures and drawings - A new graphics system gives shapes and WordArt much smoother outlines, as well as adjustable levels of transparency and true blending. Digital images now stay sharper and clearer when they are re-sized.

Digital signatures - You can apply a digital signature to a file to confirm that it has not been altered.

Save a Web page as a single file - A special Web archive file format is available which lets you save all the elements of a Web page, including text and graphics, into a single file.

Document recovery and safer shutdown - Current documents can be recovered if an Office application encounters an error or stops responding. They are displayed in the **Document Recovery** Task Pane the next time you open that program.

Office Safe Mode - Office XP programs can now detect and isolate startup problems. This lets you get round the problem, run the application in safe mode, and continue working.

Crash reporting tool - Diagnostic information about program crashes can be collected and sent to your IT department or to Microsoft itself, allowing problems to be corrected in the easiest way.

Formatting improvements - The **Styles and Formatting** Task Pane in Word can be used to create, view, select, apply, or clear formatting from text, whilst the **Reveal Formatting** Task Pane lets you display text formatting attributes. Word also marks formatting inconsistencies with blue, wavy underlines.

AutoCorrect and Paste Options buttons appear directly in your document to help you fine-tune these tasks without having to click a toolbar button or use a dialogue box.

Collaborative document creation - An improved Reviewing toolbar can be used for document collaboration.

Handwriting recognition - You can write with a handwriting input device (such as a graphics tablet) and use handwriting recognition in Word to enter the text into a document. The natural handwriting can be converted to typed characters or left as hand-written text, such as a signature.

Improved table and list formatting - Word now offers drag-and-drop copying of tables, custom table and list styles, and improved sorting. You can also format bullets or numbers independently of the text in a list.

Enhanced AutoComplete - The name of any person you send e-mail to in Outlook 2002 will later be recognised in Word and used as an AutoComplete suggestion.

Simplified mail merge - Word now uses a Task Pane to provide a new way to connect to your data source and create form letters, mailing labels, envelopes, directories, and mass e-mail and fax distributions.

Drawing Canvas - The new Drawing Canvas helps you easily insert, position, layer, and re-size drawing objects.

Improved watermarks - It is now easy to select a picture, logo, or text to use as the background to a printed document.

Filtered HTML - To reduce the size of Web pages and e-mail messages in HTML format, you can now save them in filtered HTML so that the tags used by Microsoft Office programs are removed.

The various applications within *Microsoft Office XP* can either be used by themselves or made to share information. This book introduces each application by itself, with sufficient detail to get you working, then discusses how to share information between them. No prior knowledge of this package's applications is assumed.

The book was written with the busy person in mind. It is not necessary to learn all there is to know about a subject, when reading a few selected pages can usually do the same thing quite adequately. With the help of this book, it is hoped that you will be able to come to terms with Microsoft Office and get the most out of your computer in terms of efficiency, productivity and enjoyment, and that you will be able to do it in the shortest, most effective and informative way.

If you would like to purchase a Companion Disc for any of the listed books by the same author(s), apart from the ones marked with an asterisk, containing the file/program listings which appear in them, then fill in the form at the back of the book and send it to Phil Oliver at the stipulated address.

About the Authors

Noel Kantaris graduated in Electrical Engineering at Bristol University and after spending three years in the Electronics Industry in London, took up a Tutorship in Physics at the University of Queensland. Research interests in Ionospheric Physics, led to the degrees of M.E. in Electronics and Ph.D. in Physics. On return to the UK, he took up a Post-Doctoral Research Fellowship in Radio Physics at the University of Leicester, and then in 1973 a lecturing position in Engineering at the Camborne School of Mines, Cornwall, (part of Exeter University), where between 1978 and 1997 he was also the CSM Computing Manager. At present he is IT Director of FFC Ltd.

Phil Oliver graduated in Mining Engineering at Camborne School of Mines in 1967 and since then has specialised in most aspects of surface mining technology, with a particular emphasis on computer related techniques. He has worked in Guyana, Canada, several Middle Eastern countries, South Africa and the United Kingdom, on such diverse projects as: the planning and management of bauxite, iron, gold and coal mines; rock excavation contracting in the UK; international mining equipment sales and international mine consulting for a major mining house in South Africa. In 1988 he took up a lecturing position at Camborne School of Mines (part of Exeter University) in Surface Mining and Management. He retired from full-time lecturing in 1998, to spend more time writing, consulting and developing Web sites for clients.

Acknowledgements

We would like to thank the staff of Microsoft Press Centre for providing the software programs on which this work was based.

Trademarks

Arial and **Times New Roman** are registered trademarks of The Monotype Corporation plc.

HP and LaserJet are registered trademarks of Hewlett Packard Corporation.

IBM is a registered trademark of International Business Machines, Inc.

Intel is a registered trademark of Intel Corporation.

Microsoft, **MS-DOS**, **Windows**, **Windows NT**, and **Visual Basic**, are either registered trademarks or trademarks of Microsoft Corporation.

PostScript is a registered trademark of Adobe Systems Incorporated.

TrueType is a registered trademark of Apple Corporation.

All other brand and product names used in the book are recognised as trademarks, or registered trademarks, of their respective companies.

Contents

1

Package Overview

Microsoft Office XP is a collection of powerful, full-featured, programs with the same look and feel that work together as if they were a single program. Office XP was specifically designed to allow you to work with your information data, either by yourself or to share such data with others, if you so wish, quickly and efficiently.

Microsoft Office XP comes in four flavours, each one of which contains a different mixture of applications (for an explanation on what these applications can do, see overleaf). The four sets are: Standard with 4 applications, Professional with 5 applications, Professional Special Edition with 9 applications, and Developer with 6 applications. The various mixtures of applications for these four sets are as follows:

Office XP Unique Sets	Office XP Applications								
	Outlook 2002	Word 2002	Excel 2002	PowerPoint 2002	Access 2002	SharePoint Team S.	FrontPage 2002	Publisher 2002	IntelliMouse Expl.
Standard	☺	☺	☺	☺					
Professional	☺	☺	☺	☺	☺				
Professional Special Edition	☺	☺	☺	☺	☺	☺	☺	☺	☺
Developer	☺	☺	☺	☺	☺	☺	☺		

The various Office XP applications have the following main functions:

Outlook E-mail and Personal Information Manager (PIM) - provides a full set of multi-user, group-scheduling PIM functions, including a multi-account e-mail client.

Word Word processor - offers almost every imaginable feature, including background spelling and grammar checking, integrated drawing tools, WYSIWYG editing views, Smart Tags and Task Panes.

Excel Electronic spreadsheet - allows the creation of a 3D super-spreadsheet by using multi-page workbooks which support 3D *drill-through* formulae, and includes a long list of 'goal-seeking', 'what-if?' analysis tools and an excellent set of database capabilities.

PowerPoint Presentation graphics - allows creation of slide shows for training, sales and other presentations, and includes, amongst other capabilities, object animation, speaker notes, and recorded voice-overs.

Access Database management - includes a full set of WYSIWYG design tools for database, forms, queries and reports, plus a full Visual Basic derived programming language for developing specific applications.

SharePoint T. S. Allows the sharing of information between Office applications and your team Website. Each member of the team can access documents, participate in discussions and add content to the shared Website.

FrontPage	Gives users tools to create and manage Websites, whether personal or corporate Web pages on intranet or Internet sites.
Publisher	Allows the design and creation of printed documents with the help of publication templates. You can auto-fit text to frame sizes, provides inter-frame text flow options, and auto-wraps text around irregular images.
IntelliMouse Expl.	Allows the use of its built-in scrolling and zooming capabilities.

All Office XP applications have a built-in consistency which makes them easier to use. For example, they all have standardised toolbars and consistent menus, commands, and dialogue boxes. Once you become familiar with one application, it is far easier to learn and use the others.

Microsoft Office XP applications are the most integrated to date. Just like their predecessors, Office XP applications make use of what is known as IntelliSense, which anticipates what you want to do and helps you to produce the correct result. Amongst other common code, first introduced in Office 95, then improved in Office 97 and Office XP, are the Wizards which can help you simplify everyday and/or complex tasks, and the support for Microsoft Visual Basic for Applications, which gives you a powerful and flexible development platform with which to create custom solutions.

New in Office XP's guessing ability are Smart Tags and Task Panes. Smart Tags anticipate what you might want to do next and pop up a button near where you are working, offering relevant suggestions. For example, when copying then pasting text into a document causes a Paste Options Smart Tag to pop up giving you the opportunity to select a style. Other context sensitive Smart Tags allow you to access names, addresses and telephone numbers from your Outlook folder which can save you time and bother. These provide a welcome addition to Word's ability to recognise Web links and e-mail addresses.

Task Panes utilise the screen space available when writing portrait-orientated documents to provide an area in the right-hand side of your screen where information relevant to what you are doing at the time is given. For example, when you first start working within an application, you are offered options to open new documents or search for existing documents. As the type of work changes, the contents of the Task Pane change to reflect the type of work you are doing at the time.

Another innovative feature in Office XP is Document Recovery. Gone are the days when unless you saved your work every second you lost everything when a program error occurred. Now Office XP gives you the opportunity to save your work immediately after a program error occurs.

Other new features in Office XP include the ability to Send for Review documents which you have created. For example, if you are involved in a team project, you can allocate different review mark-up and changing privileges to your colleagues so that you can see the changes applied by everyone. You are then in a position to accept or reject these changes.

To take advantage of the SharePoint Services of Office XP, you require connection to a Windows 2000 (or later) server. This enables colleagues to create task and contact lists, calendars and planners, discussion groups and easy accessibility to common documents.

Finally, Office XP is the first Microsoft product to use the new activation system, shortly to be followed by Windows XP. Whether this remains a permanent feature of Microsoft software, only time will tell! To use Office XP more than 50 times, you must register it via the Internet or by telephone. In addition to entering the product code during installation, the Microsoft system examines your PC's configuration and produces a code from part of the serial numbers of around 15 hardware components. This code is then merged with the code given to you by Microsoft to produce a 'specific to your system' activation code. Any more than three changes to your hardware components, or reformatting your hard disc, will require you to apply to Microsoft for a reactivating code!

Hardware and Software Requirements

If Microsoft Office is already installed on your computer, you can safely skip this and the next section of this chapter.

To install and use Microsoft Office XP, you need an IBM-compatible PC equipped with Intel's Pentium processor. Microsoft suggests a 133 MHz or higher processor. In addition, you need the following:

*   Windows 98/98SE/Me (or higher), or Windows NT/2000 as the operating system. If you have an earlier version of Windows you must first upgrade to one of the above versions before you can install Office XP.

*   Random access memory (RAM) required is 32-128 MB and depends on the operating system in use.

    With Windows 98 or 98SE you require a minimum of 24 MB of RAM plus an additional 8 MB for each Office application running simultaneously.

    With Windows Me or NT you require 32 MB of RAM plus an additional 8 MB for each Office application running simultaneously.

    With Windows 2000 you require 64 MB of RAM plus an additional 8 MB for each Office application running simultaneously.

*   Hard disc space required for Microsoft Office XP is at least 115 MB (up to 245 MB) if the default installation is selected.

*   CD-ROM drive.

*   Super VGA (800x600) or higher resolution video adapter with a minimum of 256 colours.

*   Microsoft Mouse, IntelliMouse, or compatible pointing device.

*   For sound and other multimedia effects, a multimedia compliant PC is required, including a Windows compatible sound card.

Realistically, to run Office XP with multimedia support you will need 100 MB of additional hard disc space. With reasonable sized application documents, and speech recognition, you will also need an MMX 400 MHz Pentium II PC with at least 128 MB of RAM. To run Microsoft Office XP from a network, you must also have a network compatible with your Windows operating environment, such as Microsoft's Windows 98/Me (or higher), or Windows NT/2000.

Finally, if you are connected to the Internet, you can take advantage of Word's advanced editing and formatting features when working with e-mail messages. Word can be used as an alternate e-mail editor for Outlook 2002, and now takes advantage of custom backgrounds and themes, as well as supporting auto signatures. However, before you can do so, you must have Outlook installed on your computer and in that program have Word 2002 selected as your e-mail editor.

Installing Microsoft Office XP

Installing Office on your computer's hard disc is made very easy using the SETUP program, which even configures Office automatically to take advantage of the computer's hardware. One of SETUP's functions is to convert compressed Office files from the CD-ROM, prior to copying them onto your hard disc.

Note: If you are using a virus detection utility, disable it before running SETUP, as it might conflict with it.

To install Microsoft Office, place the distribution CD in your CD drive and close it. The auto-start program on the CD will start the SETUP program automatically. If that does not work, click the **Start** button, and select the **Run** command which opens the Run dialogue box, as shown here.

Next, type in the **Command Line** box:

    j:\setup

In our case we used the CD-ROM in the J: drive; yours could be different. Clicking the **OK** button, starts the installation of Microsoft Office XP. SETUP first displays a screen informing you that the program is preparing the Office XP Installation Wizard, then displays the following screen:

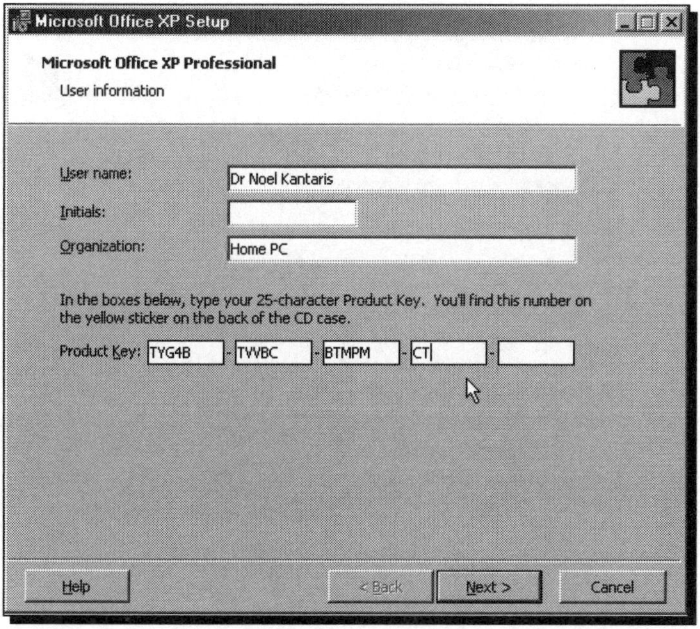

Fig. 1.1 User Information Screen.

We suggest that you follow the instructions displayed on the screen. Clicking the **Next** button, causes SETUP to go through the following procedure:

- Asks you to accept the licence agreement.

- Asks you whether to Upgrade now or keep your current installation and choose an install type. If you choose the latter option it prompts you to supply the new path to the directory where you want to install Office XP, and then checks your system and the available hard disc space.

- Searches your system's discs for installed Office components and asks you whether older versions of Office applications should be removed or not - we selected to keep them, but Microsoft Outlook has to be removed before Outlook 2002 can be installed.

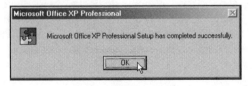

Microsoft Office XP Setup

Microsoft Office XP Professional
Remove previous versions of Office applications

Setup has detected the following previous version of Office applications installed on your machine. Setup can remove all previous versions, or you may choose to keep some or all of them.

○ Remove all previous versions.

◉ Remove only the following applications:

☐ Microsoft Access
☐ Microsoft Excel
☑ Microsoft Outlook
☐ Microsoft PowerPoint
☐ Microsoft Word

Previous versions of Outlook must be removed to install Microsoft Outlook 2002.

Help   < Back   Next >   Cancel

Fig. 1.2 Removing Previous Versions of Office Applications.

- Displays a dialogue box specifying the choices you have made. Clicking the **Install** button starts copying files to your computer's hard disc.

Note: Next, in our case, we were asked to insert the CD of the previous version of Office. To avoid an error being generated, click the **Cancel** button of the displayed box.

When all necessary files are copied successfully, the following screen is displayed:

Microsoft Office XP Professional

Microsoft Office XP Professional Setup has completed successfully.

OK

Next the Office XP Activation Wizard starts up, displaying the following screen in our case:

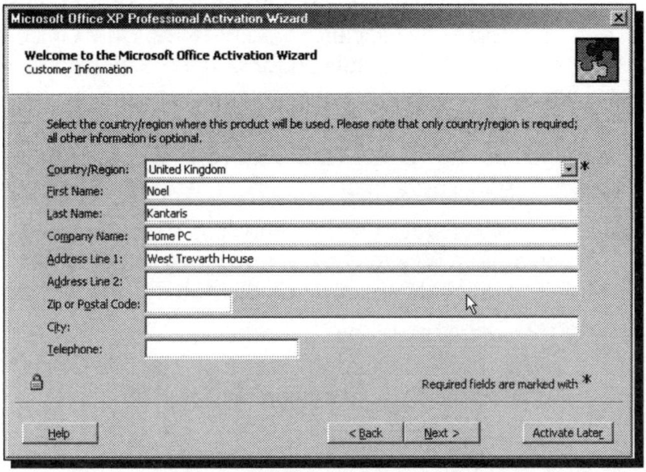

Fig. 1.3 The Office Activation Wizard Screen.

In the next Wizard screen you can choose the method of activation; via the Internet, or by telephone. If you are connected to the Internet, you are asked whether you want Microsoft to inform you of upgrades, etc., in which case you are asked to insert your e-mail address. Pressing the **Submit** button, connects you to the Internet and a few seconds later the final Wizard screen is displayed, as shown in Fig. 1.4.

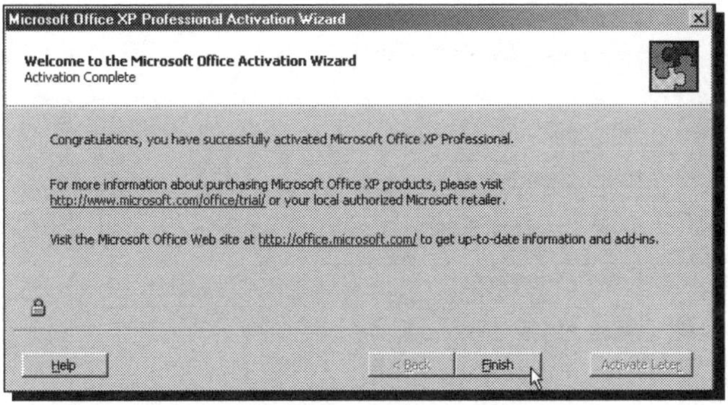

Fig. 1.4 The Final Office XP Activation Screen.

The Office Shortcut Bar

During installation, if you already use the Office Shortcut Bar, it will be updated automatically to point to the new Office XP applications. Any additional buttons (also referred to as icons) which you might have assembled on it will be preserved. To activate the Office Shortcut Bar, double-click its filename in the **C:\WINDOWS\Start Menu\Programs\ Microsoft Office Tools** folder.

The Microsoft Office Shortcut Bar, provides a convenient way to work with your documents and the Office applications by complementing the Windows **Start** cascade menu.

The buttons on the Shortcut Bar of Office XP Professional Special edition are labelled as:

New Office Document

Open Office Document

Microsoft Word

Microsoft Excel

Microsoft PowerPoint

Microsoft Outlook

Microsoft Access

Microsoft Publisher

Microsoft FrontPage

New Appointment

New Contact

New Journal Entry

New Message

New Note

New Task

Apart from the buttons which launch the four main applications in Office XP (Word, Excel, PowerPoint, and Access), the function of the other buttons is as follows:

New Office Document: Allows you to select in the displayed dialogue box the tab containing the type of document you want to work with. Double-clicking the type of document or template you want, automatically loads the appropriate application.

Open Office Document: Allows you to work with an existing document. Opening a document, first starts the application originally used to create it.

Microsoft Outlook: Launches the desktop manager used to manage your e-mail, contact lists, tasks and documents.

Microsoft Publisher: Launches the desktop publishing program that allows the design and creation of documents suitable for marketing or sales material, such as professional-looking brochures, sales letters, business stationery, and even whole Websites.

Microsoft FrontPage: Launches the Web design program.

New Appointment: Allows you to add a new appointment in your management system. This caters for all-day or multiple-day events and a meeting planner, including meeting request processing and attendance lists.

New Contact: Allows you to enter a new contact in Outlook's database, or to send an e-mail message direct from the contact manager and use hyper-links for direct access to a contact's home page on the Internet.

New Journal Entry: Allows you to make a New Journal.

New Message: Allows you to type a New Message.

New Note: Allows you to type a new Note.

New Task: Allows you to add a new task in your management system, including automatic composition of an e-mail message summarising a task and automatic tracking of tasks sent to other users.

Changing the Office Shortcut Bar

You have the option of changing the buttons on the Office Shortcut Bar. To do so, left-click on an empty part of the Shortcut bar to display the available options, as shown here to the left.

Here, we show the 'Programs' option ticked, which we find most useful for quickly launching a selection of programs. Clicking this option, replaces the original Office Shortcut Bar with the one shown here to the right. However, clicking the **Office** button (top left), changes the Shortcut Bar back to the original Office Shortcut Bar. In this way, you can flick between selected Shortcut Bars.

Adding/Deleting Buttons

You can add buttons to the Shortcut Bar by dragging them there. To find the application you want to add to this bar, use the Windows **Start**, **Find** command.

To delete a button, right-click on an empty part of the Shortcut Bar, select **Customize** from the displayed menu, then click the Buttons tab, select the unwanted button and click **Delete**. But beware, this also deletes the folder that holds the application! It may be better to hide it.

Hiding/Displaying Buttons

To hide a button from the Shortcut Bar (without deleting it),

right-click on the button and select the **Hide Button** option on the displayed menu, shown here to the left. To display previously hidden buttons, right-click the Shortcut Bar, use the **Customize** option on the displayed menu and click the Button tab. Clicking on the check box of the required button makes it visible on the Shortcut Bar. Clicking again, clears its check mark and hides it.

Adding or Removing Office Applications

To add or remove an Office application, left-click the **Start** button at the bottom left corner of the screen, point to **Settings**, then click the **Control Panel** option on the Windows pop-up menu, as shown in Fig. 1.5 below.

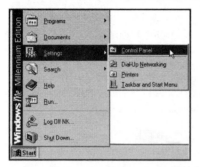

Fig. 1.5 The Windows
Pop-up Menu.

This opens the Control Panel dialogue box. Next, double-click the **Add/Remove Programs** icon, shown here to the left, to open the dialogue box shown in Fig. 1.6. Click the Install/Uninstall tab and select the Microsoft Office XP program, and then click the **Add/Remove** button.

Add/Remove
Programs

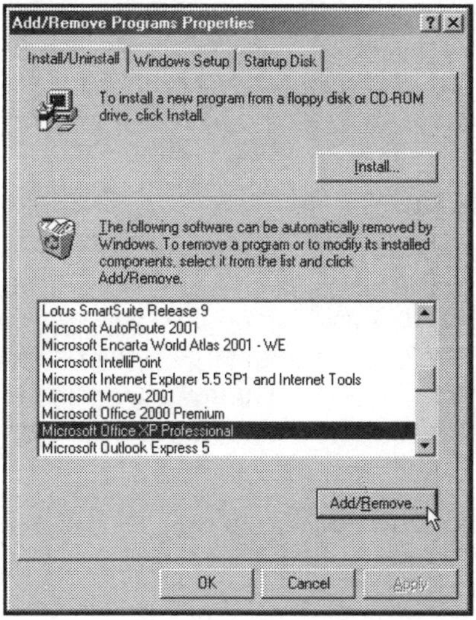

Add/Remove Programs Properties   ? ☒

Install/Uninstall | Windows Setup | Startup Disk |

To install a new program from a floppy disk or CD-ROM drive, click Install.

         Install...

The following software can be automatically removed by Windows. To remove a program or to modify its installed components, select it from the list and click Add/Remove.

Lotus SmartSuite Release 9
Microsoft AutoRoute 2001
Microsoft Encarta World Atlas 2001 - WE
Microsoft IntelliPoint
Microsoft Internet Explorer 5.5 SP1 and Internet Tools
Microsoft Money 2001
Microsoft Office 2000 Premium
Microsoft Office XP Professional
Microsoft Outlook Express 5

         Add/Remove...

OK   Cancel   Apply

Fig. 1.6 The Add/Remove
Properties Dialogue Box.

This causes SETUP to display the Maintenance Mode Options dialogue box, shown in Fig. 1.7:

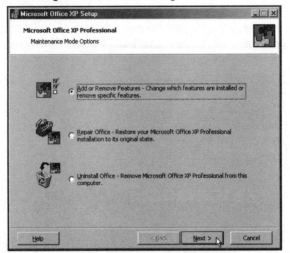

Fig. 1.7 The Office XP Maintenance Mode Options Dialogue Box.

Selecting the **Add or Remove Features** option and pressing the **Next** button opens up the dialogue box of Fig. 1.8. A plus (+) sign to the left of an application indicates sub-features which you can add or remove from the Office installation, or change how the feature is installed by clicking its symbol and then selecting another symbol from the list that appears.

Fig. 1.8 Installation Options for Office Applications.

Note the **Repair Office** button on the screen of Fig. 1.7. Use this to reinstall the whole of Office XP, or to find and fix any errors in your original installation.

The Mouse Pointers

In Office XP applications, as with all other graphical based programs, using a mouse makes many operations both easier and more fun to carry out.

Office XP makes use of the mouse pointers available in Windows, some of the most common of which are illustrated below. When an Office application is initially started up the first you will see is the hourglass, which turns into an upward pointing hollow arrow once the individual application screen appears on your display. Other shapes depend on the type of work you are doing at the time.

🕛 The hourglass which displays when you are waiting while performing a function.

 The arrow which appears when the pointer is placed over menus, scrolling bars, and buttons.

I The I-beam which appears in normal text areas of the screen. For additional 'Click and Type' pointer shapes, specific to Office XP applications, see the table overleaf.

✛ The 4-headed arrow which appears when you choose to move a table, a chart area, or a frame.

↔ The double arrows which appear when over the border of a window, used to drag the side and alter the size of the window.

 The Help hand which appears in the Help windows, and is used to access 'hypertext' type links.

Office XP applications, like other Windows packages, have additional mouse pointers which facilitate the execution of selected commands. Some of these are:

↓   The vertical pointer which appears when pointing over a column in a table or worksheet and used to select the column.

➡   The horizontal pointer which appears when pointing at a row in a table or worksheet and used to select the row.

⇗   The slanted arrow which appears when the pointer is placed in the selection bar area of text or a table.

◄║►   The vertical split arrow which appears when pointing over the area separating two columns and used to size a column.

⇕   The horizontal split arrow which appears when pointing over the area separating two rows and used to size a row.

+   The cross which you drag to extend or fill a series.

✐   The draw pointer which appears when you are drawing freehand.

Word 2002 also has the following Click and Type pointer shapes which appear as you move the I-beam pointer into a specific formatting zone; their shape indicating which formatting will apply when you double-click.

I≡	Align left	≡I	Align right
I≡	Centre	I≝	Left indent
I≡◳	Left text wrap	◲I	Right text wrap

Fig. 1.9 The Click and Type Pointer Shapes in Word 2002.

If you don't see the Click and Type pointer shapes, check that the facility is turned on. You can do this by using the **Tools**, **Options** command, then click the Edit tab and select the **Enable click and type** check box, and press **OK**.

Getting Help in Office XP

No matter how experienced you are, there will always be times when you need help to find out how to do something in the various Office applications. Office is after all a very large and powerful suite of programs with a multitude of features. As we shall see, there are several ways to get help now, including the Office Assistant, or Clippy as he is called by Microsoft, although by default it is switched off.

Ask a Question Box

To quickly access Help, you can use the Ask a Question box on the menu bar. You type a question in this box, as we show in Fig. 1.10, and press the <Enter> key.

Fig. 1.10 The Ask a Question Box.

A list of help topics is then displayed, as shown here. To see more topics, left-click the small triangle at the bottom of the list with the caption 'See more'. Once you select an option from the list and click on it, the Help system is opened and you should quickly be able to find the answers you need. In fact it works the same way as the Assistant, but without the constant 'distractions'.

It seems to be better to type a full question in the Ask a Question box, rather than just a keyword. The options presented can then be more relevant. When you use the feature several times, the previous questions can be accessed by clicking the down-arrow to the right of the text box. However, the list is cleared whenever you exit the Office application you are using at the time.

The Office Assistant

The Office Assistant is turned off by default in this version of Office and may not even be installed unless you specifically request it. When activated, it first appears as we show on the left, and automatically provides Help topics and tips on tasks you perform as you work. To find out how it works, start an Office application (we used Word) and use the **Help**, **Show the Office Assistant** menu command to open Clippy. Now left-click him to open the 'What would you like to do?' box, shown in Fig. 1.11.

To get help you simply type your query here and click the **Search** button. From then on the procedure is the same as with the Ask a Question box.

If you like, you can customise the Assistant, and decide if you want it to automatically display tips, messages, and alerts, make sounds, move when it's in the way, and guess a Help topic that it thinks you may need.

Fig. 1.11 Using the Office Assistant.

You can also switch it off once you have mastered a particular Office application, or cannot cope with its intrusions any more! All of these features are controlled from the box shown in Fig. 1.12 which is opened by clicking the **Options** button shown in Fig. 1.11.

To change the shape of your Office Assistant (there are eight shapes to choose from), either left-click the Gallery tab of the dialogue box shown in Fig. 1.12, or right-click the Office Assistant and select the **Choose Assistant** option from the displayed menu, as shown here to the left.

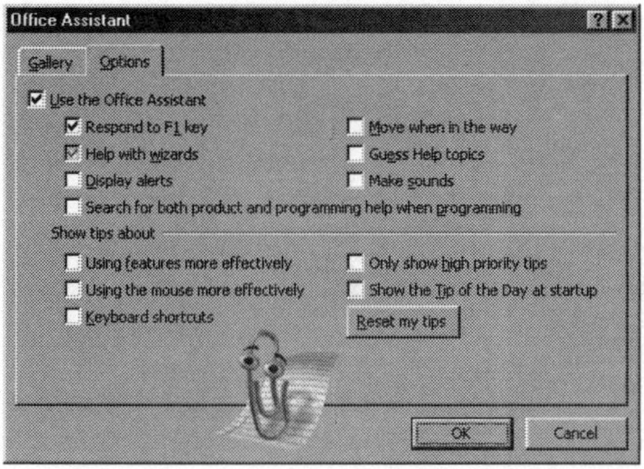

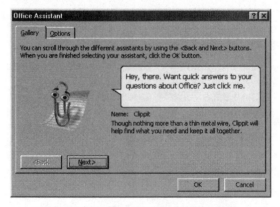

Fig. 1.12 The Office Assistant Options Box.

Either of these actions displays the following dialogue box (Fig. 1.13) in which you can select your preferred Assistant shape by left-clicking the **Next** button.

Fig. 1.13 The Office Assistant Gallery Box.

The eight shapes of the available Assistants are shown in Fig. 1.14 on the next page. We find the Office Assistant's animated characters to be very clever and amusing, but must admit that like most people we prefer to work with the facility turned off. To do this, make sure the **Use the Office Assistant** option is not selected in the Options box shown in Fig. 1.12.

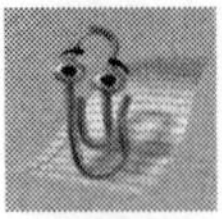 Clippit	 The Dot	 F1
 Merlin	 Office Logo	 Mother Nature
 Links	 Rocky	

Fig. 1.14 The Office Assistant Shapes.

The Main Help System

To illustrate the Main Help System we will use here the word processing application (Word 2002) in Office XP. If you turn the Office Assistant completely off (as described on the previous page) and press the **F1** function key, or click the **Help** toolbar button shown here, or use the **Help**, **Microsoft Word Help** menu command, Help will be accessed directly through the Help window. This is the way we prefer to use it.

When first opened, the Microsoft Word Help Center will be displayed in the right-hand pane as shown in Fig. 1.15 on the next page. This gives a quick way to get information on **What's New** with Word 2002, the **Microsoft Office Web Site** and about **Getting Help** itself. Each of these has a very colourful button you can press.

Below these is a listing of 'hypertext links' to some of the help topics Microsoft thought you were most likely to use first. Clicking any of these opens the relevant Help page, without you having to look for the item itself.

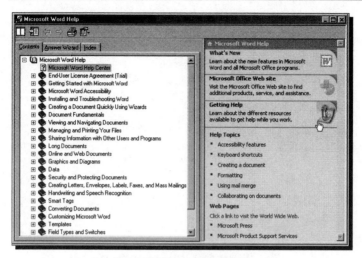

Fig. 1.15 Microsoft Word Help.

As can be seen here, the left pane of the Help window has three tabbed sections.

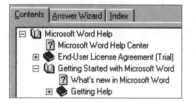

Fig. 1.16 Help Contents List.

The **Contents** tab of the Help screen opens up an impressive list of topics relating to the Word 2002 program. Clicking a '+' at the left of an item, or double-clicking a closed book icon, opens a sublist; clicking a '-', or double-clicking an open book icon, will close it again. Clicking a list item, with the ? mark as shown, opens the help text in the right-hand pane.

To type a question in the Help window, you click the **Answer Wizard** tab. When you want to search for specific words or phrases, you click the **Index** tab. For example, click the **Answer Wizard** tab, and type the text *How do I open a document* in the **What would you like to do?** text box. Then click the **Search** button and you should see something like the screen in Fig. 1.17 on the next page.

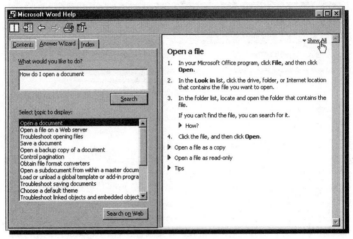

Fig. 1.17 Using the Help Answer Wizard.

Clicking an item in the list of topics opens the relevant Help page in the right pane. A new feature with Office XP is that the Help pages are opened in an 'outline' view. Clicking a blue link item with a ▶ symbol to its left, opens up more detail, whereas clicking the ▾ **Show All** link in the top-right corner will fully expand the page. This is very useful if you want to print or copy the Help information.

The Help Toolbar

Note the Web browser type buttons at the top of the Help screen. These allow you to carry out the following functions:

▯▯	**Auto Tile** - click this button to tile the Help window on the screen next to the main Word window.
⇦▤	**Show** - click this button to display the help screen tabs which allow you to access Help's Contents, Answer Wizard, and Index.
⇦	**Back** - if more than one help screen has been opened, click this button to go back to the previously opened help screen.

⇨	**Forward** - if you have moved back to a previous help screen, click this button to move forward through opened help screens.
🖨	**Print** - click this button to print the contents of the current help screen.
🗐	**Options** - click this button to open up a menu of options which control all of the above facilities plus the ability to select the Internet Options dialogue box.

The Word Help system is very comprehensive but it is not always easy to find the information you are looking for. It usually pays to select the feature, or object, you want details on before accessing Help, you may then get exactly the right information straight off. Do spend some time here to learn, particularly what is new in the Office application you are using. Other topics can always be explored later.

ScreenTips

If you want to know what a menu command or button does, or if you want to know more about an option in a dialogue box, you can also get ScreenTips help. These can be accessed in three ways:

- For help with a menu command, toolbar button, or a screen region, click **What's This?** on the **Help** menu, or <Shift+**F1**>, and then click the feature you want help on.

- In a dialogue box, click the Help button 🔳 in the top right corner of the box, and then click the option.

- To see the name of a toolbar button, rest the pointer . over the button and its name will appear.

Help on the Internet

If all else fails, you can connect to several Microsoft Web sites with the **Help**, **Office on the Web** menu command. You must obviously have an Internet connection for this to work, though!

1 Package Overview

2

Microsoft Outlook 2002

Microsoft's Outlook 2002 is a powerful personal information manager (PIM) - a kind of Filofax - that supports a full set of multi-user, group scheduling PIM functions. Outlook 2002 can be made the centre of activity for all the other Office XP applications; it can be used *online* or *off-line*. Outlook 2002 continues to support a multiple-account e-mail client, compatible with Microsoft's Exchange messaging server as well as Internet-based POP3, HTTP (Web mail, such as Hotmail) and IMAP.

To work online, your computer must be connected to a shared network resource, which is imperative if you are planning to use Outlook's group-scheduling features. In that case, your computer must have a connection to a *post office* which is a list of Mail users on the system. Outlook 2002 can do the following:

- Manage information such as your appointments, contacts, tasks, and files, and if your computer is connected to a network, manage your e-mail, use group scheduling, and public folders.

- Browse and find Office files from within Outlook.

- Share information across the World Wide Web, provided you are connected to the Internet and have a browser, such as Microsoft's Explorer or Netscape.

A major example of integration of Outlook 2002 with the rest of the Office suite is the Journal, which automatically tracks the use of the other Office applications. It can be customised to monitor as many or as few entries of activity as required, for example, to record an entry every time you open, save or print a document from any of Office XP's applications. The result can be a time map of the user's activity.

Starting Outlook 2002

Outlook 2002 is started in Windows either by clicking on the **Microsoft Outlook** button on the Office Shortcut Bar, or by

clicking any of the six buttons 'New Appointment' 'New Contact', 'New Journal Entry', 'New Message', 'New Note', or 'NewTask', also to be found on the Office Shortcut Bar. Once you have created an Outlook file, you can also start the program by clicking the **Open Office Document** button on the Office Shortcut Bar and double-clicking the relevant Outlook file.

If you are not using the Office Shortcut Bar, then you can start Outlook 2002 by clicking one of the shortcuts placed on the desktop and Taskbar, shown here to the right.

When you start Outlook 2002 the program momentarily displays its opening screen, shown in Fig. 2.1 below, and then displays the Personal Folders screen shown in Fig. 2.2.

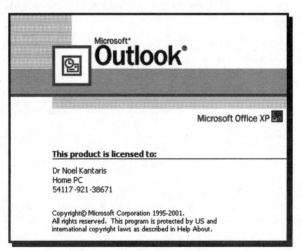

Fig. 2.1 Outlook's Opening Screen.

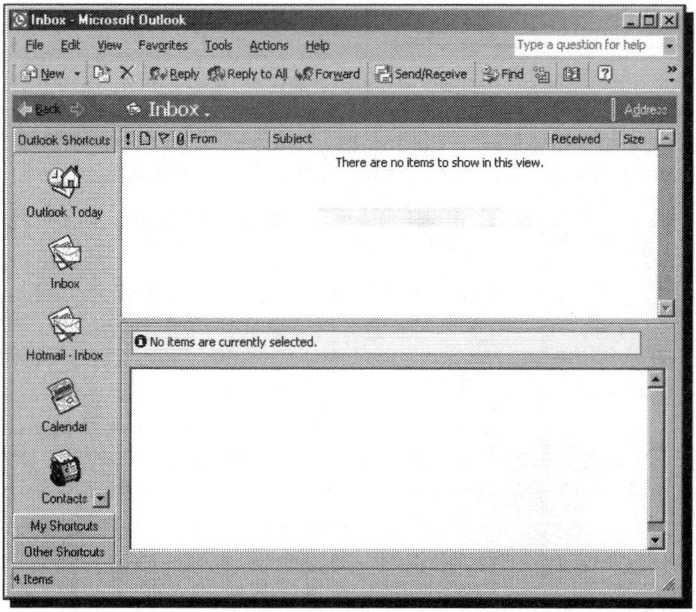

Fig. 2.2 The Inbox Folder of Outlook.

Other Outlook folders can be reached by clicking the small triangle (pointed to in Fig. 2.3) which opens up a list of available items. Most of these folders are self-explanatory, with Inbox being the folder containing all the received e-mails, Outbox being the folder containing the e-mails you have prepared off-line ready to be sent when you connect to the Internet, while Draft is the folder in which you save the e-mails under preparation that you intend to complete later.

Fig. 2.3 Available Outlook Folders.

Some of these folders will also be found in the **My Shortcuts** list which will be discussed shortly together with other lists of shortcuts.

Managing Information

You can use Outlook to effectively manage information whether it is personal or business. The Outlook screen provides you with the means to manage information on three general topics: Outlook Shortcuts, My Shortcuts, and Other.

Outlook Shortcuts provides the following tools:

Outlook Today - gives you a snapshot of your day. It lists your appointments for the week, your tasks, and how many new e-mail messages you have.

Inbox - used to send and receive messages, preview messages before you open them, and manage your e-mail folders (see next chapter).

Calendar - used to keep track of your schedule and plan meetings with others. Use the TaskPad to see the day's tasks.

Contacts - used to keep your personal and business contact information up to date. Sort and file contacts any way you want, and go directly to their Web page.

Tasks - used to organise your personal and business to-do list in one easy-to-manage place.

Notes - used to write down notes on anything you like, or drop text in notes that you want to reuse in other places.

Deleted Items - used to find deleted items and reinstate them.

Clicking each of the two buttons at the bottom of the screen lists additional shortcuts, as shown on the next page.

My Shortcuts provides the following options:

Drafts - used to locate the folder in which unfinished messages have been saved.

Outbox - used to configure the way you send messages by delaying their delivery, or make them unavailable after a specified date.

Sent Items - used to manage mail you have sent to others, a copy of which is saved in the sent items folder. Items can be sorted in any way you like.

Journal - used to record Outlook items, such as e-mail messages and files that are important, and to record and track activities of all types.

Outlook Update - used to update Outlook from the Microsoft Website.

Other Shortcuts provides the following tools:

My Computer - used to search drives and folders for a file you want to view, use, or perform housekeeping operations on, such as delete it or rename it.

My Documents - used to store Office documents, worksheets, databases, and presentations that you are working on inside the same folder.

Favorites - used to insert shortcuts to frequently used folders.

In general, you can use Outlook to open, view, and share other Office program files and use its various tools to help you work more efficiently.

Parts of the Outlook Screen

Before we go any further, take a look at the **Outlook Today**

screen which can be displayed by clicking the first button on the Outlook Shortcuts Option Bar shown to the left. The screen contains three distinct areas, **Calendar**, **Tasks** and **Messages**.

Left-clicking any one of these, takes you to the appropriate option the first two of which can also be reached from the Outlook Option Bar (see Fig. 2.4).

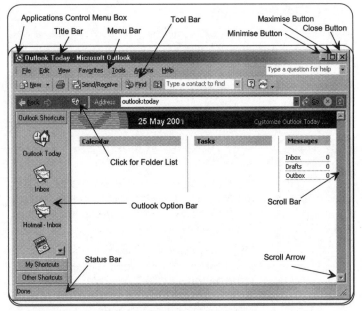

Fig. 2.4 The Outlook Today Screen.

Clicking the **Messages** option or the **Inbox** icon on the Outlook Option Bar, displays the screen shown in Fig. 2.2.

To find out more about Outlook in general, and its new features in particular, left-click the Help button on the Toolbar shown to the left, to display the help screen in Fig. 2.5 on the next page.

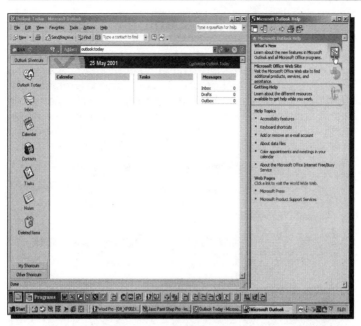

Fig. 2.5 The Outlook Help Screen.

To display information on any of the listed topics, simply move the mouse pointer onto one of the link icons and when the pointer changes to a hand, click the left mouse button. Items on the Help list displaying in blue are also hypertext links which when left-clicked display more information.

Another useful link is the **Customize Outlook Today** pointed to below. Clicking this displays a screen in which you

can specify whether to go directly to Outlook Today at **Startup**, the folders to be displayed under **Messages**, and the number of days to be displayed in your **Calendar**. You can also select which **Tasks** should be displayed and how they should be sorted, as well as the style in which Outlook Today should be displayed. If you alter any of these settings, click the **Save Changes** link, otherwise click **Cancel**.

Importing Data into Outlook

If you already hold personal or business information, such as contacts or tasks to perform, on another program, now is the time to import these into Outlook. To begin the process, use the **File, Import and Export** command which starts the Import and Export Wizard, the first screen of which is shown in Fig. 2.6.

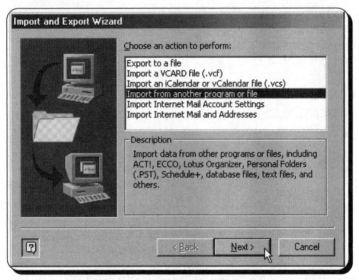

Fig. 2.6 The Import and Export Wizard Screen.

Next, highlight the 'Import from another program or file' entry and press **Next**, which causes the Wizard to display a list of possible organiser-type formats that it can handle by displaying the screen in Fig. 2.7.

We will attempt to import information from Lotus Organizer 5.0, our previously used scheduler. Selecting the type of file you want to convert and pressing the **Next** button displays the next Wizard screen in which you are asked to locate the file to be converted, as shown in Fig. 2.8.

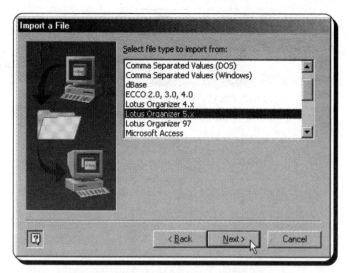

Fig. 2.7 Selecting a File Type to Import.

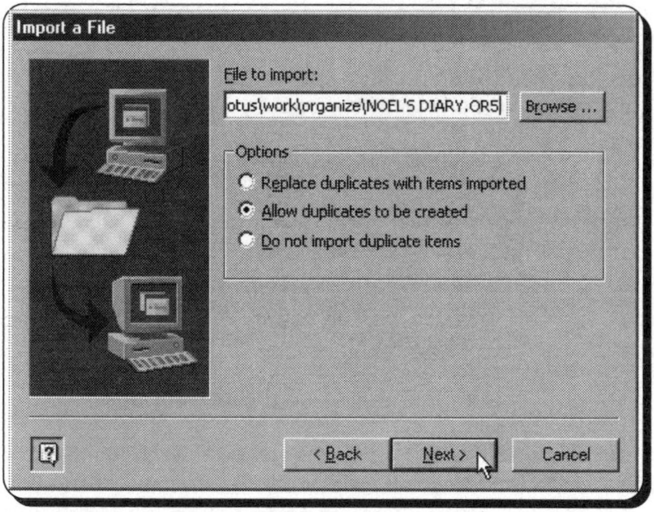

Import a File

File to import:
otus\work\organize\NOEL'S DIARY.OR5   Browse ...

Options
○ Replace duplicates with items imported
● Allow duplicates to be created
○ Do not import duplicate items

< Back   Next >   Cancel

Fig. 2.8 Locating the File to Import.

In our case the Wizard found the required file and proposed to carry out five actions, as detailed below. In your case these will most certainly be different.

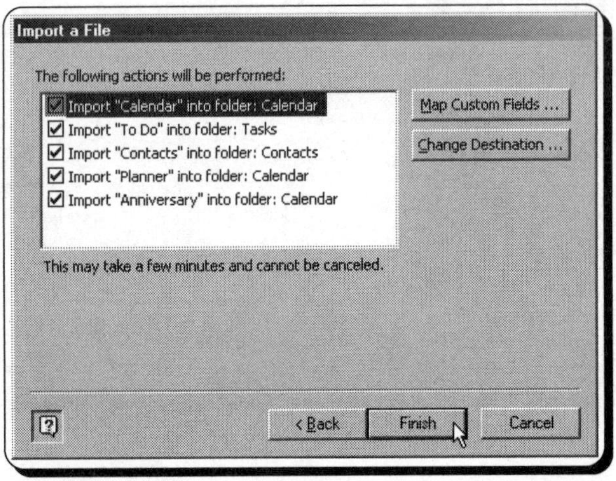

Fig. 2.9 Proposed Actions to be Taken During Data Conversion.

Pressing the **Finish** button, starts the conversion process, during which you are informed exactly what is going on.

In our experience the data conversion was faultless. We were particularly impressed that the extensive information in our **Contacts** folder was converted fully and accurately. Obviously we cannot show you the complete outcome of this process, as it contains private and sensitive information, but you will see some conversion entries as we examine the individual sections of Outlook.

Using the Calendar

Before we start entering information in our Calendar, let us take a look at its opening screen.

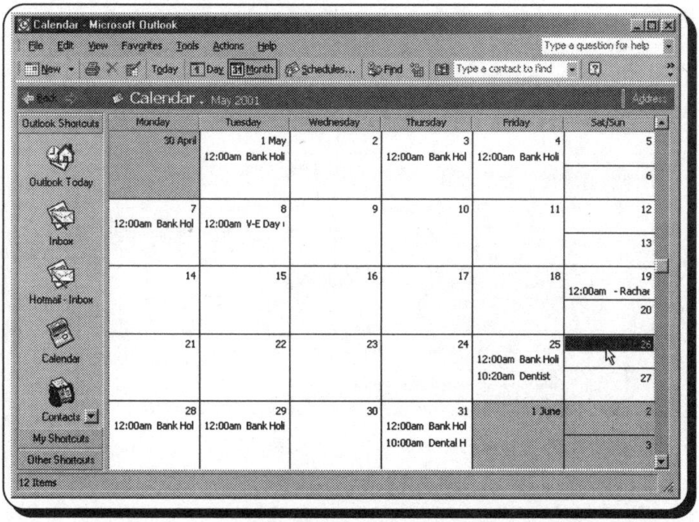

Fig. 2.10 The Opening Calendar Screen in Monthly View.

As you can see, certain information was transferred from our previous organiser and is shown here in Fig. 2.10. Changing the month you are viewing could not be simpler; just click the scroll buttons of the vertical scroll bar - clicking the upper scroll button displays earlier months, while clicking the lower scroll button displays later months. The days in the current month are shown in white, with the current day highlighted, while the days of earlier and later months are shown in grey.

To see the Calendar in daily or weekly view, simply click the appropriate button on the Calendar Toolbar, shown below.

Or use the **View** command, then select **Day**, **Work Week**, or **Week**.

Viewing Appointments

All the details of appointments, events or meetings can be viewed in Outlook whether you are in the Daily, Weekly, or Monthly view; you can see the date, time, and the description. You also have the facility to use symbols to indicate whether the appointment is recurring, tentative, or private, and whether a reminder has been set, shown by a small bell, or other users have been invited (to be discussed next). In Fig. 2.11 the Calendar is displayed in Daily View.

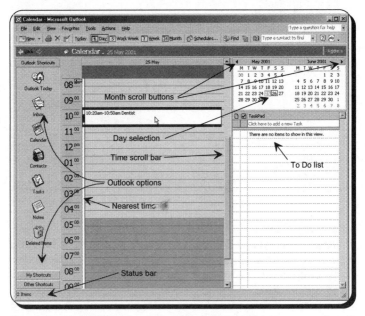

Fig. 2.11 The Calendar Display in Daily View.

To look at another day, left-click on the day you want to look at on the monthly calendar at the top right of the screen.

Information relevant to an appointment or meeting is also displayed in the Appointment dialogue box (to see one, double-click on a day on the Calendar - again, this will be discussed next). To organise a meeting, however, you will need to click the Scheduling tab of the Appointment dialogue box.

Appointments, Meetings, and Events

Before you start scheduling an appointment, meeting or event, it is necessary to look at the following definitions:

- An appointment does not involve other colleagues or resources, and can be recurring, that is, it can be repeated on a regular basis.

- A meeting is an appointment that involves other people and possibly resources, and can also be recurring.

- An event is an activity that lasts one day, or more, such as attendance at an exhibition or conference. An annual event occurs yearly on a specific date. Events and annual events do not occupy blocks of time in your Calendar; instead, they appear as a banner below the current day heading.

Entering Appointments

To start with, let us type in a recurring appointment to, say, meet Section Managers, that takes place on Thursday every four weeks starting at 10:00 a.m. on 7 June and lasts for 2 hours. To do so, click on 7 June on the calendar to the right of the entry area, move the cursor to 10:00 a.m. and click the

Make a New Appointment button shown here. This opens the Appointment dialogue box displayed in Fig. 2.12 on the next page in which you can type 'Managers' meeting' in the **Subject** box, and 'My Office' in the **Location** box, set the **End time** to 12.00, click the **Reminder** box and select 15 minutes, and then press the **Recurrence** button on the Toolbar.

In the Appointment Recurrence dialogue box (Fig. 2.13), click the **Weekly** radio button and in the **Recur every** box, pointed to by the mouse pointer on our screen dump, type '4', fill in the rest of the information as shown, and click **OK**. Finally, click the **Save and Close** button located at the top of the first dialogue box.

Fig. 2.12 Entering Information in the Appointment Dialogue Box.

Fig. 2.13 The Appointment Recurrence Dialogue Box.

Your Calendar now shows the latest entry, including location of meeting, together with the **Reminder** icon and the Recurring symbol.

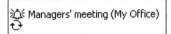

If you want to make any changes to the newly created appointment, point to it and right-click it. You can use the options on this drop-down menu to print, edit, or delete the appointment. Choosing the **Edit Series** option, opens the Recurring Appointment dialogue box where you can make the required changes.

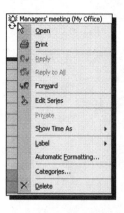

Next, let us now assume that you also have a special lunch appointment with your mother on the 5th of July each year, as it is her birthday. To enter this information click on 5 July on the calendar to the right of the Daily entry area, and create a yearly appointment 'Lunch with mother' for 1:00 p.m., for 1½ hours, as shown in Fig. 2.14 below. Add as a note the reminder 'Birthday lunch'.

Fig. 2.14 Entering a Yearly Appointment.

Note that the meeting with the Managers is also shown on the same day, as it is four weeks since the last meeting. This information also appears on the Weekly and the Monthly view. Try it!

Printing Information

Information held in a diary can be printed on paper. Simply use the **File, Print** command to open the dialogue box below.

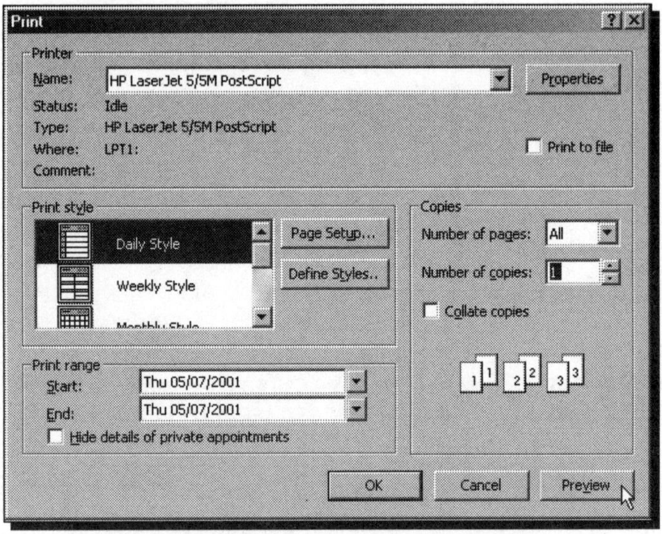

Fig. 2.15 The Calendar Print Dialogue Box.

In the Printer **Name** box, at the top of the dialogue box, click the down arrow to select from one of the installed printers under Windows. Next, choose an appropriate item from the **Print Style** list and use the **Page Setup** button to see the format, page size, and header/footer options of the selected print style.

In Fig. 2.16 on the next page, we show the Page Setup dialogue box with the Header/Footer tab selected. Note the five icon buttons below the Footer text boxes, also shown

here. These can be used to insert page number, total number of pages, date, time, and user's name, respectively, in both headers and footers. To do so, simply place the insertion cursor on one of the text boxes, then click the appropriate button.

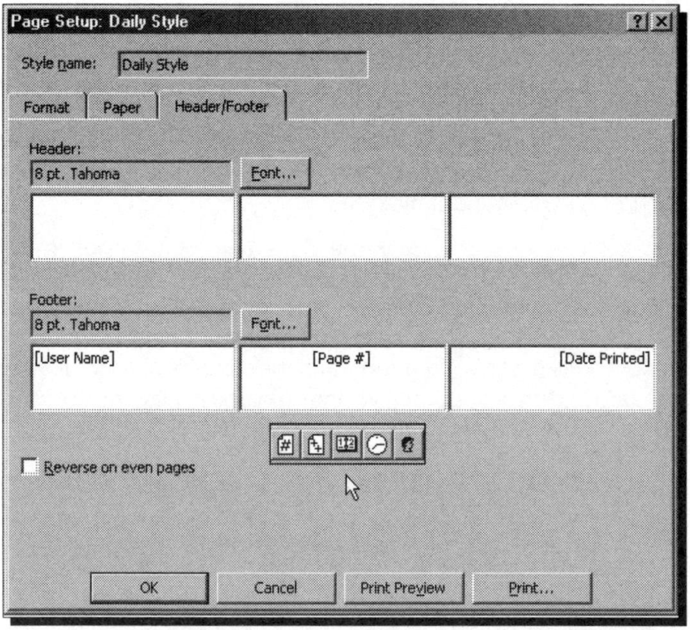

Fig. 2.16 Inserting a Footer in the Page Setup Dialogue Box.

In the above footer set-up, we have inserted the user's name in the left panel of the footer, the page number in the middle panel, and the date printed in the right panel. If you decide to show such information on your printout, it is entirely up to you where you choose to insert it. In addition, you can change the font type and font size of the information appearing on a header or footer.

If you want to change the font type and font size of the text appearing on the actual body of your printout, click the Format tab of the above dialogue box, and make appropriate selections under the displayed **Fonts** section. Pressing the **OK** button on the Page Setup dialogue box returns you to the Print dialogue box.

However, before committing anything to paper, use the **Preview** button and save a few trees!

Planning a Meeting

Suppose we decide to invite other people into the meeting with the Managers on 7 June. First, locate the date of the meeting on the Calendar display and double-click the entry in question. In the displayed 'Open Recurring Item' screen, click the **Open this occurrence** radio button to display the Recurring Appointment dialogue box.

In this dialogue box, click the Scheduling tab to obtain the screen in Fig. 2.17, in which we typed the names of two colleagues we would like to be present at the meeting. If you had a Contacts list (see next section), you could also select one or more persons to attend this meeting by simply clicking the **Add Others** button on the dialogue box below and selecting from the displayed list.

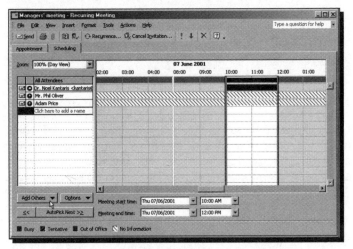

Fig. 2.17 Scheduling Colleagues to Attend a Meeting.

From here, you can organise meetings and send requests to participants and then track the status of their response provided, of course, you are either connected to a local network or know their e-mail address. You can even give other Outlook users permissions to view your diary and to plan meetings with you at times when you are not so busy, but still be able to maintain private information in your diary.

Below we list several new options available to Outlook 2002 on group Scheduling. The list can be found in Outlook's Help system under New Features, but we included it here for convenience.

- Ability to receive counter proposals for alternate meeting times. If allowed by the meeting organiser, invited colleagues can propose an alternate meeting time.

- Ability to view the schedules of multiple people or resources on a single calendar. The calendar contains a detailed graph of when each user is free and busy and also shows details of their appointments (except for those that they have marked private). When you rest the mouse pointer over an appointment, the details of that appointment are visible.

- Ability to use the Microsoft Office Internet Free/Busy Service to publish the blocks of time when you are free and when you are busy to a shared Internet location. This is convenient for people who don't normally have access to your Calendar but who do have Internet access. The service works with Microsoft Outlook 2002 or later so that the times published to the service also display in an Outlook meeting request when someone is trying to schedule a meeting with you. Anyone who isn't a member of the service and who you haven't specifically authorised to view your free/busy times won't be able to access the information you publish to the service. (Requires Microsoft Internet Explorer 5 or later.)

Other Outlook Facilities

Apart from 'Calendar', the Outlook Shortcuts tab on the opening screen contains all the other elements needed to give you an effective time-management tool. These elements are accessed, as we have already seen, by appropriate icons situated on the left edge of the screen.

Contacts

The **Contacts** icon displays your contacts in a combined business card and list view. You can change the way information is displayed by using the **View, Current View** command. What is shown below is the Address Cards view format - you have the choice of six additional types of views.

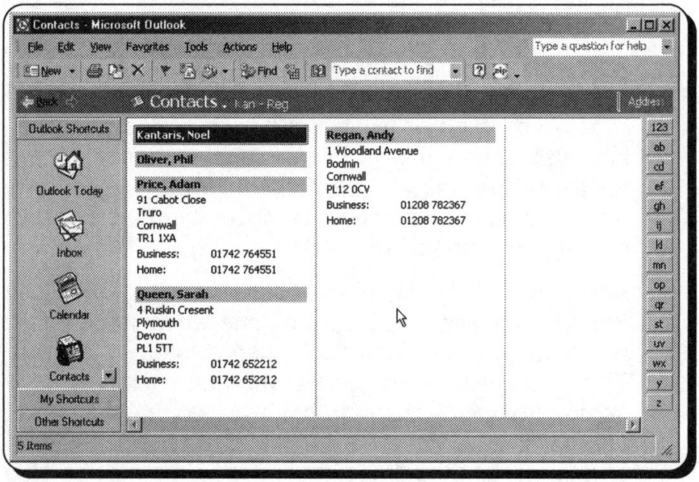

Fig. 2.18 The Contacts Screen in Outlook.

To add a new contact, click the **New** button, shown here, or to edit an existing entry, double-click on the contact name. Either action displays a multi-tab dialogue box, shown in Fig. 2.19 on the next page, in which you type relevant information. We have only ever bothered to type details in the General tab sheet, but if you are so inclined, you can include someone's whole history by filling in the other tab sheets. Once this is done, the name, address, telephone numbers, and e-mail address from the General tab sheet are displayed in Outlook's Contact list.

Contact lists can be saved under different group names, so that you can have one list for your friends, and another for your business.

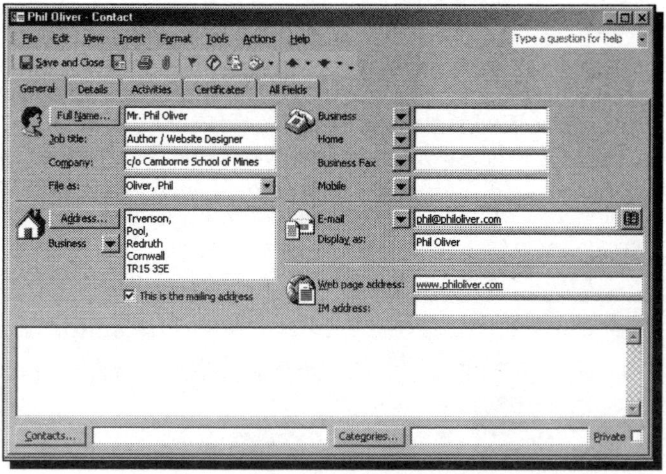

Fig. 2.19 Adding or Editing Contact Information.

The task of filling in such detailed information about an individual might be daunting at first, but you will find it very useful later. For example, you only have to left click on the Web page address to be automatically connected to that Web page (of course, you will have to be connected to the Internet for that facility to work - see next chapter). Equally, you could click on the phone icon on the toolbar to display the AutoDialer, as shown in Fig. 2.20. Pressing the **Start Call** button connects you to your contact via the modem, provided you have a voice capable modem and a handset or microphone attached to it.

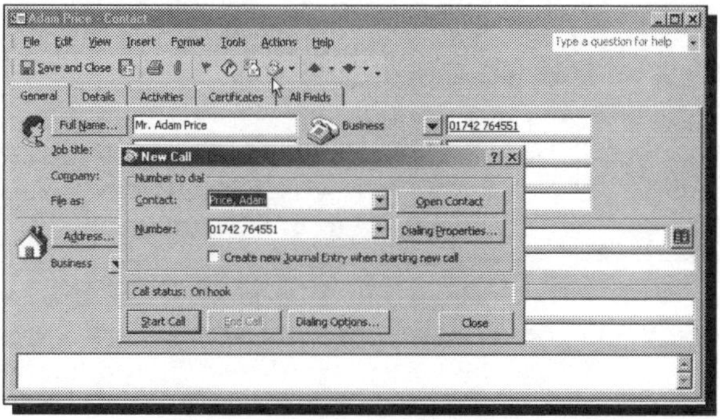

Fig. 2.20 Using Outlook's AutoDialer Facility.

Tasks

Tasks appear in the daily and weekly views of Calendar, or can be displayed by clicking on the **Task** icon of the Outlook Options Bar. Tasks are used to organise your personal to-do list, as well as keep track of your business. In Fig. 2.21 we show a list of personal tasks, with their due date of completion. Completed tasks are shown with a line through them.

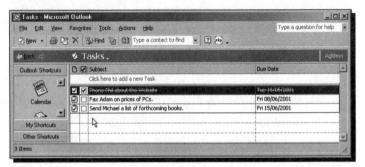

Fig. 2.21 The Task List in Outlook.

Tasks can be assigned to other people within your organisation, and can help you keep track of progress on work that other people do for you or in co-operation with you. For example, you might assign a task to a colleague, or a colleague might assign a task to you in a group effort.

A task assignment requires at least two people: one to send a task request and another to respond to it. When you send a task request, you give up ownership of the task, but can keep an updated copy of it in your task list and receive status reports, but you cannot change information in it. The person that receives the task request is the temporary owner of the task until acceptance of the task, in which case that person becomes the new, permanent owner of that task. Only temporary or permanent owners of a task can update that task. If a task is declined, ownership of the task is returned to the person who sent the task request.

To find out how to use the various functions appearing on a Tasks list, use the Outlook Help system and search for 'tasks'. On the displayed list, first click the 'Create a Task' link then the 'Create a task from scratch' link to obtain the screen in Fig. 2.22.

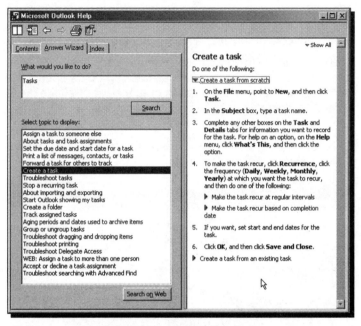

Fig. 2.22 Using the Outlook Help System.

Look through the various topics listed in the left panel of the above Help screen, and work through all of them. Using Help in this way, you will learn quickly how to sort and give priority to tasks, track task progress, enter recurring tasks once, assign tasks to others, and keep complex task lists organised.

Finally, try creating your own task list. The easiest way to do this is to click the **New** button, which displays a multi-tab dialogue box in which you type relevant information.

Journal

In Journal you can select to automatically record actions relating to specified contacts and to place the actions in a Timeline view. In addition to tracking Microsoft Outlook items, such as e-mail, or other Microsoft Office documents, such as Microsoft Word or Microsoft Excel files, you can keep a record of any interaction you want to remember, such as a telephone conversation or a letter you mailed or received.

Use Journal to record the dates and times of your interactions with contacts, such as tracking hours spent on a particular account. If you want to create a list of all the items related to a contact, use activity tracking, instead, to link the items to that contact.

To start Journal, click the **Journal** icon on the Outlook Options Bar, to display the screen in Fig. 2.23.

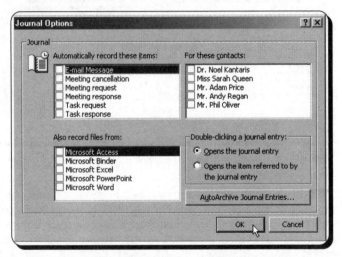

Fig. 2.23 The Journal Options Dialogue Box.

To find out how to use the various functions appearing on a Journal list, use the Office Help system and search for 'Journal'. Go through all the displayed help options in a similar manner to that for Tasks. Try it, you will learn a lot.

3

E-mail with Outlook 2002

In what follows, it is assumed that your computer is capable of being connected to the Internet, or a local area network (LAN), so that you can receive e-mail. A connection to the Internet is usually made via a modem and a telephone line, an ethernet card to a LAN which itself is connected to the Internet, or an ISDN direct line. The latter provides faster connection, at present, but is more expensive than the alternatives. Finally, you may also need to find, and possibly subscribe to, a suitable Internet Service Provider (ISP) which is a company that allows you to connect to its Internet host.

There are many such providers in the UK. Most can be found in an Internet based PC magazine, your telephone directory, or possibly in adverts in one of the many computer magazines. Be careful though before committing yourself to one provider as the quality of service and costs can vary considerably. One thing we can't do here is make specific recommendations, but try and find someone who uses the company you decide on, or have a trial period with them.

All ISPs offer an e-mail address and mailbox facility to their customers; a mailbox being a storage area which holds your incoming messages until you connect to your ISP and download them to your computer so that you can read them. As long as your computer can access the Internet, you can use e-mail to keep in touch with friends and colleagues, anywhere in the world, provided they have their own e-mail address. The whole procedure of connecting to your ISP, downloading e-mail, filtering unwanted junk e-mail, saving and managing e-mail and other information, such as addresses of Web sites, can be done very easily in Outlook's Inbox - we will step you through the procedure later.

The Inbox Toolbar

You must have noticed by now that, apart from the symbols that appear on the screen of the various Outlook 2002 options, the buttons on the Toolbar also change from one option to the other.

Below, we show the Inbox toolbar buttons, before Outlook 2002 is configured for sending and receiving e-mail, with an explanation of their function.

Icon	Function
New ▾	New Mail Message. Click the arrow to get ⇩
	Print
	Move to Folder
	Delete
Reply	Reply
Reply to All	Reply to All
Forward	Forward
Send/Receive	Send/Receive
Find	Find
	Organise
	Address Book
	Office Help

Fig. 3.1 The New Menu Options

Left-clicking an icon button can display a drop-down menu, (as shown in Fig. 3.1), action a command (such as displaying the Folder List), or open an appropriate dialogue box so that you can, for example, access the address book or search for items, such as folders or files.

Note that when you first open a drop-down menu similar to the one shown in Fig. 3.1, only the most frequently used options are visible. However, a few seconds later, or when you place the mouse pointer on the down-arrow appearing at the bottom of the menu, additional options are displayed. The latter are the less frequently used options, but once you select one, it joins the frequently used ones.

Configuring Outlook

If you are using a modem to connect to the Internet, you must check that Windows is configured correctly for this type of communication medium. Usually, after connecting your modem and starting your computer, Windows will auto-detect its presence using its Plug and Play capability.

Next, you need to check that the correct driver (a small program that allows your computer to communicate with the modem) has been selected. To do this, click the Windows **Start** button and select **Settings, Control Panel** from the

cascade menu. This displays various Control Panel options from which you should double-click the **Modems** icon, shown here, to start the relevant program.

If in the Modems Properties dialogue box, shown in Fig. 3.2, the name of your actual modem is not displayed, then click the **Add** button to start the Install New Modem Wizard. Next, click the **Don't detect my modem; I will select it from a list** box, and press the **Next** button. Windows then searches your system and displays all the installed modem drivers.

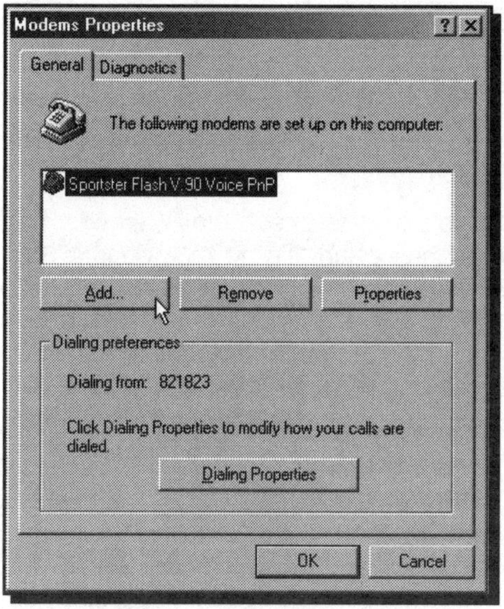

Fig. 3.2 The Modems Properties Dialogue Box.

If your modem's Manufacturer or Model does not appear on the displayed list, insert in your computer's appropriate drive the disc or CD that came with your modem and click the **Have Disk** button, as shown in Fig. 3.3.

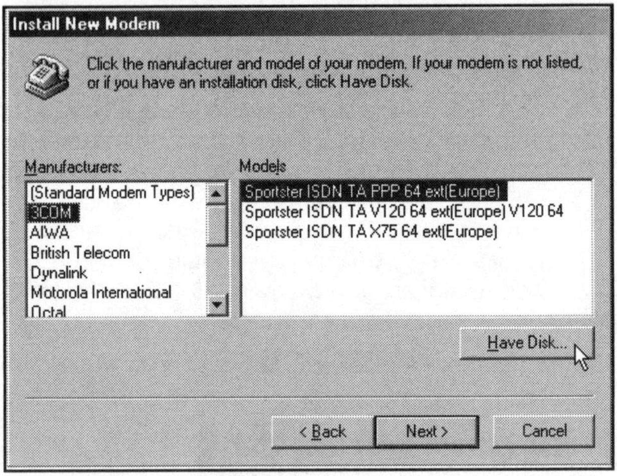

Fig. 3.3 The Install New Modem Dialogue Box.

Finally, select the displayed modem driver and press the **OK** button to finish the installation.

The next step to be taken is to check that Windows has the correct communications set-up. To do this, double click the **Network** icon in the Control Panel, shown here to the left, which opens the Network dialogue box shown in Fig. 3.4 on the next page. Make sure that all the displayed entries appear in that dialogue box (in our case these are under Windows Me - under different versions of Windows the list could be slightly different).

If you can see or suspect that some items are missing from the list, then double-click the **Add/Remove Programs** icon in the Control Panel, also shown here to the left, to open its Properties dialogue box. In that box, click the Windows Setup tab and check that all the components under **Communications** are installed, as shown in Fig. 3.5 on the next page.

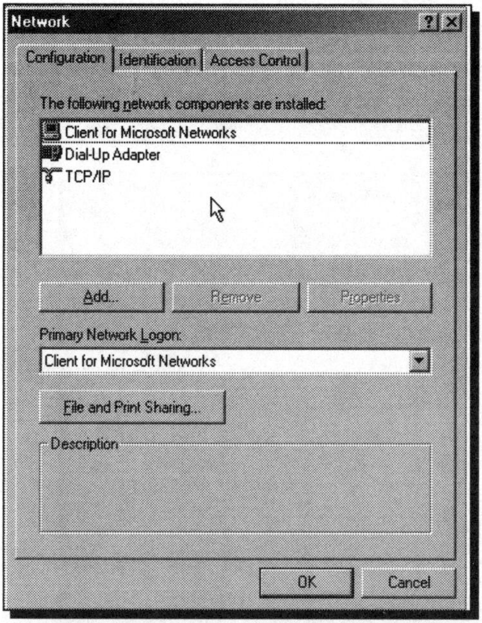

Network ? ×

Configuration | Identification | Access Control

The following network components are installed:

- Client for Microsoft Networks
- Dial-Up Adapter
- TCP/IP

[Add...] [Remove] [Properties]

Primary Network Logon:

Client for Microsoft Networks ▼

[File and Print Sharing...]

Description

[OK] [Cancel]

Fig. 3.4 The Network Dialogue Box.

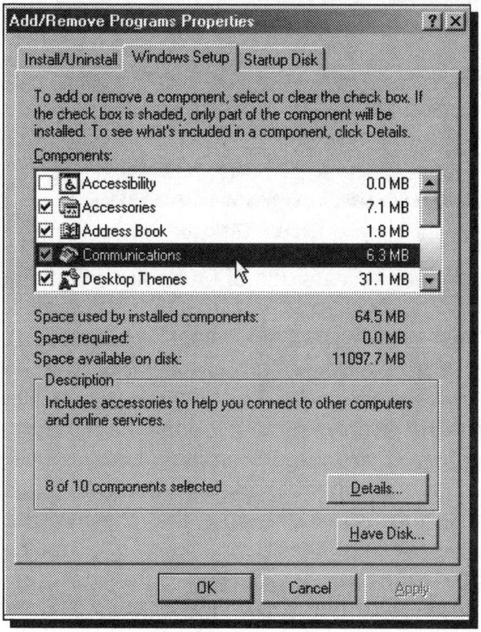

Add/Remove Programs Properties ? ×

Install/Uninstall Windows Setup Startup Disk

To add or remove a component, select or clear the check box. If the check box is shaded, only part of the component will be installed. To see what's included in a component, click Details.

Components:

☐ Accessibility	0.0 MB
☑ Accessories	7.1 MB
☑ Address Book	1.8 MB
☑ Communications	6.3 MB
☑ Desktop Themes	31.1 MB

Space used by installed components: 64.5 MB
Space required: 0.0 MB
Space available on disk: 11097.7 MB

Description

Includes accessories to help you connect to other computers and online services.

8 of 10 components selected [Details...]

[Have Disk...]

[OK] [Cancel] [Apply]

Fig. 3.5 The Add/ Remove Programs Properties Box.

E-mail Settings

To configure Outlook 2002 to send and receive e-mail, use the **Tools, Send/Receive Settings, Define Send/Receive Groups** command to open the dialogue box in Fig. 3.6.

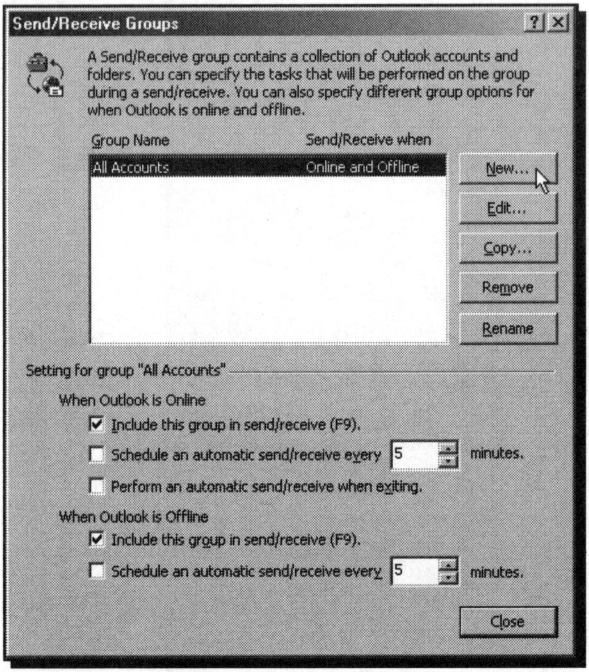

Fig. 3.6 The Send/Receive Groups Dialogue Box.

If you have been using earlier versions of Outlook or Outlook Express, the program copies across your existing connection settings, but you must specify that you want to be able to receive your e-mail within a given group, whether the All Accounts group or a new one. For the first case click the **Edit** button, while for the second case click the **New** button and supply a Group Name (we used 'Family Group'). Either of these moves opens the appropriate Send/Receive Settings dialogue box shown in Fig. 3.7. Make sure that the **Include account in this send/receive group** is ticked (it is not by default), then click the **Account Properties** button to open the Internet E-mail Settings screen shown in Fig. 3.8.

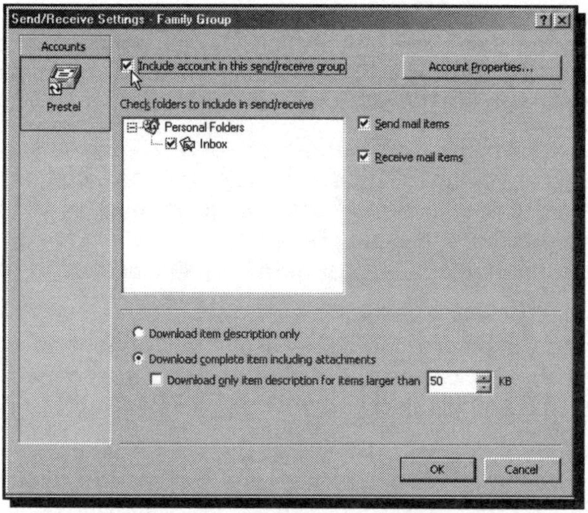

Fig. 3.7 The Send/Receive Settings Dialogue Box.

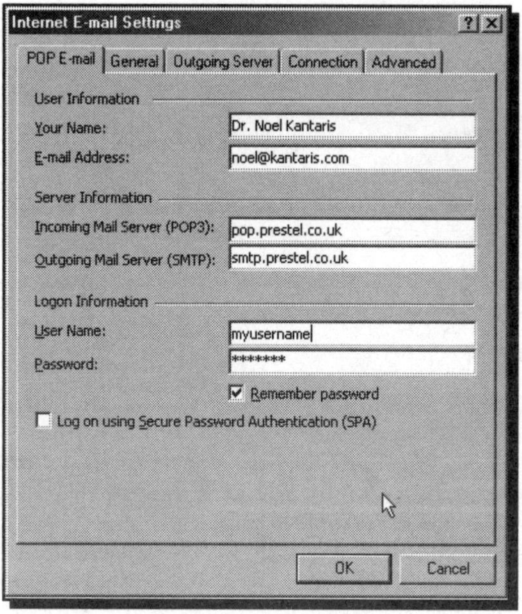

Fig. 3.8 The Internet E-mail Settings Dialogue Box.

If you have been connected to the Internet previously and have been using the e-mail facility, your details (similar to those in Fig. 3.8) will have been transferred automatically, otherwise you will have to type them in. You must provide:

(a) Your name. (b) Your e-mail address - this is supplied to you by your ISP when you join their services. (c) The name of the 'Incoming' and 'Outgoing' mail server - this information is also supplied to you by your ISP. (d) Your 'account name' and 'password' - again supplied to you by your ISP.

In the Connection tab sheet, click the **Connect using my phone line** radio button (if that is how you are connected to the Internet), and select your ISP for your Dial-Up Networking connection.

You are now in a position to send and receive e-mail, but before we do so, we need to add to the configuration so that each e-mail you send shows your signature. To do this, use the **Tools, Options** command, press the Mail Format tab of the displayed dialogue box, and click the **Signatures** button at the bottom of the Options dialogue box. This displays the Create Signature dialogue box shown (partially obscured) in

Fig. 3.9. Clicking the **New** button displays the Create New Signature Box. Give your signature a name, such as 'Signature 1', then press the **Next** button to open the Edit Signature dialogue box shown in Fig. 3.10 in which you can type what you want to appear at the bottom of each e-mail you send.

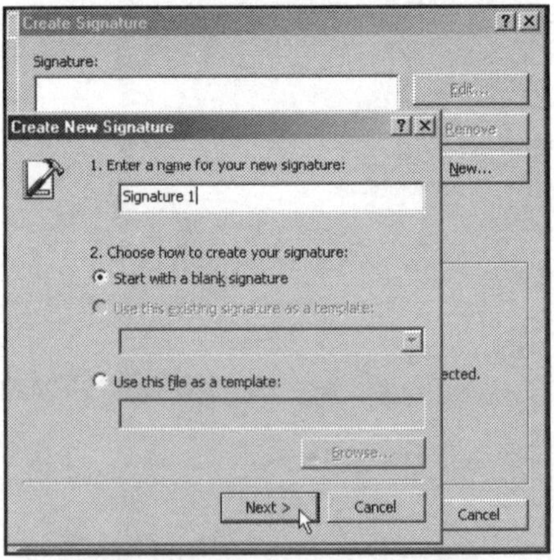

Fig. 3.9 The Create New Signature Box.

This information for one of us is as shown on the next page.

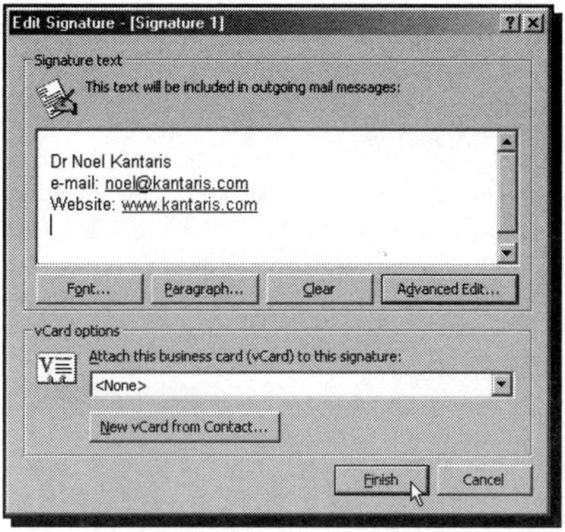

Fig. 3.10 Creating an E-mail Signature.

It is only polite to supply your name and e-mail address at the bottom of each electronic mail. In addition, you could create another signature which could include your telephone number and/or your full address. In fact, you could create several signatures, each one with different content to be used depending on whether your e-mail is casual, formal, or professional, and switch between them as required.

Sending and Receiving E-mail

Clicking the **Inbox** icon opens a screen which will probably contain one or more messages from Microsoft. It is worthwhile reading these, as they can demonstrate some of the features of Outlook and show you how decorative your e-mail can be.

If the displayed screen has only one pane, use the **View**, **Preview Pane** menu command to toggle on the preview pane so that the Inbox screen displays in two panes with the message titles appearing on the top pane. Clicking on a message highlights it and opens a Preview of it on the lower pane. Double-clicking on a message title opens the message in its own window.

In Fig. 3.11, we show an empty Inbox screen with the Preview pane toggled on.

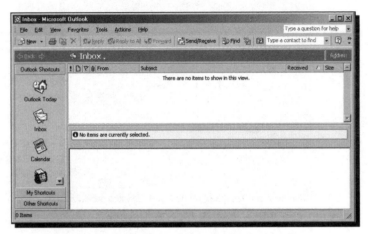

Fig. 3.11 The Outlook Inbox Screen with Preview Pane.

To check your mail, click the **Send/Receive** toolbar button which will download any new messages from your mailbox to your hard disc. You can then read and process your mail at your leisure without necessarily being still connected to the Internet.

The best way to test out new e-mail features is to send a test message to your own e-mail address. This saves wasting somebody else's time, and the message can be very quickly checked to see the results.

So, to start, click the **New** button to open the New Message dialogue box in which we compose a short message, as shown in Fig. 3.12.

Note the address in the **To...** box is shown underlined. This was automatically done by Outlook after we typed in the text string and moved to the **Subject:** box, because 'my-address' was associated with an e-mail address in the Address Book and Outlook picked it up. We could, of course, have typed the full e-mail address in the **To...** box, but the above method is a much easier and neater way.

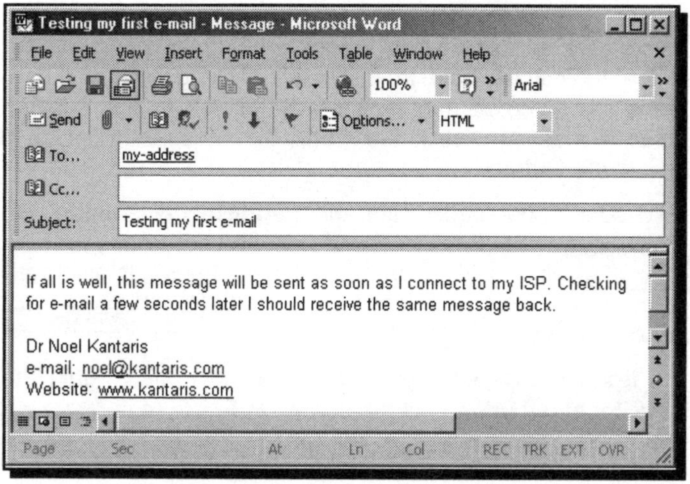

Fig. 3.12 Testing the E-mail System.

Each e-mail should have a short subject which is what will appear on the upper Inbox panel when the message is received by the recipient. The **Cc...** box is where you include the address of additional persons that you would like to receive a copy of the same message. To send the message, simply press the **Send** button which causes the New Message box to close down. What has happened here is that the message has been placed in Outlook's Outbox, waiting for you to perhaps compose another e-mail.

To see that your message is waiting in the Outbox, click the **Inbox** button, pointed to in Fig. 3.13, which opens up a list of folders. As you can see, the Outbox folder is marked with one (1) item.

Fig. 3.13 The Outlook List of Folders.

Should you want to edit a message in the Outbox, double-click its folder which opens an Outbox window listing all the messages held in it. Double-clicking one of these, opens the selected message ready for you to edit. Having edited a message, click the **Send** button again to place it back in the Outbox.

To send a message, click the **Send/Receive** button and follow the connection procedure to your ISP. Verification of what is happening is displayed at the bottom right corner of Outlook's screen.

A few seconds later (sometimes longer), click again the **Sent/Receive** button until the screen in Fig. 3.14 is revealed. This is the very message we sent a few seconds earlier which came back to us at the speed of light, well almost!

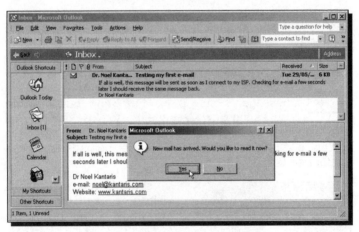

Fig. 3.14 An Incoming E-mail Message.

As you can see, the first few lines of the received message are displayed in the message titles pane, and the full message is displayed in the preview pane. Further, Microsoft Outlook asks you in an information box whether you would like to read the new message. If you click **Yes**, the received message opens in its own window. A bit of an overkill you might think!

Having previewed your messages, the Inbox screen changes slightly - It now lists your received message titles only, without any accompanying text, as shown in Fig. 3.15.

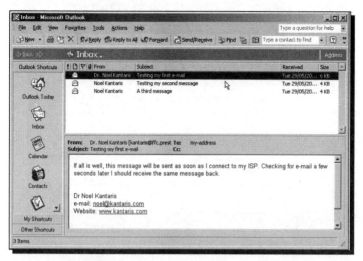

Fig. 3.15 List of Received E-mail Messages in Inbox.

Highlighting a message displays its contents on the lower pane of the Inbox screen, while double-clicking it, opens the message in its own window. Looking at messages without opening them, can be used to transfer them to preselected folders, using the **Move to Folder** toolbar button; you could, for example, have a folder for each of the most important persons in your private or business life, thus keeping their messages together.

If you have received a message that you don't want to keep, then highlight it and press the **Delete** toolbar button. Deleted items are held in a folder,

in case you want to resurrect them. To empty this folder, click the **Deleted Items** button on the Outlook Shortcuts menu bar to reveal all the items held in this folder. To permanently delete an item, left-click it to select it, then either press the **Delete** button or the **Del** keyboard key. You will be asked to confirm deletion before the action is carried out.

Formatting your E-mail

Apart from sending messages in HTML (the default Hyper Text Markup Language used to format most documents on the Web), Outlook 2002 allows you to format your e-mail in Rich Text, or Plain Text. To select one of these, use the **Tools**, **Options** command to open the dialogue box in Fig. 3.16.

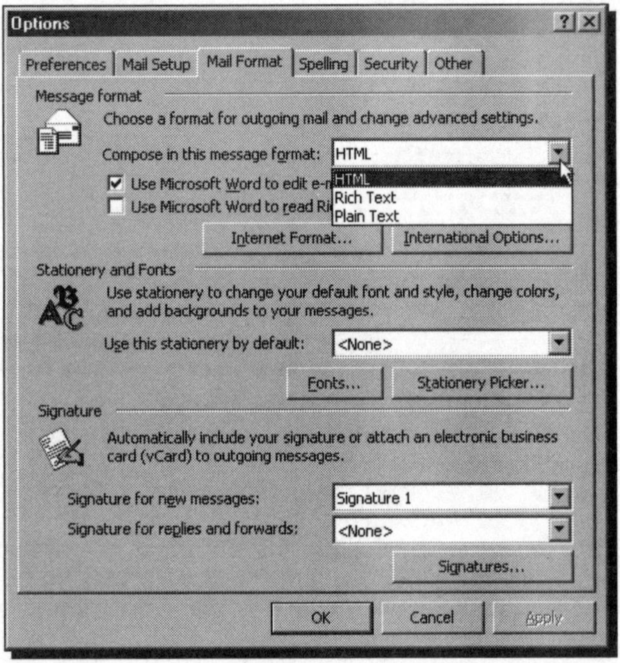

Fig. 3.16 The Mail Format Tab Screen of the Options Dialogue Box.

You can also select in the above dialogue box whether to use Microsoft Word as your default e-mail editor. Any of the above mentioned formats can be used with either Outlook or Word as your e-mail editor. Furthermore, you can use the **Actions**, **New Mail Message Using** command to create a single message in a format, or e-mail editor, other than the defaults that you have selected by choosing the message format or e-mail editor from the displayed menu shown in Fig. 3.17.

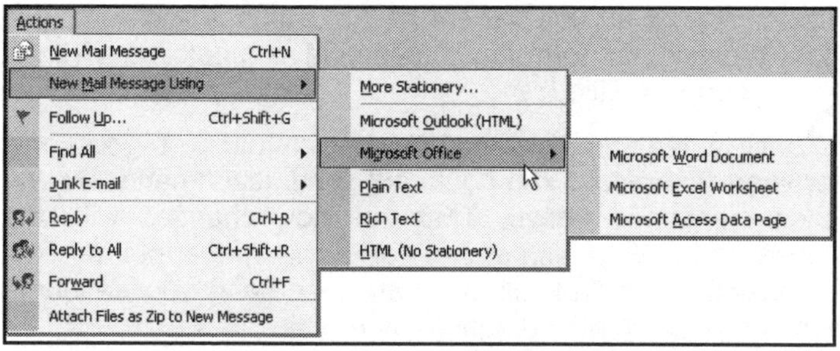

Fig. 3.17 The Actions, New Mail Message Using Cascade Menu.

However, remember that not everyone will be able to read the work you spent ages creating! There are still some people out there who use e-mail programs that are only capable of receiving plain text. So, it might be safer to avoid excessive text enhancements. The same can be said for Outlook's pre-formatted stationery under the HTML option.

Using E-mail Attachments

Sometimes, when you receive an e-mail with Outlook 2002, you might find at the bottom of the main text area, a file displayed, as shown in Fig. 3.18.

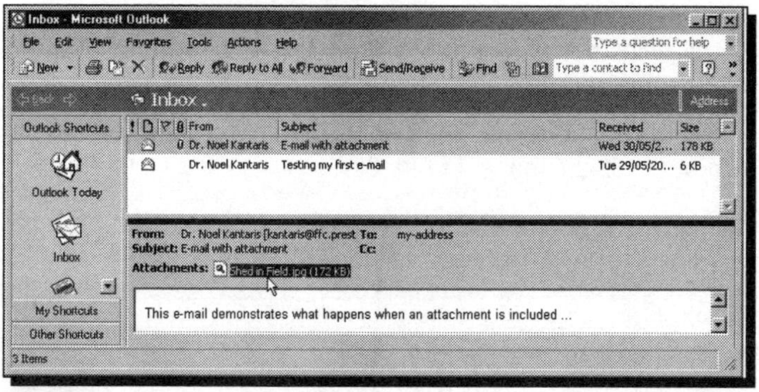

Fig. 3.18 The Display of an Attachment Received with an E-mail.

This indicates an attachment to the e-mail which can be a drawing, another formatted document, a photo, or even a sound and video file.

Until fairly recently, e-mail on the Internet was good only for short text notes. You could not send attachments like the ones mentioned above. That has now changed with the advent of MIME, which stands for Multipurpose Internet Mail Extension. With Outlook you can even send your favourite Web page as an attachment to an e-mail.

To view or save an attachment file, right-click its icon and choose to **Open**, or **Save As** from the drop-down menu. You can also view the attachment by double-clicking its icon.

Adding Attachments to your E-mail

If you want to include an attachment to your main e-mail message, you simply click the **Insert File** toolbar button

shown here, and select the file to attach. This opens the Insert File dialogue box, for you to select the file, or files, you want to go with your message.

Before you start sending attachments with your e-mail, make sure that the person you are sending your message to has e-mail software capable of decoding them. In our experience some people seem to stick to their tried and trusted 'old' software that does not. If that is the case, only include one attachment per e-mail and mention in the text area of your e-mail what software you used to create the attachment; it will help the recipient to decipher it.

In Outlook 2002 the attached files are 'placed' below the **Subject** box, as shown in Fig. 3.19.

⊟ Send	𝕌 ▾	᠍ ᠍ ✓	! ↓ ▼	᠍ Options... ▾	HTML ▾
᠍ To...	my-address
᠍ Cc...	
Subject:	Sending E-mail Attachments
Attach...	᠍ Shed in Field.jpg (172 KB); ᠍ Smokey Light.jpg (143 KB)

Fig. 3.19 Two Attachments Selected for Transmission.

Viewing and Sending Web Pages

You can use the Outlook Today option to view Web pages by clicking sites listed under the **Favorites** menu command, or create shortcuts to Web pages that you visit frequently and add them to the list.

Even more interesting is the ease with which you can send a Web page as an e-mail. We will demonstrate the process by left-clicking one entry from our **Favorites** list which connects us to the Internet and displays the relevant Web page, as shown in Fig. 3.20.

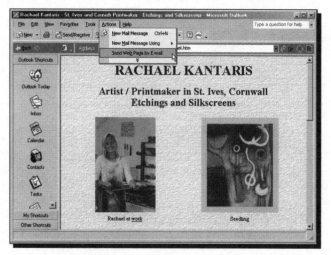

Fig. 3.20 Attaching a Web Page to an E-mail.

Next, click the **Actions** menu command and select the **Send Web Page by E-Mail** option from the drop-down menu, as shown in Fig. 3.20. This opens a New Mail Message screen for you to type the recipient's address and e-mail subject. In

the main body of the e-mail, Outlook automatically includes the **Attachment** icon shown to the left, below which you can add your text.

To preview such a file, double-click this attachment link.

Spell Checking

Some people do not seem to read their e-mail before clicking the **Send** button. With Outlook this could be avoided, as the program is linked to the spell checker that comes with Microsoft's Office. To try it out, prepare a message in the New Message window, but make an obvious spelling mistake, maybe like ours below. Pressing the **F7** function key, or using the **Tools**, **Spelling and Grammar** command, will start the process.

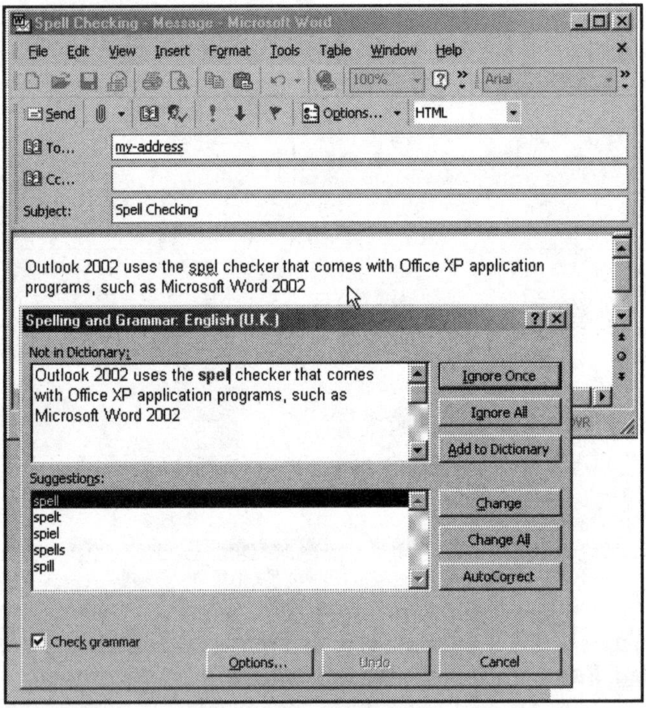

Fig. 3.21 Spell Checking an E-mail.

Any words not recognised by the spell checker will be flagged up as above. If you are happy with the word just click one of the **Ignore** buttons, if not, you can type a correction at the insertion point, or accept one of the **Suggestions**, and then click the **Change** button.

Selecting Options Settings

Now that we have finished experimenting with sending and receiving e-mail, it is a good idea to make some permanent changes to Outlook's settings. Use the **Tools, Options** command to open the Options dialogue box.

We suggest you make the following options selections:

- Click the Spelling tab and select the **Always check spelling before sending** option, so that every message you write is checked before it is sent.

- Click the Mail Setup tab and perhaps select **Hang up when finished sending, receiving, or updating** option, so that you don't forget to disconnect your phone.

- Click the Preferences tab and click the **E-mail Options** button. In the **When replying to a message** box you can select to include or not include the original message with your reply. If you choose to include it, make sure you edit it first - it is pointless making your reply longer by including the whole of the original message. If, on the other hand, you choose not to include it, make sure you refer to the points made in it; don't just answer 'yes' or 'no'.

- Click the Other tab and check the **Empty the Deleted Items folder upon exiting** box.

Obviously there are a lot more selections you could make, but we leave these to you. Very soon, after you have been using Outlook 2002 for a while, you will know yourself what options and preferences to choose.

Web Mail Access

If you have a Web-based e-mail client, such as Hotmail, you can now use Outlook 2002 to send and receive e-mail messages with the click of a button. This has become possible because Outlook now supports the HTTP proxy.

In what follows, we will step through the procedure of creating a Hotmail account in Outlook. However, before we start you must either be an existing Hotmail user or register your personal account at www.hotmail.com. Next, use the **Tools, E-mail Accounts** command and in the displayed dialogue box click the **Add a new e-mail account** radio button, as shown in Fig. 3.22, and click **Next**.

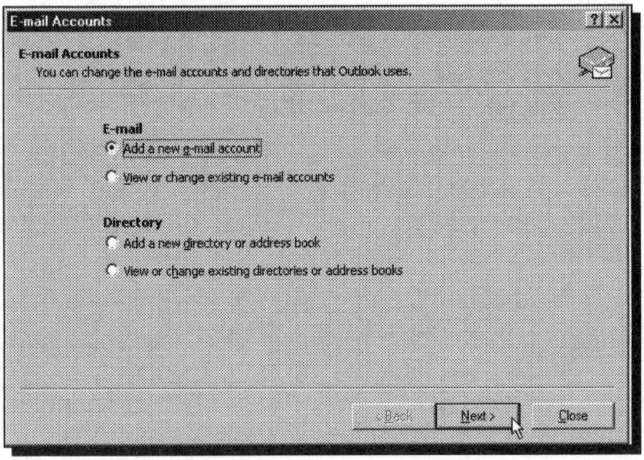

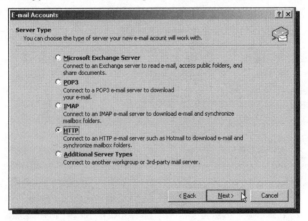

Fig. 3.22 Creating a New E-mail Account in Outlook.

In the second E-mail Accounts dialogue box select the **HTTP** Server Type, as shown in Fig. 3.23, and click **Next**.

Fig. 3.23 Selecting the Server Type for the New E-mail Account.

In the third dialogue box, enter your Hotmail account details, as shown in Fig. 3.24. Pressing the **Next** button causes Outlook to connect to the Internet, create a separate folder in the Folder List and display a **Hotmail - Inbox** button on the Outlook Shortcuts bar, as shown in Fig. 3.25, so that you can easily switch between your regular mail and Hotmail.

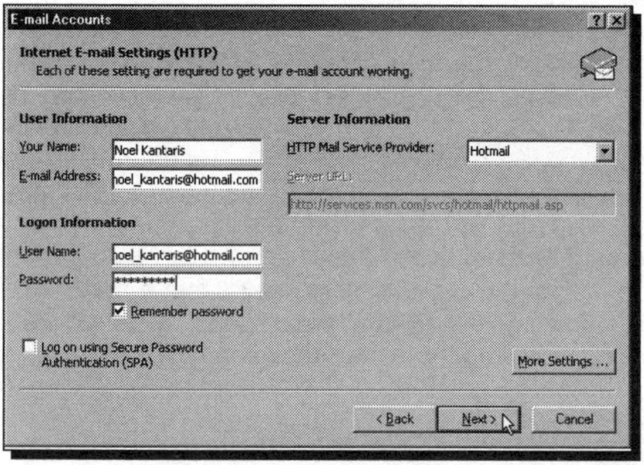

Fig. 3.24 Entering your Hotmail Account Details.

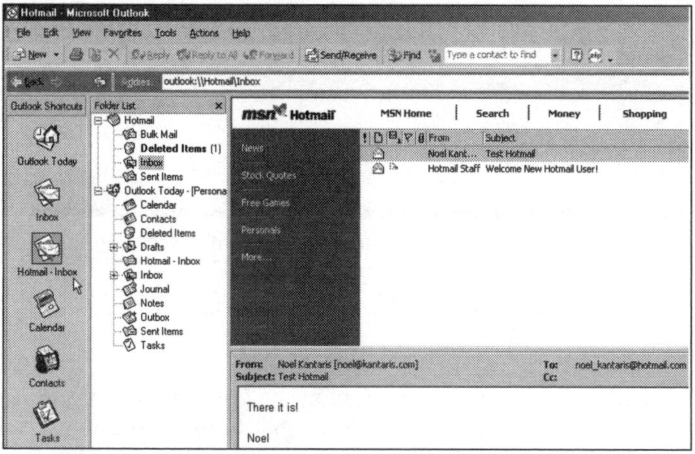

Fig. 3.25 Connecting to your Hotmail Account from Outlook.

Security Measures

Microsoft has implemented some welcomed security measures in Outlook 2002. It is now impossible to view or

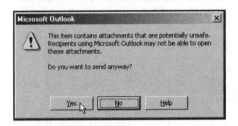

open attachment files with extensions such as **.exe** (executable), **.bat** (batch), **.vbs** (visual Basic script), or **.js** (Java script). If you attempt to send such attachments, Outlook will warn you, as shown here, that the recipient may not be able to open them, depending on the e-mail program they are using. If you do send yourself a test e-mail with, say, a **.bat** attachment, as we have done, you will receive something similar to the e-mail shown in Fig. 3.26.

Fig. 3.26 Receiving an E-mail with Blocked Attachment.

* * *

Outlook has many more features, far too numerous to discuss in the space allocated in this book. What we have tried to do, is give you enough basic information so that you can have the confidence to explore the rest of Outlook's capabilities by yourself. Have fun!

4

Microsoft Word 2002 Basics

Microsoft's Word 2002 is part of the Office XP package and is without doubt the best Windows word processor so far. As you would expect, it is fully integrated with all the other Office XP applications. This version of Word, like its predecessors, has particularly strong leanings towards desk top publishing which offers fully editable WYSIWYG (what you see is what you get) modes that can be viewed in various zoom levels. Couple this with the ability to include and manipulate full colour graphics and to easily create Web pages and you can see the enormous power of the program. You will find using Word 2002 to be even more intuitive and easy than earlier versions and you will soon be producing the type of word processed output you would not have dreamt possible.

In many situations Word 2002 will attempt to anticipate what you want to do and will probably produce the correct result most of the time. For example, AutoCorrect and AutoFormat can, when active, correct common spelling mistakes and format documents automatically. Other Wizards can help you with everyday tasks and/or make complex tasks easier to manage.

Word uses Object Linking and Embedding (OLE) to move and share information seamlessly between Office XP applications. For example, you can drag information from one application to another, or you can link information from one application into another. Similarly, Hyperlinks can be used from any of the Office XP applications to access other Office documents, files on an internal or external Web or FTP (File Transfer Protocol) site, or HTML (Hypertext Markup Language) files. Hyperlinks help you use your documents with the Internet.

Finally, writing macros in Visual Basic gives you a powerful development platform with which to create custom solutions.

Starting the Word Program

Word is started in Windows either by clicking the **Start** button then selecting **Programs** and clicking on the **Microsoft Word** icon on the cascade menu, clicking the **Word** button, or the **Open Office Document** button on the Office Shortcut Bar, or by double-clicking on a Word document file. In the latter case the document will be loaded into Word at the same time.

When you start Word 2002 the program momentarily displays its opening screen, shown in Fig. 4.1, and then displays the first page of a new document (more about this shortly).

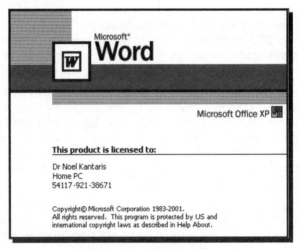

Fig. 4.1 Word's Opening Screen.

Whether you have used a previous version of Word or not, the first time you use the program, it might be a good idea to click the **Microsoft Word Help** button, shown here, and click the *What's new* link in the right pane of the Help screen.

This displays the Help screen shown in Fig. 4.2. Start by looking at the 'Key new features in Microsoft Word' option, from which you can find out differences between this version of Word and previous versions of the program. As you click each hypertext link, Word displays several topics on the subject. After looking at these options, have a look at the other options displayed in the Help screen. We suggest you spend a little time here browsing through the various topics before going on.

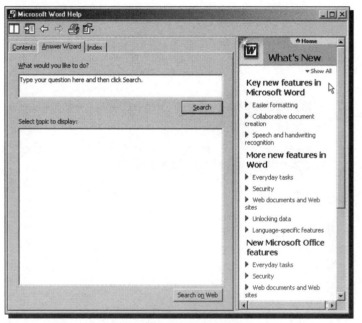

Fig. 4.2 The Microsoft Word Help Screen.

For additional Help topics, click the Contents tab of the above screen, then double-click the displayed Microsoft Word Help book to open a list of books covering various topics.

The Word Screen

The opening 'blank' screen of Word 2002 is shown below. It is perhaps worth spending some time looking at the various parts that make up this screen. Word follows the usual Microsoft Windows conventions and if you are familiar with these you can skip some of this section, but even so, a few minutes might be well spent here.

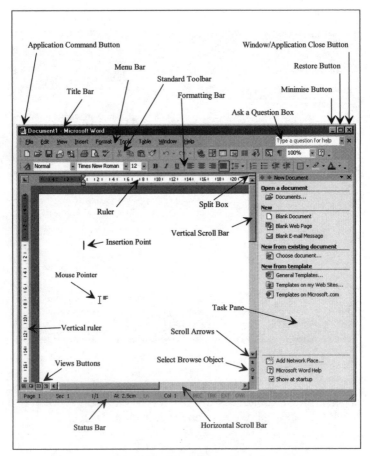

Fig. 4.3 The Word Screen Layout.

The layout as shown is in a window, but if you click on the application restore button, you can make Word take up the full screen area available. Using a window can be useful when you are running several applications at the same time and you want to transfer between them with the mouse.

Note that in this case, the Word window displays an empty document with the title 'Document1', and has a solid 'Title bar', indicating that it is the active application window. Although multiple windows can be displayed simultaneously, you can only enter data into the active window (which will always be displayed on top, unless you view them on a split screen). Title bars of non-active windows appear a lighter shade than that of the active one.

The Word screen is divided into several areas which have the following functions:

Area	*Function*
Command buttons	Clicking on the command button, (see upper-left corner of the Word window), displays a pull-down menu which can be used to control the program window. It allows you to restore, move, size, minimise, maximise, and close the window.
Title Bar	The bar at the top of a window which displays the application name and the name of the current document.
Minimise Button	When clicked on, this button minimises Word to an icon on the Windows Taskbar.
Restore Button	When clicked on, this button restores the active window to the position and size that was occupied before

it was maximised. The restore button is then replaced by a Maximise button, as shown here, which is used to set the window to full screen size.

Close button

The extreme top right button that you click to close a window.

Menu Bar

The bar below the Title bar which allows you to choose from several menu options. Clicking on a menu item displays the pull-down menu associated with that item.

Ask a Question Box

The text box at the far right of the menu bar. You can type in a help query and press the Return key to get a listing of matching topics.

Standard Toolbar

The bar below the Menu bar which contains buttons that give you mouse click access to the functions most often used in the program.

Formatting Bar

The buttons on the Formatting Bar allow you to change the attributes of a font, such as italic and underline, and also to format text in various ways. The Formatting Bar contains three boxes; a style box, a font box and a size box to give instant access to all the installed styles, fonts and character sizes.

Rulers

The horizontal and vertical bars where you can see and set page margins, tabulation points and indents.

Split Box	The area above the top vertical scroll button which when dragged allows you to split the screen.
Task Pane	A new pane which presents formatting options and other relevant controls on the right-hand side of the Word screen. It has its own button bar for instant control.
Scroll Bars	The areas on the screen that contain scroll boxes in vertical and horizontal bars. Clicking on these bars allows you to control the part of a document which is visible on the screen.
Scroll Arrows	The arrowheads at each end of each scroll bar which you can click to scroll the screen up and down one line, or left and right 10% of the screen, at a time.
Insertion pointer	The pointer used to indicate where text will be inserted.
Views Buttons	Clicking these buttons changes screen views quickly.
Status Bar	The bottom line of the document window that displays status information.

The Toolbars

There are nineteen different toolbars available in Word 2002. To see the full list you can use the **View**, **Toolbars** menu command, or more easily, right-click in the toolbar area. In this list active bars are shown with a blue tick to their left. Clicking on a list entry will toggle that toolbar on or off. By default, only two bars are active, the Standard and the Formatting toolbars.

When Word is first opened these two bars will probably be placed alongside each other, which means that not all the buttons will be visible. To see the other available buttons click the toolbar options button ⁞ at the right end of each bar, as shown in Fig. 4.4.

Clicking any of the buttons now displayed will action that function. For our screen layout of Fig. 4.3 we have clicked the **Show Buttons on Two Rows** option. We find it easier to work with both toolbars almost fully open. You might feel differently.

To 'complicate' matters further, Word automatically customises both toolbars and menus, based on how often you use their commands. As you work, they adjust so that only the buttons and commands you use most often are shown. Thus your screen may not display the same features as ours.

Fig. 4.4 Toolbar Options.

The Standard Toolbar

As we show it, this is located below the Menu bar at the top of the Word screen and contains command buttons. As you move the mouse pointer over a button it changes to an 'active' blue colour and a banner opens to indicate the button's function. Left-clicking the button will then action that function or command.

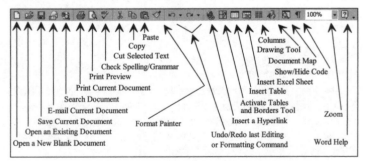

Fig. 4.5 Standard Toolbar Functions.

The Formatting Bar

This is located to the right of, or below, the Standard Toolbar, and is divided into sections that contain command buttons, as shown in Fig. 4.6 below.

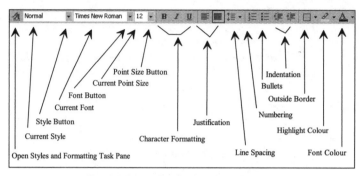

Fig. 4.6 Formatting Toolbar Functions.

The first option displays the name of the current style (Normal) in a box. Clicking the down-arrow against this box, opens up a menu of default paragraph styles with their font sizes. The Current font box shows the current typeface. Clicking on the down-arrow button to the right of it allows you to change the typeface of any selected text. The Current point size box shows the size of selected characters which can be changed by clicking on the down-arrow button next to it and selecting another size from the displayed list.

Next, are three character formatting buttons which allow you to enhance selected text by emboldening, italicising, or underlining it. The next buttons allow you to change the justification of a selected paragraph, control the Line spacing and set the different types of Numbering and Indentation options. The last three buttons allow you to add an Outside Border to selected text or objects, and change the highlight and font colour of selected text.

The Status Bar

This is located at the bottom of the Word window and is used to display statistics about the active document.

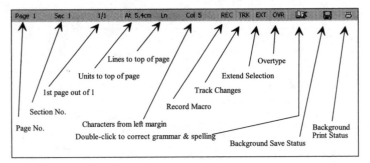

Fig. 4.7 The Word Status Bar.

For example, when a document is being opened, the Status bar displays for a short time its name and length in terms of total number of characters. Once a document is opened, the Status bar displays the statistics of the document at the insertion point; here it is on Page 1, Section 1, and 5 characters from the left margin.

Double-clicking the left of the status bar displays the Find and Replace dialogue box, as shown in Fig. 4.8. This is shown with the **Go To** tab selected. You can choose which page, section line, etc., of the document to go to, or you can use the other tabs to **Find** and **Replace** text (more about this later). Double-clicking the other features on the Status bar will also activate their features.

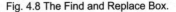

Fig. 4.8 The Find and Replace Box.

The Menu Bar Options

Each menu bar option has associated with it a pull-down sub-menu. To activate the menu, either press the <Alt> key, which causes the first option of the menu (in this case the **File** menu option) to be selected, then use the right and left arrow keys to highlight any of the options in the menu, or use the mouse to point to an option. Pressing either the <Enter> key, or the left mouse button, reveals the pull-down sub-menu of the highlighted menu option. The sub-menu of the **File** option is shown below.

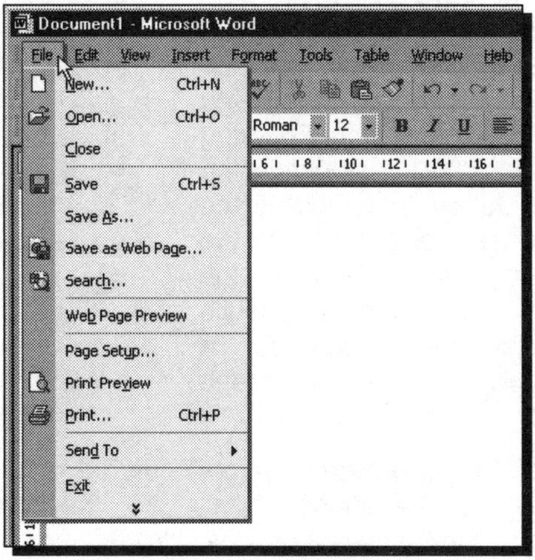

Fig. 4.9 The File Sub Menu.

Note that as in the previous version of Word, the drop-down sub-menu displays only the most important options, but you have the option to view the full sub-menu by highlighting the double arrowheads at the bottom of it, by either pointing to that part of the sub-menu with the mouse or using the down-arrow cursor key to move the highlighted bar down.

The full sub-menu of the **File** menu option is displayed here in Fig. 4.10 on the next page. However, the order of your sub-menu options in both the short and the full version of the sub-menu could differ from ours. This is because

Word learns from your actions and automatically promotes the items you choose from menu extensions on to the shortened version of the sub-menu.

Menu options can also be activated directly by pressing the <Alt> key followed by the underlined letter of the required option. Thus, pressing <Alt+F>, opens the pull-down **File** sub-menu. You can use the up and down arrow keys to move the highlighted bar up and down a sub-menu, or the right and left arrow keys to move along the options in the menu bar. Pressing the <Enter> key selects the highlighted option or executes the highlighted command. Pressing the <Esc> key once, closes the pull-down sub-menu, while pressing the <Esc> key for a second time, closes the menu system.

Fig. 4.10 The Full File Sub Menu.

Some of the sub-menu options can be accessed with 'quick key' combinations from the keyboard. Such combinations are shown on the drop-down menus, for example, <Ctrl+S> is the quick key for the **Save** option in the **File** sub-menu. If a sub-menu option is not available at any time, it will display in a grey colour. Some menu options only appear in Word when that tool is being used.

To get more details about any of the above menu options, simply highlight the option and use the <Shift+F1> key combination. This opens a pop-up box like that shown here for the **Tools**, **Options** menu.

Options (Tools menu)

Modifies settings for Microsoft Office programs such as screen appearance, printing, editing, spelling, and other options.

Shortcut Menus

Context-sensitive shortcut menus are now one of Windows' most useful features. If you click the right mouse button on any screen feature, or document, a shortcut menu is displayed with the most frequently used commands relating to the type of work you were doing at the time. In this version of Word, Microsoft have also combined 'smart tags' as part of the shortcut menu system. These automatically link related features or data to the situation involved.

The composite screen dump in Fig. 4.11 below shows in turn the shortcut menus that open when selected text, or the Toolbar area is right-clicked. In the first shortcut menu the **Cut** and **Copy** commands only become effective if you have text selected.

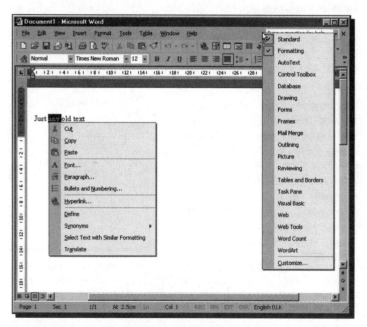

Fig. 4.11 Example Shortcut Menus.

So, whatever you are doing in Word, you have rapid access to a menu of relevant functions by right-clicking your mouse.

Left-clicking the mouse on an open menu selection will choose that function, while clicking on an area outside the shortcut menu (or pressing the <Esc> key), closes down the shortcut menu. If you are wondering about the smart tags we mentioned, don't worry we will get round to them a little later on.

Task Panes

Some of the common tasks in Word 2002 can now be carried out in new Task Panes that display on the right side of your document. You can quickly create new documents or open files using the Task Pane that appears when you first start the program. The **Search**
Task Pane gives you easy access to Word's file search facilities, or you can visually pick from a gallery of items in the Office **Clipboard** Task Pane.

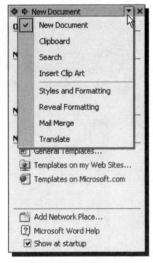

Fig. 4.12 shows the **New Document** Task Pane with its control buttons on top. The left and right arrows let you quickly move between the Task Panes you have open, the down arrow opens a drop-down list of the available tasks, as shown here. The **x** button lets you close the pane. To reopen it you use the **View**, **Task Pane** menu command.

Fig. 4.12 The Task Pane List.

We must admit to having reservations about this new feature of Office XP, but once you get used to the panes, they 'become less of a pain' and at times can make some of Word's features much easier and quicker to access. Each type of pane will be discussed in more detail as they are encountered throughout the book.

5

Creating Word Documents

When the program is first used, all Word's features default to those shown in Fig. 4.3. It is quite possible to use Word in this mode, without changing any main settings, but obviously it is possible to customise the package to your needs, as we shall see later.

Entering Text

In order to illustrate some of Word's capabilities, you need to have a short text at hand. We suggest you type the memo below into a new document. At this stage, don't worry if the length of the lines below differ from those on your display.

As you type in text, any time you want to force a new line, or paragraph, just press <Enter>. While typing within a paragraph, Word sorts out line lengths automatically (known as 'word wrap'), without you having to press any keys to move to a new line.

MEMO TO PC USERS
Networked Computers
The microcomputers in the Data Processing room are a mixture of IBM compatible PCs with Pentium processors running at various speeds. They all have 3.5" floppy drives of 1.44MB capacity, and most also have CD-ROM drives. The PCs are connected to various printers via a network; the Laser printers available giving best output.

The computer you are using will have at least a 10.0GB capacity hard disc on which a number of software programs, including the latest version of Windows, have been installed. To make life easier, the hard disc is highly structured with each program installed in a separate folder.

Moving Around a Document

You can move the cursor around a document with the normal direction keys, and with the key combinations listed below.

To move	*Press*
Left one character	←
Right one character	→
Up one line	↑
Down one line	↓
Left one word	Ctrl+←
Right one word	Ctrl+→
To beginning of line	Home
To end of line	End
To paragraph beginning	Ctrl+↑
To paragraph end	Ctrl+↓
Up one screen	PgUp
Down one screen	PgDn
To top of previous page	Ctrl+PgUp
To top of next page	Ctrl+PgDn
To beginning of file	Ctrl+Home
To end of file	Ctrl+End

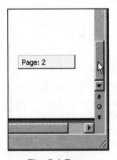

Fig. 5.1 Page
Change Controls.

To move to a specified page number in a multi-page document, either drag the vertical scroll bar up or down until the required page number is shown, as in Fig. 5.1, or use the **Edit**, **Go To** command (or <Ctrl+G>), as described on page 80.

To easily step from page to page you can also click the **Previous Page** ▓ and **Next Page** ▓ buttons, shown in Fig. 5.1.

Obviously, you need to become familiar with these methods of moving the cursor around a document, particularly if you spot an error in a document which needs to be corrected, which is the subject of the latter half of this chapter.

Templates and Paragraph Styles

As we saw under the Formatting Bar section earlier, when you start Word for the first time, the Style box contains the word **Normal**. This means that all the text you have entered, at the moment, is shown in the Normal paragraph style which is one of the styles available in the NORMAL template. Every document produced by Word has to use a template, and NORMAL is the default. A template contains both the document page settings and a set of formatting instructions which can be applied to text.

Changing Paragraph Styles

To change the style of a paragraph, first open the **Styles and Formatting** Task Pane by clicking its toolbar button, as shown here. Place the cursor in the paragraph in question, say the title line and select the **Heading 1** style from the **Pick formatting to apply** list in the Task Pane. The selected paragraph reformats instantly in bold, and in Arial typeface of point size 16.

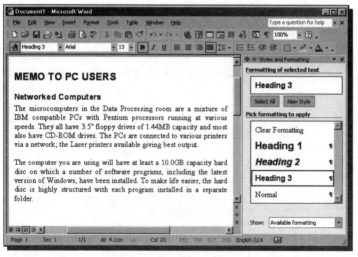

Fig. 5.2 Using the Styles and Formatting Task Pane.

Now with the cursor in the second line of text, select **Heading 3** which reformats the line in Arial 13. Your memo should now look presentable, and be similar to Fig. 5.2 on the previous page.

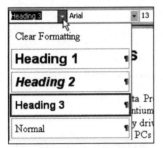

Fig. 5.3 Using the Style Box.

The other way of setting these styles is from the Style box on the Word Formatting toolbar, as shown here in Fig. 5.3. This was the usual way in the previous version of Word, which did not have Task Panes.

If you try both methods you will find that in the long run the Task Pane method is better. As we shall see later, you can carry out most, if not all, of your style format work from the Task Pane without having to resort to dialogue boxes. Microsoft have included Task Panes to make the features of Word more accessible, and this is a good example.

Document Screen Displays

Fig. 5.4 View Menu.

Word provides four display views, **Normal**, **Web Layout**, **Print Layout**, and **Outline**, as well as the options to view your documents in a whole range of screen enlargements by selecting **Zoom**. You control all these viewing options with the **View** sub-menu, shown here, and when a document is displayed you can switch freely between them. When first loaded the screen displays in Print Layout view.

The main view options have the following effect, and can also be accessed by clicking the **Views** buttons on the left of the Status bar.

Normal Layout

A view that simplifies the layout of the page so that you can type, edit and format text quickly. In normal view, page boundaries, headers and footers, backgrounds, drawing objects, and pictures that do not have the **'In line with text'** wrapping style do not appear.

Web Layout

A view that optimises the layout of a document to make online reading easier. Use this layout view when you are creating a Web page or a document that is viewed on the screen. In Web layout view, you can see backgrounds, text is wrapped to fit the window, and graphics are positioned just as they are in a Web browser.

Print Layout

Provides a WYSIWYG (what you see is what you get) view of a document. The text displays in the typefaces and point sizes you specify, and with the selected attributes.

This view is useful for editing headers and footers, for adjusting margins, and for working with columns and drawing objects. All text boxes or frames, tables, graphics, headers, footers, and footnotes appear on the screen as they will in the final printout.

Outline Layout

Provides a collapsible view of a document, which enables you to see its organisation at a glance. You can display all the text in a file, or just the text that uses the paragraph styles you specify. Using this mode, allows you to quickly rearrange large sections of text. Some people like to create an outline of their document first, consisting of all the headings, then to sort out the document structure and finally fill in the text.

With large documents, you can create what is known as a master document by starting with an Outline View, and then designate headings in the outline as sub-documents. When you save the master document, Word assigns names to each sub-document based on the text you use in the outline headings.

Document Map

This view displays a separate pane with a list of document headings. You can quickly navigate through the document, when you click a heading Word jumps to that place in the document and displays the heading at the top of the window.

Full Screen

Selecting the **View**, **Full Screen** command, displays a clean, uncluttered screen; the Toolbars, Ruler, Scroll bars, and Status bar are removed. To return to the usual screen, click the **Close Full Screen** button on the icon which appears at the bottom of your screen when in this mode.

Zoom

The **Zoom** command opens the Zoom dialogue box, in which you can change the screen viewing magnification factor from its default value of 100%.

Changing Word's Default Options

Modifying Margins

It is easy to change the standard page margins for your entire document from the cursor position onward, or for selected text (more about this later).

Select the **File, Page Setup** command, click the left mouse button on the **Margins** tab of the displayed dialogue box, shown in Fig. 5.5 below, and change any of the margin or gutter settings in the **Margins** boxes.

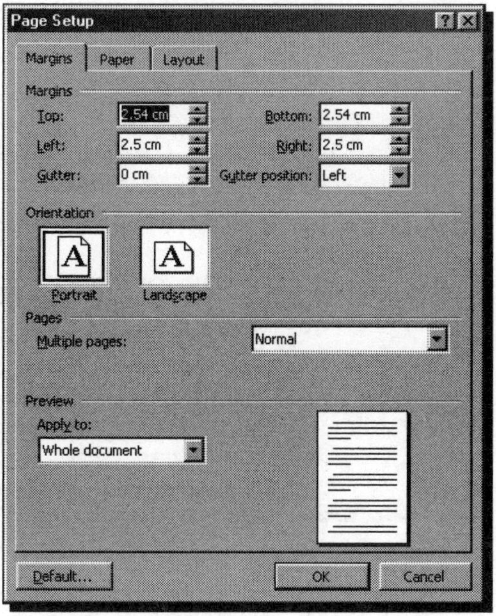

Fig. 5.5 Margins Sheet of the Page Setup Box.

The **Preview** page at the bottom of the box shows how your changes will look on a real page. The orientation of the printed page is normally **Portrait** where text prints across the page width, but you can change this to **Landscape** which prints across the page length, if you prefer.

Changing the Default Paper Settings

To change the default paper settings from those set during installation you do the following.

As before, select the **File, Page Setup** command, but click the **Paper** tab on the Page Setup dialogue box. Click the down-arrow against the **Paper size** box to reveal the list of available paper sizes, as shown in Fig. 5.6. Change the page size to your new choice.

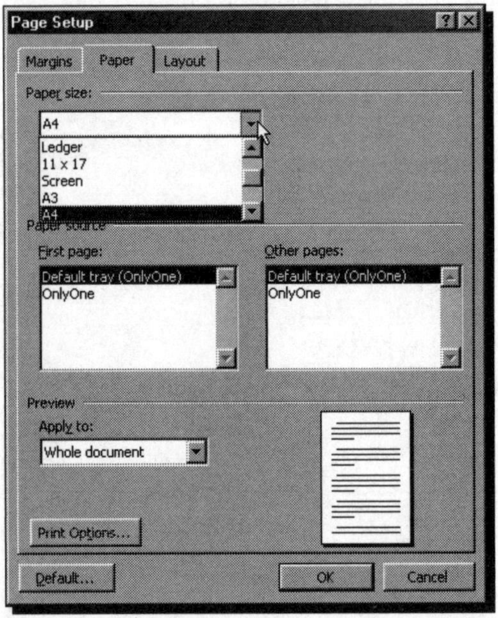

Fig. 5.6 Paper Sheet of the Page Setup Box.

Any changes you can make to your document from the Page Setup dialogue box can be applied to either the whole document or to the rest of the document starting from the current position of the insertion pointer. To set this, click the down-arrow button against the **Apply to** box and choose from the drop-down list. To make any of the new settings you make 'permanent', press the **Default** button and confirm that you wish this change to affect all new documents based on the Normal template.

The Paper source section of the Page Setup box lets you set where your printer takes its paper from. You might have a printer that holds paper in trays, in which case you might want to specify that the **First page** (headed paper perhaps), should be taken from one tray, while **Other pages** should be taken from a different tray.

Modifying the Page Layout

Clicking the last Page Setup tab displays the Layout box, part of which is shown here. From this dialogue box you can set options for headers and footers, section breaks, vertical alignment and whether to add line numbers or borders.

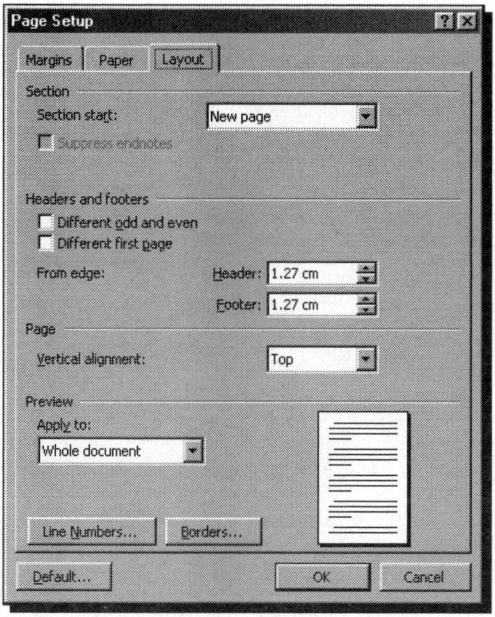

Fig. 5.7 Layout Sheet of the Page Setup Box.

The default for **Section Start** is 'New Page' which allows the section to start at the top of the next page. Pressing the down arrow against this option, allows you to change this choice.

In the Headers and Footers section of the dialogue box, you can specify whether you want one header or footer for even-numbered pages and a different header or footer for odd-numbered pages. You can further specify if you want a different header or footer on the first page from the header or footer used for the rest of the document. Word aligns the top line with the 'Top' margin, but this can be changed with the **Vertical alignment** option.

Changing Other Default Options

You can also change the other default options available to you in Word 2002, by selecting the **Tools, Options** command. This opens the Options dialogue box displayed in Fig. 5.8 below.

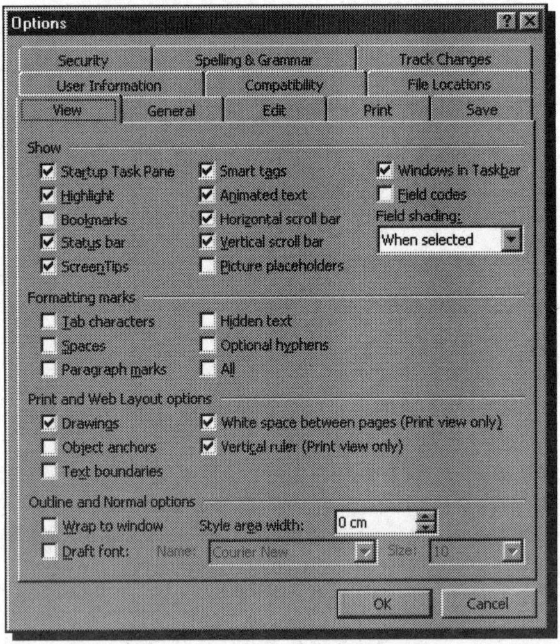

Fig. 5.8 The Word Options Dialogue Box.

As can be seen, this box has eleven tabbed sheets which give you control of most of the program's settings.

You can, amongst other things, do the following:

* Specify the default **View** options. For example, you can select whether non-printing formatting characters, such as Tabs, Spaces, and Paragraph marks, are shown or not.

* Adjust the **General** Word settings, such as background re-pagination, display of the recently used file-list, and selection of units of measurement.

* Adjust the **Print** settings, such as allowing background printing, reverse print order, or choose to print comments with documents.

* Change the **Save** options, such as selecting to always create a backup copy of your work.

Saving to a File

To save a document to disc, use either of the commands:

* **File, Save** (or click the **Save** toolbar button) which is used when a document has previously been saved to disc in a named file; using this command saves your work under the existing filename automatically without prompting you.

* **File, Save As** command which is used when you want to save your document with a different name from the one you gave it already.

Using the **File, Save As** command (or with the very first time you use the **File, Save** command when a document has no name), opens the dialogue box shown in Fig. 5.9 on the next page.

Note that the first 255 characters of the first paragraph of a new document are placed and highlighted in the **File name** field box, with the program waiting for you to over-type a new name.

Fig. 5.9 The File Save As Box.

Any name you type must have less than 255 characters and will replace the existing name. Filenames cannot include any of the following keyboard characters: /, \, >, <, *, ?, ", |, :, or ;. Word adds the file extension **.doc** automatically and uses it to identify its documents.

You can select a drive other than the one displayed, by clicking the down arrow against the **Save in** text box at the top of the Save As dialogue box. You can also select a folder in which to save your work. The large buttons on the left of the box give rapid access to five possible saving locations. If you do not have a suitably named folder, then you can create one using the **Create New Folder** button, as shown below.

Fig. 5.10 Creating a New Folder.

We used this facility to create a folder called **Word Docs** within the **Documents** folder. To save our work currently in memory, we selected this folder in the **Save in** field of the Save As dialogue box, then moved the cursor into the **File name** box, and typed **PC Users1**. We suggest you do the same.

By clicking the **Save as type** button at the bottom of the Save As dialogue box, you can save the Document Template, or the Text Only parts of your work, or you can save your document in a variety of 29 formats, including Rich Text, and several Web Page options.

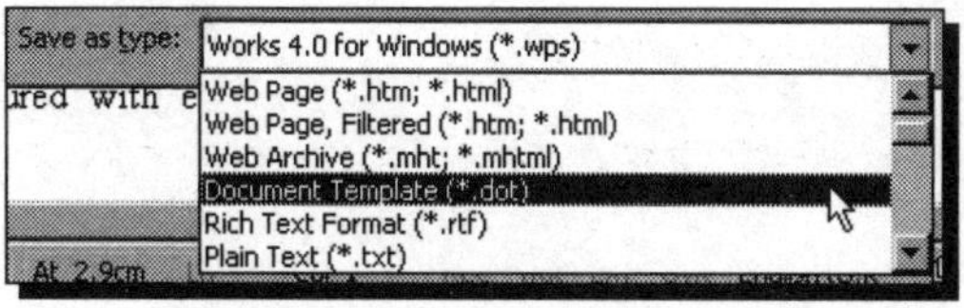

Fig. 5.11 Saving a Document as a Different File Type.

Selecting File Location

You can select where Word automatically looks for your document files when you first choose to open or save a document, by selecting the **Tools, Options** command, click the File Locations tab of the displayed Options dialogue box, (Fig. 5.8), and modify the location of the document files, as shown on the next page in Fig. 5.12.

As you can see, the default location of other types of files is also given in this dialogue box.

Microsoft suggests that you store documents, worksheets, presentations, databases, and other files you are currently working on, in the **My Documents** folder, which is easily accessed from the Desktop by clicking the special **Documents** button. This, of course, is a matter of preference, so we leave it to you to decide. We prefer to create sub-folders within **My Documents** to group our files more closely.

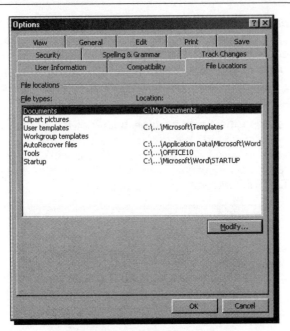

Fig. 5.12 Setting Word's File Locations.

To change the default folder for any of the file types listed above, simply select the type and click the **Modify** button.

Fig. 5.13 Menu.

This opens a dialogue box very similar to the Save As box for you to locate or even create the folder you want to select.

While any of the file opening, saving and location dialogue boxes are open you can use them to generally manage your files and folders. You do this by right-clicking on the name of a file or folder you want to manipulate. A context sensitive menu is opened like ours in Fig. 5.13. All of these options may not be available on your system, but the common ones of Open, New, Print, Cut, Copy, Create Shortcut, Delete, Rename and Properties should always be there.

Document Properties

A useful feature in Word is the facility to add document properties to every file by selecting the **File, Properties** command. A Properties box, as shown in Fig. 5.14 below, opens for you to type additional information about your document.

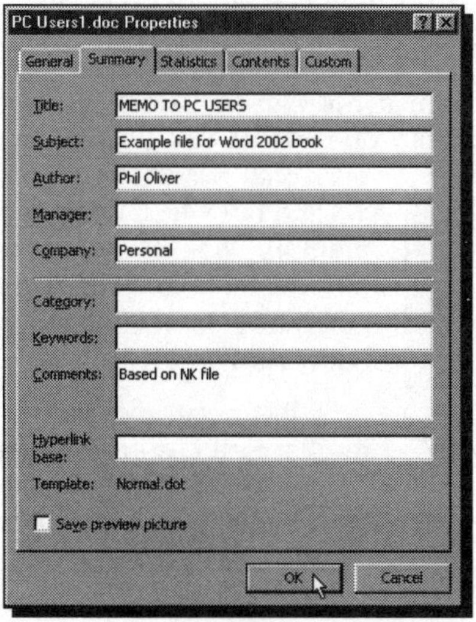

Fig. 5.14 The Document Properties Box.

One of the most useful features in this box is the Statistics tabbed page.

Statistic name	Value
Pages:	1
Paragraphs:	4
Lines:	13
Words:	107
Characters:	538
Characters (with spaces):	641

Fig. 5.15 Document Statistics.

As we show in Fig. 5.15, this gives a listing of the document statistics, including the number of pages, paragraphs, lines, words and even characters. Very useful for writing papers and reports, where the size is important.

To use this feature on a more regular basis, make sure that the **Prompt for document properties** box appears ticked on the Save tabbed sheet of the Options dialogue box (use the **Tools, Options** command and click the Save tab).

Closing a Document

There are several ways to close a document in Word. Once you have saved it you can click its **x** close button, or double-click on the **Document Control** button at the left end of the menu bar, or use the **File, Close** menu command.

If the document (or file) has changed since the last time it was saved, you will be given the option to save it before it is removed from memory.

If a document is not closed before a new document is opened, then both documents will be held in memory, but only one will be the current document. To find out which documents are held in memory, look at the Windows Taskbar, (see note below) or use the **Window** command to reveal the menu options shown in Fig. 5.16.

Window	Help
New Window	
Arrange All	
Split	
1 Fred letter.doc	
✓ 2 PC Users1.doc	
3 Practice file.doc	

Fig. 5.16 Window Menu.

In this case, the second document in the list is the current document, and to make another document the current one, either type the document number, or point at its name and click the left mouse button.

To close a document which is not the current document, use the **Window** command, make it current, and close it with one of the above methods.

Note - With Word 2002 it is now possible to limit what is shown on the Taskbar. By default all your open Word windows (or documents) will each have an entry on the Taskbar. But you can change this so that only the current, or active, document is shown there. This can be useful to save clutter if you have several programs open at the same time.

To do this, open the View tab sheet of the **Tools, Options** dialogue box, shown in Fig. 5.8, and uncheck the **Windows in Taskbar** option.

Opening a Document

 You can use the Open dialogue box in Word, shown in Fig. 5.17 below, to open documents that might be located in different locations. As we saw earlier, this is opened by clicking the **Open** toolbar button, or with the **File**, **Open** command, or the <Ctrl+O> keystrokes.

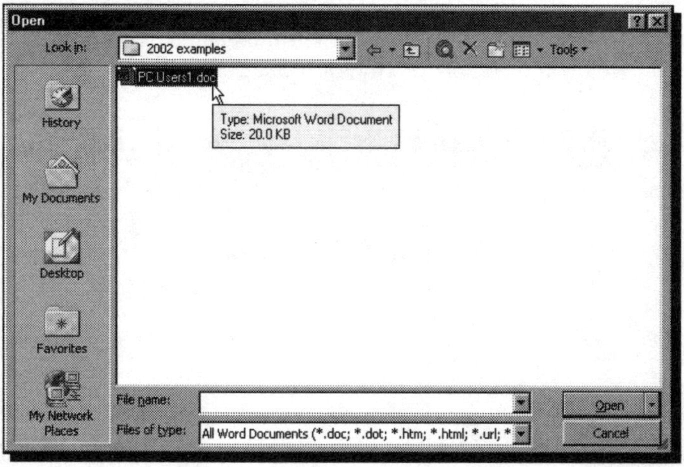

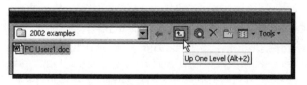

Fig. 5.17 The File Open Box.

For example, you can open a document which might be on your computer's hard disc, or on a network drive that you have a connection to. To locate other drives and folders, simply click the **Up One Level** button pointed to in Fig. 5.18 below.

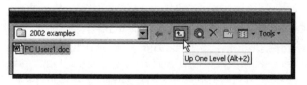

Fig. 5.18 The Up One Level Button.

Having selected a drive, you can then select the folder within which your document was saved, select its filename and click the **Open** button on the dialogue box.

As in older versions of Word, the last few files you worked on are also listed at the bottom of the **File** menu, as shown in Fig. 5.19 below. Selecting one of these will reopen that file.

If you do not have any past files displayed, as described above, open the General tab sheet of the **Tools**, **Options** dialogue box, and make sure the **Recently used file list** option is checked. In the **entries** box next to it you can choose to have up to the last nine files listed. The default is four, which is probably plenty for most people.

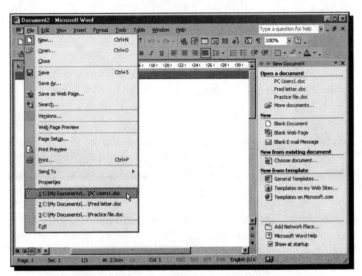

Fig. 5.19 Opening the Last Used Documents.

The New Document Task Pane

The **New document** Task Pane, shown above, is another way of opening both new and recently used documents. If it is not open, simply use the **View**, **Task Pane** command.

The **Open a document** section at the top, lists the last few files you have used. Simply clicking on one will open it. The **More documents** option displays the Open dialogue box, seen in Fig. 5.17, for you to find and select an existing file to open.

The **New** section offers several options for opening new documents of different kinds. **Blank Document** opens a new empty document using the Normal template (the same as clicking the **New** toolbar button). **Blank Web Page** opens a blank page in Web layout view, for you to build a Web page. The **Blank E-mail Message** option lets you use Word to write an e-mail which you can then send using Outlook.

The **New from existing document** section is a very welcome new feature which lets you create a document based on the features of an existing one. You can click **Choose document** to open an existing file, maybe a letter with all your address and salutation details, and make any changes you want to it. When you click the **Save** toolbar button, however, the Save As dialogue box is opened with a new filename suggested. It was so easy before this to overwrite the old file accidentally during the saving process.

The last section **New from Template** lets you open a template to use for your document. Microsoft have produced 'hundreds' of templates for particular types of documents. These make it very easy for a 'newish' user to produce very professional documents. Once opened you just change the existing text to your own, print it and wait for the admiring comments - maybe. The **General Templates** option accesses those that came with Word, as shown in Fig. 5.20.

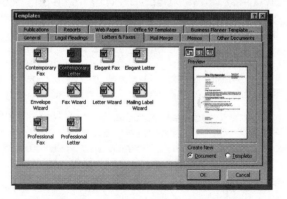

Fig. 5.20 Some of the Templates Available in Word.

These templates are well worth exploring as you may save yourself an awful lot of work. In the example below we opened a new document with the Contemporary Letter template from the Letters & Faxes sheet.

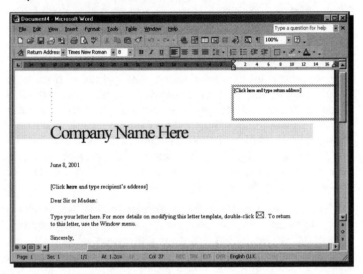

Fig. 5.21 Using a Microsoft Template.

This letter has instructions in it that tell you what to customise and how. Once you have entered your name and address it is a good idea to save the document again, but as a template, so that you can use it again in the future. To do this, select Document Template in the **Save as type** box of the Save As dialogue box and rename the document. It will then be available in the General tabbed section of the Templates box, for you to use again and again.

The other two template options on the **New Document** Task Pane let you access templates from your own Web space, maybe a company intranet, or from Microsoft's own Web sites. That should keep you busy for a while!

As long as the **Show at startup** option is checked at the bottom of the pane, this list should always be available whenever you start up Word.

6

Editing Word Documents

Microsoft have built some very clever editing facilities into Word 2002, and we will introduce some of them here. When you enter text you will notice that some basic errors are automatically corrected and that misspelled words are unobtrusively underlined in a red wavy line and ungrammatical phrases are similarly underlined in green.

AutoCorrect

To demonstrate these, use the **File, New** command (or click ☐) to create a new file, and type the words 'teh computor is brukn', exactly as misspelled here.

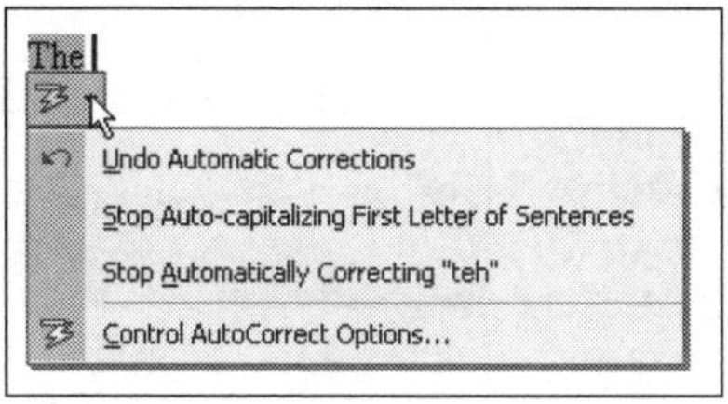

Fig. 6.1 The AutoCorrect Option Button.

As soon as you press the space bar after entering the first 'word', it will be changed to 'The', as shown in Fig. 6.1. This is the **AutoCorrect** feature at work, which will automatically detect and correct typing errors, misspelled words, and incorrect capitalisation. If you agree with the change made, as in our example, all is well. If not, you can move the pointer over the corrected word until a blue box is shown below it. This changes to the **AutoCorrect Options** button when you point to it, and clicking it opens the menu shown above.

Selecting the first menu option **Undo Automatic Corrections** will cancel the correction for you. The other options give you control of how the feature works in the future.

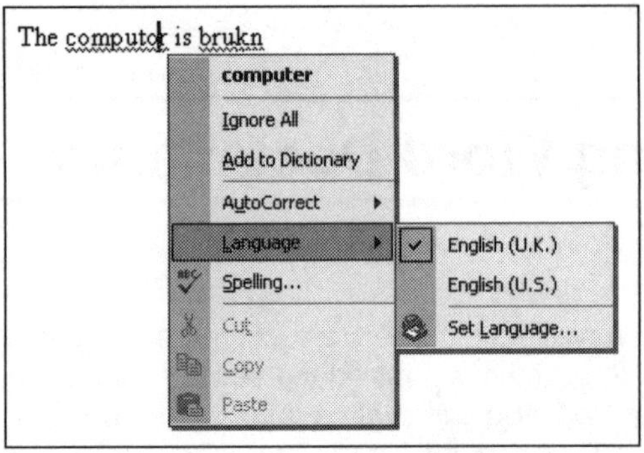

Fig. 6.2 Correcting Spelling Mistakes.

What should appear on your screen is shown in Fig. 6.2, with the two misspelled words underlined in a red wavy line.

Right-clicking the first misspelled word allows you to correct it, as shown above. To do this, left-click the **Computer** menu option. You even have a choice of **Language** to use. This is possibly the most timesaving enhancement in editing misspelled words as you type.

During this process the status bar will indicate your 'state of play'. As shown in Fig. 6.3, the active language is displayed, English (UK) in our case. To the right of this, the small 'book' icon has three forms. In Fig. 6.3 it is ticked to indicate

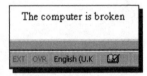

Fig. 6.3 The Status Bar.

that spell checking is completed. If there are errors to correct, it has a red cross on it, and during the actual checking process it displays an active pencil as shown here to the left. If you double-click this icon when it displays a cross, the full spell and grammar checker is opened which will be discussed later in more detail.

If you really have a problem spelling particular words you can add them to the AutoCorrect list yourself. To do this, select the **AutoCorrect** option from the menu in Fig. 6.2 (or the **Tools**, **AutoCorrect Options** menu command) to open the AutoCorrect box shown in Fig. 6.4 on the next page.

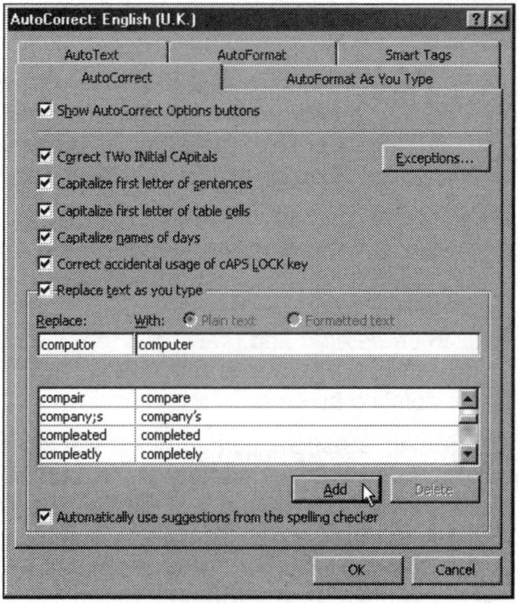

Fig. 6.4 Controlling AutoCorrections.

This dialogue box lets you control all of Word's automatic text, formatting and correction features, as well as the new Smart Tags feature we will encounter later on. Make sure the AutoCorrect tabbed sheet is active, as shown above, and have a good look at the ways you can control how it works for you. We suggest you scroll through the very long list of common misspellings at the bottom to see which ones will automatically be corrected.

In our example we have chosen to have the program always **Replace** the word 'computor' **With** the correct spelling of 'computer' as soon as we type the word. Clicking the **Add** button will add these to the AutoCorrect list.

The top fifteen options on the list are not corrections, but give you a rapid way to enter some common symbol characters by typing in a series of keyboard strokes. For example, if you type the three characters '(c)' AutoCorrect will change them to the copyright symbol '©'.

Editing Text

Other editing could include deleting unwanted words or adding extra text in the document. All these operations are very easy to carry out. For small deletions, such as letters or words, the easiest method is to use the <Del> or <BkSp> keys.

With the <Del> key, position the cursor on the left of the first letter you want to delete and press <Del>. With the <BkSp> key, position the cursor immediately to the right of the character to be deleted and press <BkSp>. In both cases the rest of the line moves to the left to take up the space created by the deleting process.

Word processing is usually carried out in the insert mode. Any characters typed will be inserted at the cursor location (insertion point) and the following text will be pushed to the right, and down, to make room. To insert blank lines in your text, place the cursor at the beginning of the line where the blank line is needed and press <Enter>. To remove the blank line, position the cursor on it and press <Del>.

When larger scale editing is needed you have several alternatives. You could first 'select' the text to be altered, then use the **Cut**, **Copy** and **Paste** operations available in the **Edit** sub-menu, or more easily, click on their Toolbar button alternatives shown here.

Another method of copying or moving text is to use the 'drag and drop' facility which requires you to highlight a word, grab it with the left mouse button depressed, and drop it in the required place in your text.

These operations will be discussed shortly in more detail.

Selecting Text

The procedure in Word, as with most Windows based applications, is first to select the text to be altered before any operation, such as formatting or editing, can be carried out on it. Selected text is highlighted on the screen. This can be carried out in two main ways:

A. *Using the keyboard, to select:*

* A block of text.

  Position the cursor on the first character to be selected and hold down the <Shift> key while using the arrow keys to highlight the required text, then release the <Shift> key.

* From the present position to the end of the line.

  Use <Shift+End>.

* From the present cursor position to the beginning of the line.

  Use <Shift+Home>.

* From the present cursor position to the end of the document.

  Use <Shift+Ctrl+End>.

* From the present cursor position to the beginning of the document.

  Use <Shift+Ctrl+Home>.

* Select the whole document.

  Use <Ctrl A>

B. With the mouse, to select:

• A block of text.

Press down the left mouse button at the beginning of the block and while holding it pressed, drag the cursor across the block so that the desired text is highlighted, then release the mouse button.

• A word.

Double-click within the word.

• A line.

Place the mouse pointer in the selection bar (just to the left of the line, when it changes to an arrow ⇗) click once. For multiple lines, drag this pointer down.

• A sentence.

Hold the <Ctrl> key down and click in the sentence.

• A paragraph.

Place the mouse pointer in the selection bar and double-click (for multiple paragraphs, after selecting the first paragraph, drag the pointer in the selection bar) or triple-click in the paragraph.

• The whole document.

Place the mouse pointer in the selection bar, hold the <Ctrl> key down and click once.

With Word 2002 you can now select non-contiguous text and graphics (ones that aren't next to each other), by selecting the first item you want, such as a word, sentence or paragraph, holding down the <Ctrl> key and selecting any other items from anywhere in the document. You can only select text, or graphics in this way, not both at the same time.

Copying Blocks of Text

Once text has been selected it can be copied to another location in your present document, to another Word document, or to another Windows application, via the system clipboard. As with most of the editing and formatting operations there are several alternative ways of doing this, as follows:

* Use the **Edit, Copy** command sequence from the menu, to copy the selected text to the clipboard, moving the cursor to the start of where you want the copied text to be placed, and using the **Edit, Paste** command.

* Use the quick key combinations, <Ctrl+C> (or <Ctrl+Ins>) to copy and <Ctrl+V> (or <Shift+Ins>) to paste. This does not require the menu bar to be activated.

* Use the **Copy** and **Paste** Standard Toolbar buttons; you can of course only use this method with a mouse.

 To copy the same text again to another location, or to any open document window or application, move the cursor to the new location and paste it there with any of these methods.

The above operations use the system clipboard which only holds the last item cut or copied. Microsoft Office XP comes with a new extra clipboard in which you can store 24 cut or copied items until they are needed. Each item is displayed as a thumbnail on the new **Clipboard** Task Pane as shown in Fig. 6.5 on the next page.

The Clipboard Task Pane

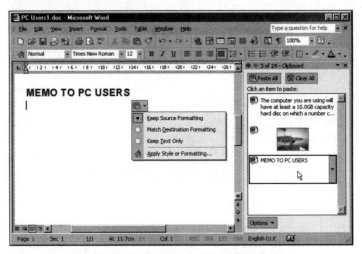

Fig. 6.5 Pasting from the Clipboard Task Pane.

The **Clipboard** Task Pane opens automatically in Word when you cut or copy for the second time, otherwise you can open it with the **Edit**, **Office Clipboard** command.

Fig. 6.5 is actually a composite, showing the **Clipboard** Task Pane on the right with two text items and a picture. The bottom item (with the selection square around it) was clicked to paste the text at the insertion point location in the main document to the left.

This also shows another new Office XP feature, a **Smart Tag** button. By default, one of these is always placed just under newly pasted text in Word 2002. Clicking this button, as shown above, opens a menu which lets you control the style and formatting of the pasted text. If you don't want to make any formatting changes to the text, just carry on and the smart tag will 'go away'.

While the **Clipboard** Task Pane is active in any Office program an icon like the one shown here is placed on the Windows Taskbar. This lets you easily access the pane, and also flags up how many items it contains.

Moving Blocks of Text

Selected text can be moved to any location in the same document by either of the following:

* Using the **Edit, Cut,** command or <Ctrl+X> (or <Shift+Del>).

* Clicking the **Cut** Toolbar button, shown here.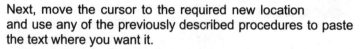

Next, move the cursor to the required new location and use any of the previously described procedures to paste the text where you want it.

The moved text will be placed at the cursor location and will force any existing text to make room for it. This operation can be cancelled by simply pressing <Esc>. Once moved, multiple copies of the same text can be produced by other **Paste** operations.

Drag and Drop Operations

 Selected text, or graphics, can be **copied** by holding the <Ctrl> key depressed and dragging the mouse with the left button held down. The drag pointer is an arrow with two attached squares, as shown here - the vertical dotted line showing the point of insertion. The new text will insert itself where placed, even if the overstrike mode is in operation. Text copied by this method is not placed on the clipboard, so multiple copies are not possible as with other methods.

 Selected text can be **moved** by dragging the mouse with the left button held down. The drag pointer is an arrow with an attached square - the vertical dotted line showing the point of insertion.

Deleting Blocks of Text

When text is 'cut' with the **Edit, Cut** command, or by clicking the **Cut** toolbar button, it is removed from the document, but placed on the clipboard. When the <Del> or <BkSp> keys are used, however, the text is not put on the clipboard.

The Undo Command

As text is lost with the delete command, you should use it with caution, but if you do make a mistake all is not lost as long as you act promptly. The **Edit, Undo** command or <Ctrl+Z> reverses your most recent editing or formatting commands.

Fig. 6.6 The Undo Cascade Menu.

You can also use the **Undo** Standard Toolbar button, shown here, to undo one of several editing or formatting mistakes (press the down arrow to the right of the button to see a list of your recent changes, as shown here).

Undo does not reverse any action once editing changes have been saved to file. Only editing done since the last save can be reversed.

Finding and Changing Text

As in previous versions, Word 2002 allows you to search for specifically selected text, or character combinations with the **Find** or the **Replace** options on the **Edit** command sub-menu.

Using the **Find** option (<Ctrl+F>), will highlight each occurrence of the supplied text in turn so that you can carry out some action on it, such as change its font or appearance.

Using the **Replace** option (<Ctrl+H>), allows you to specify what replacement is to be automatically carried out. For example, in a long article you may decide to replace every occurrence of the word 'microcomputers' with the word 'PCs'.

To illustrate the **Replace** procedure, either select the option from the **Edit** sub-menu or use the quick key combination <Ctrl+H>. This opens the Find and Replace dialogue box shown on the next page with the **More** button clicked.

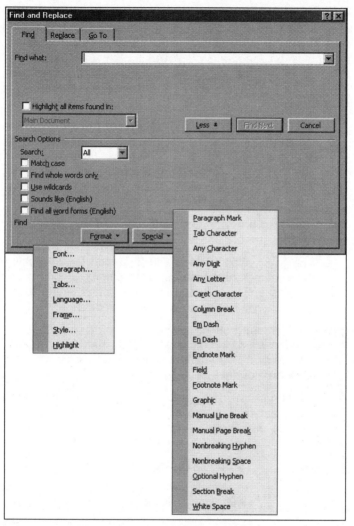

Fig. 6.7 A Composite of the Find and Replace Box.

Towards the bottom of the dialogue box, there are five check boxes; the first two can be used to match the case of letters in the search string, and/or a whole word, while the last three are used for wildcard, 'sounds like' or 'word forms' matching.

The two buttons, **Format** and **Special**, situated at the bottom of the dialogue box, let you control how the search is carried out. The lists of available options, when either of these buttons is pressed, are displayed in Fig. 6.7. You will of course only see one or the other, but not both as shown here. You can force both the search and the replace operations to work with exact text attributes. For example, selecting:

- The **Font** option from the list under **Format**, displays a dialogue box in which you select a font (such as Arial, Times New Roman, etc.); a font-style (such as regular, bold, italic, etc.); an underline option (such as single, double, etc.); and special effects (such as strike-through, superscript, subscript, etc.).

- The **Paragraph** option, lets you control indentation, spacing (before and after), and alignment.

- The **Style** option, allows you to search for, or replace, different paragraph styles. This can be useful if you develop a new style and want to change all the text of another style in a document to use your preferred style.

Using the **Special** button, you can search for, and replace, various specified document marks, tabs, hard returns, etc., or a combination of both these and text, as listed in the previous screen dump.

Below we list only two of the many key combinations of special characters that could be typed into the **Find what** and **Replace with** boxes when the **Use wildcards** box is checked.

Type	*To find or replace*
?	Any single character within a pattern. For example, searching for nec?, will find <u>neck</u>, con<u>nect</u>, etc.
*	Any string of characters. For example, searching for c*r, will find such words as <u>cellar</u>, <u>chillier</u>, etc., also parts of words such as <u>character</u>, and combinations of words such as <u>connect, cellar</u>.

A very useful new feature on the Find and Replace box is the **Highlight all items found in** option. If you tick this, your search will select all the matching words in your document at the same time. Any editing you then carry out will effect all of the selected text. This is a very rapid way of making global changes of font, size or style, etc.

The Search Task Pane

Clicking the **Search** toolbar button, shown here, opens the new **Search** Task Pane, shown in Fig. 6.8 on the right. This is really to help you locate particular files or text on your computer, but the **Find in this document** option at the bottom opens the Search and Replace dialogue box we have just looked at.

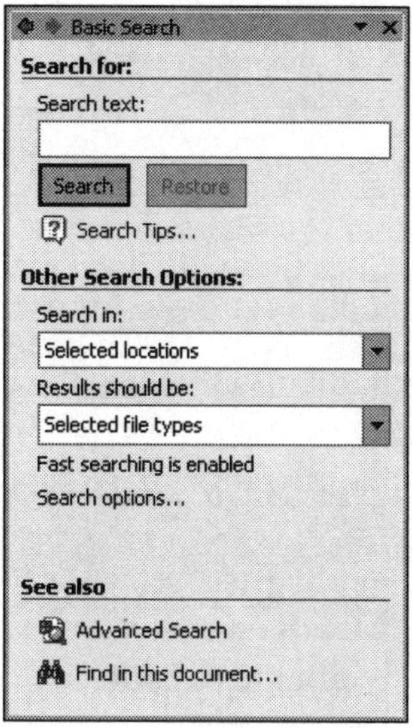

With the default **Basic Search** option this pane lets you search for files on your hard disc by name.

The **Advanced Search** option lets you search your files for particular text, particular authors, or for files with specific creation dates.

Fig. 6.8 The Search Task Pane.

If you want more help on searching for files we suggest you click the **Search Tips** option, which opens the Word Help system at the relevant page.

Page Breaks

The program automatically inserts a 'soft' page break in a document when a page of typed text is full. To force a

manual, or hard page break, either use the <Ctrl+Enter> keystrokes, or use the **Insert**, **Break** command and select **Page break** in the dialogue box, shown in Fig. 6.9.

Fig. 6.9 Break Box.

Pressing **OK** places a series of dots across the page to indicate the page break (this can only be seen in Normal View), as shown in Fig. 6.10 below. If you are in Print Layout View, the second paragraph below appears on the next page. To delete manual page breaks place the cursor on the line of dots, and press the <Del> key. In Print Layout View, place the cursor at the beginning of the second page and press the <BkSp> key.

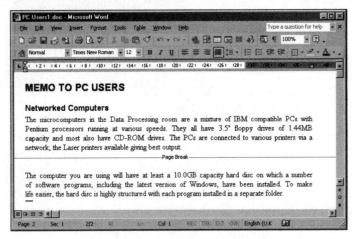

Fig. 6.10 A Hard Page Break in Normal View.

Soft page breaks which are automatically entered by the program at the end of pages, cannot be deleted.

Using the Spell Checker

The package has a very comprehensive spell checker which whenever it thinks it has found a misspelled word, underlines it with a red wavy line. To correct your document, right-click such words for alternatives, as we saw earlier.

However, the spell checker can also be used in another way. To spell check your document, either click the Spelling and **Grammar Toolbar** button, shown here, or use the **Tools**, **Spelling and Grammar** command (or **F7**) to open the dialogue box shown in Fig. 6.11 below.

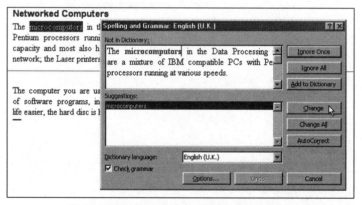

Fig. 6.11 Checking a Whole Document's Spelling.

Make sure you are using the correct dictionary by checking in the **Dictionary language** box. With us this gave an enormous list of English, French and Spanish speaking country options. If you want to check a word or paragraph only, highlight it first. Once Word has found a misspelled word, you can either correct it in the **Not in Dictionary:** box, or select a word from the **Suggestions** list.

The main dictionary cannot be edited, but you can add specialised and personal dictionaries with the facility to customise and edit them. If you choose **Add**, the specified word is added to a custom dictionary.

Using the Thesaurus

If you are not sure of the meaning of a word, or you want to use an alternative word in your document, then the thesaurus is an indispensable tool. To use the thesaurus, simply place the cursor on the word you want to look up and select the **Tools**, **Language**, **Thesaurus** command, or use the <Shift+F7> key combination. As long as the word is recognised, the following dialogue box will open.

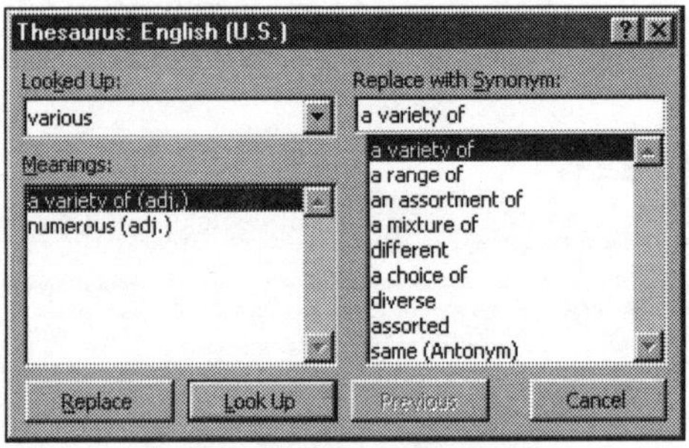

Fig. 6.12 The Thesaurus.

This is a very powerful tool; you can see information about an item in the **Meanings** list, or you can look up a synonym in the **Replace with Synonym** list. To change the word in the **Looked Up** text box, select an offered word in either the **Meanings** or the **Replace with Synonym** list box, or type a word directly into the **Replace with Synonym** box, and press the **Replace** button.

You can use the thesaurus like a simple dictionary by typing any word into the **Replace with Synonym** box and clicking the **Look Up** button. If the word is recognised, lists of its meaning variations and synonyms will be displayed. Pressing the **Replace** button will place the word into the document.

A quick way to get a list of alternatives to a word in your document is to right-click it and select **Synonyms** from the drop-down menu. If you select one from the list it will replace the original word.

The Grammar Checker

We find the Grammar Checker provided with Word to be much better than that of previous versions of the package. It does not have all the pre-set styles that we are sure were never used by anyone.

To illustrate using the Grammar Checker, open the **PC Users1** file and at the end of it type the following sentence which we know will cause some reaction from the grammar checker.

'Use the My Computer utility which Microsoft have spent much time and effort making as intuitive as possible.'

Straight away the Grammar Checker underlines the word 'have' with a green wavy line as shown below in Fig. 6.13.

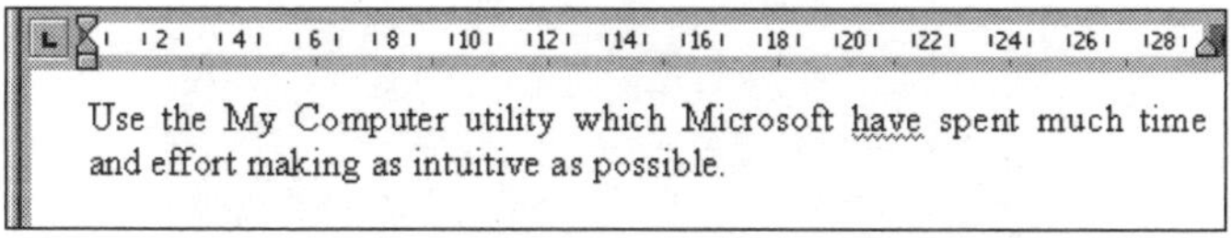

Use the My Computer utility which Microsoft have spent much time and effort making as intuitive as possible.

Fig. 6.13 Checking the Grammar of a Sentence.

Right-clicking the wavy line opens a shortcut menu and choosing the **Grammar** option displays the following:

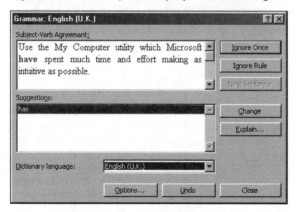

Fig. 6.14 The Grammar Checker.

The Grammar Checker has picked up what is incorrect, as expected. No other errors were flagged up in this memo. Gone are the messages about 'Passive Verb Usage' which was the obsession of the Grammar Checker in some of the older versions of Word. If you want more information on the suggested changes, try clicking the new **Explain** button.

To see the Grammar Checker settings you use the **Tools, Options** command to open the Options dialogue box, and click the Spelling & Grammar tab, as shown in Fig. 6.15.

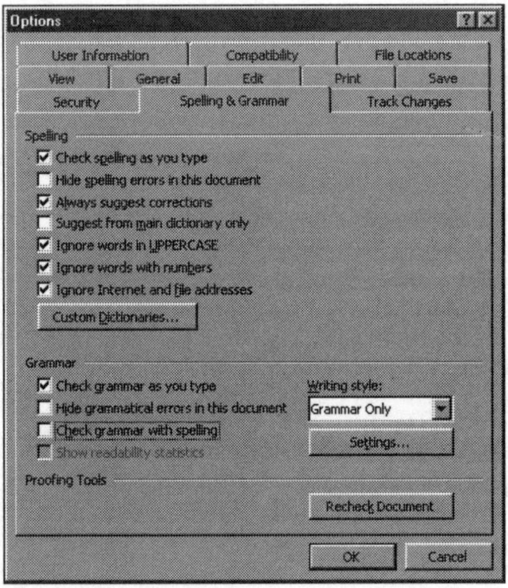

Fig. 6.15 The Spelling and Grammar Options.

As you can see, you can to a certain extent customise the way the grammar checker works. For example, clicking the **Settings** button in the above dialogue box displays the Grammar Settings dialogue box shown in Fig. 6.16 on the next page.

Do spend some time with this dialogue box to find out all the available options before going on.

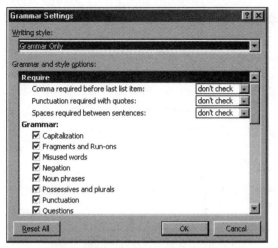

Fig. 6.16 The Grammar Settings Box.

Printing Documents

When Windows was first installed on your computer the printers you intend to use should have been selected, and the SETUP program should have installed the appropriate printer drivers. Before printing for the first time, it may be a good idea to check that your printer is in fact properly installed. To do this, click the Windows **Start** button (at the left end of the Taskbar) then select **Settings** and click the **Printers** menu option to open the Printers folder shown in Fig. 6.17 at the top of the next page.

Here, several printer drivers have been installed with the HP LaserJet 5/5M PostScript as the 'default' printer and an Acrobat Distiller 'printer' which we often use. In our case the HP LaserJet is configured to output to the printer via the parallel port LPT1 - yours may well be via a USB port. LPT1 is short for Line Printer 1 and refers to the socket at the back of your PC which is connected to your printer. Similarly, a USB port is also a socket to be found at the back of your PC.

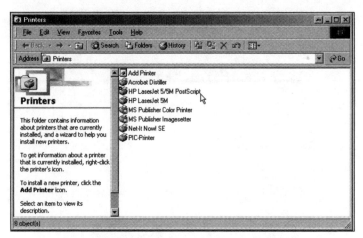

Fig. 6.17 The Windows Printers Folder.

To see how a printer is configured (whether to print to a printer port or to a file), select it by clicking its icon, use the **File, Properties** command and click the Details tab of the displayed dialogue box.

Next, return to or reactivate Word and, if the document you want to print is not in memory, either click the **Open** button on the Toolbar, or use the **File, Open** command, to display the Open dialogue box described in the previous chapter. Use this dialogue box to locate the file, or document, you want to print, which will be found on the drive and folder on which you saved it originally.

To print your document, do one of the following:

- Click the **Print** button on the Standard Toolbar, shown here, which prints the document using the default printer and current settings.

- Use the **File, Print** command which opens the Print box, shown in Fig. 6.18 on the next page.

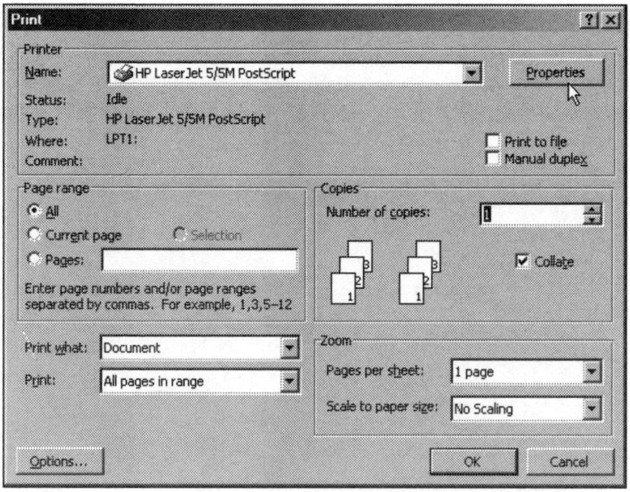

Fig. 6.18 The Print Dialogue Box.

The settings in the Print dialogue box allow you to select the number of copies, and which pages, you want printed. You can also select to print the document, the summary information relating to that document, comments, styles, etc., in the **Print what** drop-down list.

You can even change the selected printer by clicking the down arrow against the **Name** box which displays the available printers on your system.

Clicking the **Properties** button on the Print dialogue box, displays the Properties dialogue box for the selected printer, shown here, which allows you to select the paper size, orientation needed, paper source, etc.

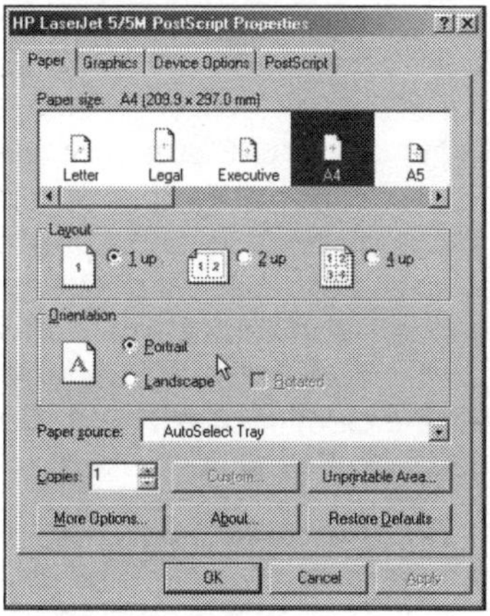

Fig. 6.19 A Printer Properties Box.

The **Options** button on the Print dialogue box, gives you access to some more advanced print options, such as printing in reverse order, with or without comments, print hidden text or field codes, etc., as shown in Fig. 6.20 below.

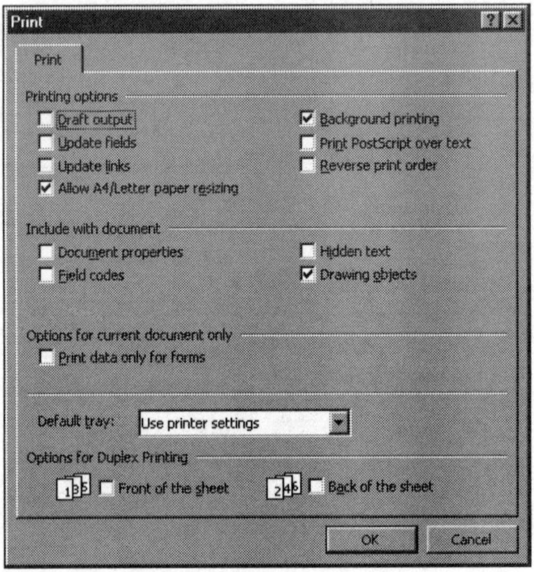

Fig. 6.20 Some Advanced Print Options.

Clicking the **OK** button on these various multilevel dialogue boxes, causes Word to accept your selections and return you to the previous level dialogue box, until the Print dialogue box is reached. Selecting **OK** on this first level dialogue box, sends print output from Word to your selection, either the printer connected to your computer, or to an encoded file on disc. Selecting **Cancel** or **Close** on any level dialogue box, aborts the selections made at that level.

Do remember that, whenever you change printers, the appearance of your document may change, as Word uses the fonts available with the newly selected printer. This can affect the line lengths, which in turn will affect both the tabulation and pagination of your document.

Print Preview

 Before printing your document to paper, click the Print **Preview** button on the Standard Toolbar, or use the **File**, **Print Preview** command, to see what your print output will look like, and how much of your document will fit on your selected page size. This depends very much on the chosen font. In Fig. 6.21 below we show a preview of our example document PC Users1.doc.

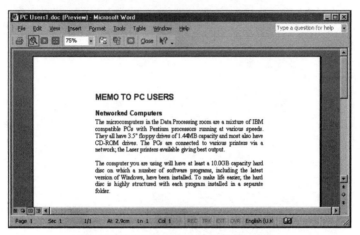

Fig. 6.21 A Print Preview of our Document.

This view allows you to see the layout of the final printed page, which could save a few trees and equally important to you, a lot of frustration and wear and tear on your printer.

The print Preview window has its own toolbar with options for magnification and number of pages actually viewed. You can even edit your document, if you want to make any last minute changes. To print the document simply click the **Print** button, or to return to your working document from a print preview display, click the **Close** button on its menu bar.

Other enhancements of your document, such as selection of fonts, formatting of text, and pagination, will be discussed in the next chapter.

7

Formatting Word Documents

Formatting involves the appearance of individual words or even characters, the line spacing and alignment of paragraphs, and the overall page layout of the entire document. These functions are carried out in Word in several different ways.

Primary page layout is included in a document's Template and text formatting in a Template's styles. Within any document, however, you can override Paragraph Style formats by applying text formatting and enhancements manually to selected text. To immediately cancel manual formatting, select the text and use the **Edit, Undo** command, or (<Ctrl+Z>). The selected text reverts to its original format. In the long term, you can cancel manual formatting by selecting the text and using the <Shift+Ctrl+N> key stroke. The text then reverts to its style format.

Formatting Text

If you use TrueType fonts, which are automatically installed when you set up Windows, Word uses the same font to display text on the screen and to print on paper. The screen fonts provide a very close approximation of printed characters. TrueType font names are preceded by ℑ in the Font box on the Formatting Bar.

If you use non-TrueType fonts, then use a screen font that matches your printer font. If a matching font is not available, or if your printer driver does not provide screen font information, Windows chooses the screen font that most closely resembles the printer font.

Originally, the title and subtitle of the **PC Users1** memo, were selected from the default Normal style as 'Heading 1' and 'Heading 3', which were in the 16 and 13 point size Arial typeface, respectively, while the main text was typed in 10 point size Times New Roman.

To change this memo into what appears on the screen dump displayed below, first select the title of the memo and format it to italics, 18 point size Arial and centre it between the margins, then select the subtitle and format it to 14 point size Arial. Both title and subtitle are in bold as part of the definition of their respective paragraph style. Finally select each paragraph of the main body of the memo in turn, and format it to 12 point size Times New Roman. Notice in each case that the Style details in the Style box on the Formatting Toolbar is changed to show the manual formatting that was added. This shows as 'Normal + 12pt' in Fig. 7.1 below.

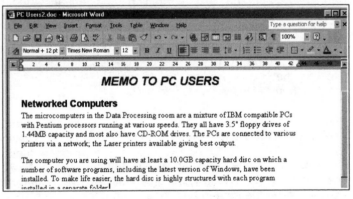

Fig. 7.1 The Reformatted PC Users Memo.

All of this formatting can be achieved by using the buttons on the Formatting Bar (see also the section entitled 'Paragraph Alignment'). Save the result under the new filename **PC Users2**, using the **File, Save As** command.

In all our screen dumps so far we show the Formatting Bar moved from its default position (to the right of the Standard Toolbar) to just below it. Although this takes up more screen space, we have done this to show more buttons on both the Toolbars.

Moving Toolbars

As we have seen, the default buttons appearing on the two Toolbars below the Menu Bar have distinctive functions. By default, the one to the left is the Standard Toolbar, while the one to the right is the Formatting Bar. Each of these two Toolbars is preceded by a vertical handle. Moving the mouse pointer onto such a handle, changes it into a four-headed 'moving' pointer, as shown here in Fig. 7.2. With the left mouse button held down you can then drag the toolbar around the screen.

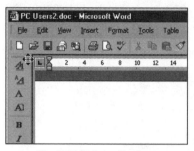

Fig. 7.2 Moving a Toolbar.

As we show here, it is possible to move Toolbars to any part of the screen, and also change the buttons contained in each (see Fig. 4.4 on page 78). Through this section of the book we have moved the Formatting Bar and placed it below the Standard Toolbar. This gives a good compromise between screen space taken up by the bars and the number of buttons displayed.

To see additional sets of Toolbars, use the **View, Toolbars** command to open up a menu of options, as shown in our previous Fig. 4.11 on page 83. You can toggle these on and off by clicking on their names. Be careful, however, how many of these you activate, as they take valuable screen space.

Text Enhancements

In Word all manual formatting, including the selection of font, point size, style (bold, italic, highlight, strike-through, hidden and capitals), colour, super/subscript, spacing and various underlines, are carried out by first selecting the text and then executing the formatting command.

With some actions the easiest way of activating the formatting commands is from the Formatting Bar. With others you have to use the **Format**, **Font** menu command, and select options from the dialogue box below.

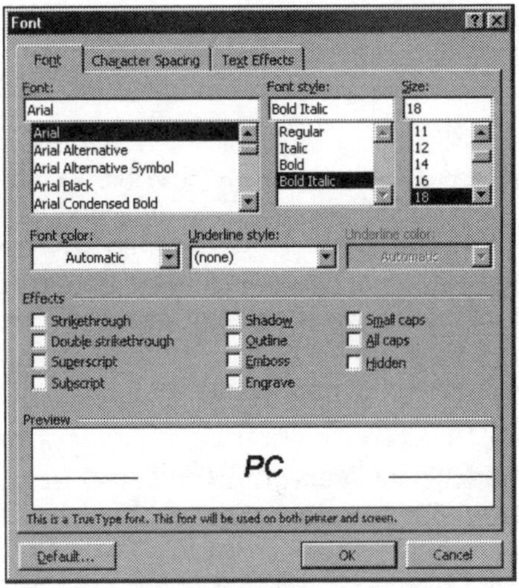

Fig. 7.3 The Font Box.

Yet another method is by using quick keys, some of which are listed below:

To Format	*Type*
Bold	Ctrl+B
Italic	Ctrl+I
Underline	Ctrl+U
Word underline	Ctrl+Shift+W

There are quick keys to do almost anything, but the ones listed here are the most useful and the easiest to remember.

Paragraph Alignment

Word defines a paragraph, as any text which is followed by a paragraph mark, which is created by pressing the <Enter> key. So single line titles, as well as sections of long typed text, can form paragraphs.

 The paragraph symbol, shown here, is only visible in your text if you have selected **Show/Hide ¶** button from the Standard Toolbar, or used <Ctrl+*>.

Word allows you to align a paragraph at the left margin (the default), at the right margin, centred between both margins, or justified between both margins. As with most operations there are several ways to perform alignment in Word. Three such methods are:

- Using buttons on the **Formatting Bar**.
- Using keyboard short cuts.
- Using the **Format, Paragraph** menu command.

The table below describes the buttons on the Formatting Bar and their keystroke shortcuts.

Buttons on Formatting Bar	*Paragraph Alignment*	*Keystrokes*
	Left	<Ctrl+L>
	Centred	<Ctrl+E>
	Right	<Ctrl+R>
	Justified	<Ctrl+J>

Fig. 7.4 below shows the dialogue box resulting from using the **F̲ormat**, **Paragraph** command in which you can specify any **L̲eft, R̲ight**, or **Special** indentation required.

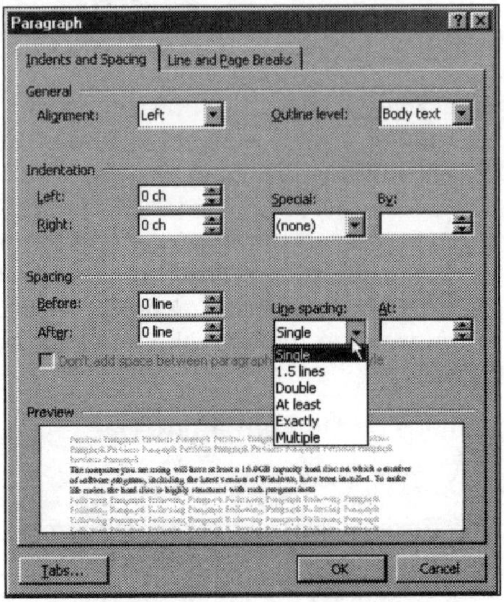

Fig. 7.4 The Paragraph Box.

Paragraph Spacing

The settings in this box will affect the current paragraph (with the insertion point in it), or any selected paragraphs. The above Paragraph dialogue box can also be used to set your paragraph line spacing to single-line, 1½-line, or double-line spacing. You can even set the spacing to any value you want by using the **At Least** option, as shown on the above screen dump, then specify what interval you want.

The available shortcut keys for paragraph spacing are as follows:

To Format	*Type*
Single-spaced lines	Ctrl+1
One-and-a-half-spaced lines	Ctrl+5
Double-spaced lines	Ctrl+2

Whichever of the above methods is used, formatting can take place either before or after the text is entered. If formatting is selected first, then text will type in the chosen format until a further formatting command is given. If, on the other hand, you choose to enter text and then format it afterwards, you must first select the text to be formatted, then activate the formatting.

Word gives you the choice of 5 units to work with, inches, centimetres, millimetres, points or picas. These can be selected by using the **Tools**, **Options** command, choosing the **General** tab of the displayed Options dialogue box, and clicking the down arrow against the **Measurement units** list box, shown open here, which is to be found at the bottom of the dialogue box. We have selected to work in the default centimetres.

Indenting Text

Most documents will require some form of paragraph indenting. An indent is the space between the margin and the edge of the text in the paragraph. When an indent is set (on the left or right side of the page), any justification on that side of the page sets at the indent, not the page border.

To illustrate indentation, open the file **PC Users2**, select the first paragraph, and then choose the **Format**, **Paragraph** command. In the **Indentation** field, select 2.5 cm for both **Left** and **Right**, as shown on the next page. On clicking **OK**, the first selected paragraph is displayed indented. Our screen dump shows the result of the indentation as well as the settings on the Paragraph dialogue box which caused it.

You can also use the Formatting Bar buttons, shown below, to decrease or increase the indent of selected text.

   Use this button to decrease indent.

   Use this button to increase indent.

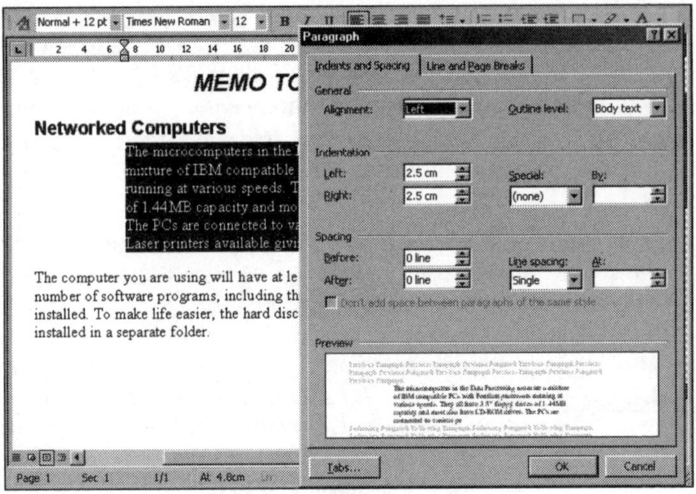

Fig. 7.5 Setting Paragraph Indentation.

The **Indentation** option in the Paragraph dialogue box, can be used to create 'hanging' indents, where all the lines in a paragraph, including any text on the first line that follows a tab, are indented by a specified amount. This is often used in lists to emphasise certain points.

To illustrate the method, use the **PC Users1** file and add at the end of it the text shown below. After you have typed the text in, save the enlarged memo as **PC Users3**, before going on with formatting the new text.

In Windows you can work with files in three different ways:

Name Description

My Computer Use the My Computer utility which Microsoft has spent much time and effort making as intuitive as possible.

Explorer Use the Windows Explorer, a much-improved version of the older File Manager.

MS-DOS Use an MS-DOS Prompt window if you prefer to and are an expert with the DOS commands.

Saving the work at this stage is done as a precaution in case anything goes wrong with the formatting - it is sometimes much easier to reload a saved file, than it is to try to unscramble a wrongly formatted document!

Next, highlight the last 4 paragraphs above, use the **Format**, **Paragraph** command, and select 'Hanging' under **Special** and 3 cm under **By**. On clicking the **OK** button, the text formats as shown in the composite screen dump below, but it is still highlighted. To remove the highlighting, click the mouse button anywhere on the page. The second and following lines of the selected paragraphs, should be indented 3 cm from the left margin.

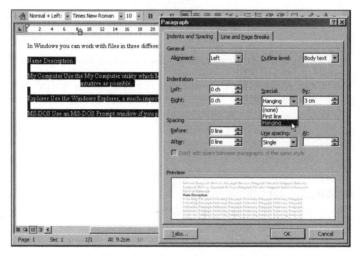

Fig. 7.6 Setting Hanging Indents Manually.

This is still not very inspiring, so to complete the effect we will edit the first lines of each paragraph as follows:

Place the cursor in front of the word 'Description' and press the <Tab> key once. This places the start of the word in the same column as the indented text of the other paragraphs. To complete the effect place tabs before the words 'Use' in the next three paragraphs, until your hanging indents are correct, as shown on the next page.

In Windows you can work with files in three different ways:

Name	Description
My Computer	Use the My Computer utility which Microsoft have spent much time and effort making as intuitive as possible.
Explorer	Use the Windows Explorer, a much-improved version of the older File Manager.
MS-DOS	Use an MS-DOS Prompt window if you prefer to and are an expert with the DOS commands.

This may seem like a complicated rigmarole to go through each time you want the hanging indent effect, but with Word you will eventually set up all your indents, etc., as styles in templates. Then all you do is click in a paragraph to produce them.

Adding a Drop Capital

Another text feature that you may want to use at times is to make the first letter of a paragraph a large dropped initial capital letter, as shown here.

With Word that is ridiculously easy. Just place the insertion point at the beginning of the existing paragraph and action the **Format**, **Drop Cap** menu command. This opens the Drop Cap dialogue box, shown in our composite Fig. 7.7. As is often the case, this gives the settings needed to produce the result shown. You would not normally see them both together.

You can choose between **Dropped** and **In margin** for the position of the initial capital letter, change the **Font** (as we have done) and select how many **Lines to drop**.

MEMO TO PC USERS

Networked Computers

The microcomputers in the Data
processors running at various s
also have CD-ROM drives. The PC
available giving best output.

The computer you are using will ha
programs, including the latest versi
highly structured with each program

In Windows you can work with file

Name	Description
My Computer	Use the My C
as intuitive as
Explorer	Use the Windows Explorer, a much-improved version of the

Drop Cap ? ✕

Position

None   Dropped   In margin

Options

Font:
Arial

Lines to drop: 2

Distance from text: 0 cm

OK   Cancel

Fig. 7.7 Setting a Dropped Capital Letter.

The new first letter is actually a graphic image now. To remove the effect if you decide you don't want it, select the image by clicking it, open the dialogue box with the **Format**, **Drop Cap** command and select **None**.

 When you finish formatting the document, save it under its current filename either with the **File, Save** command (<Ctrl+S>), or by clicking the **Save** button. This command does not display a dialogue box, so you use it when you do not need to make any changes during the saving operation.

Inserting Bullets

Bullets are small characters you can insert, anywhere you like, in the text of your document to improve visual impact. In Word there are several choices for displaying lists with bullets or numbers. As well as the two Formatting Bar buttons, others are made available through the **Format, Bullets and Numbering** command, which displays the following dialogue box.

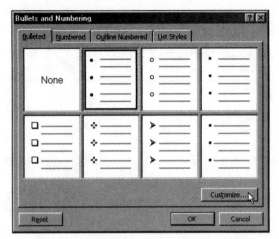

Fig. 7.8 Setting Bullets and Numbering Styles.

You can select any of the bullets shown here, or you could click the **Cus_tomize** button to change the shape, font and size of the bullet, choose a character, and set the indentation in the Customize Bulleted List box shown on the left in Fig. 7.9.

Further, by pressing the **Picture** button on the Customized Bulleted List dialogue box you can select from an enormous number of bullet pictures, as shown on the right of Fig. 7.8. If none of these images suit, you can even **Import** a graphic image yourself to use as bullets. Very comprehensive.

If you select the **Numbered** or **Outline Numbered** tabs, shown in Fig. 7.8, similar dialogue boxes are displayed, giving you a choice of several numbering or outline (multilevel) systems.

Once inserted, you can copy, move or cut a bulleted paragraph in the same way as any other text. However, you can not delete a bullet with the <BkSp> or <Del> keys. To do this, you need to place the insertion point in the line and click the **Bullets** Toolbar button, shown here. Once you have set up a customised bullet, clicking this button in a paragraph will use it.

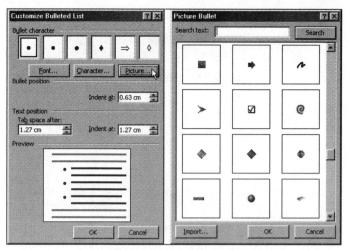

Fig. 7.9 Choosing Custom Bullet Pictures.

Inserting Date and Time

You can insert today's date, the date the current document was created or was last revised, or a date or time that reflects the current system date and time into a document. Therefore, the date can be a date that changes, or a date that always stays the same. In either case, the date is inserted in a date field.

To insert a date field in your document, place the cursor where you want to insert the date, select the **Insert**, **Date and Time** command and choose one of the displayed date formats which suits you from the dialogue box shown in Fig. 7.10 on the next page.

Highlighting '15 June, 2001' (or whatever date is current), and pressing **OK**, inserts the date in your document at the chosen position.

As before, the screen in Fig. 7.10 is a composite of the operation required and the result of that operation.

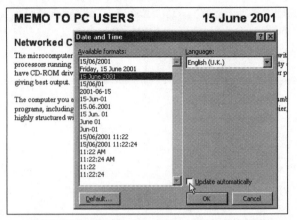

Fig. 7.10 Inserting Dates and Times in a Document.

If you save a document with a date field in it and you open it a few days later, the date shown on it will be the original date the document was created. Most of the time this will probably be what you want, but should you want the displayed date to always update to the current date whenever the document is opened, check the **Update automatically** box, pointed to in Fig. 7.10, and then click the **OK** button.

You may have noticed that many of Word's dialogue boxes have a **Default** button on them, as above. If you click this button you will make the settings active in the box at the time the default ones in any future documents opened with the Normal template. In our case the date would always be presented in the above format.

Comments and Tracked Changes

Another powerful feature of Word is the facility to add comments and to track changes made to a document. Comments are notes, or annotations, that an author or reviewer adds to a document and in Word 2002 they are displayed in balloons in the margin of the document or in the Reviewing Pane, as shown in Fig. 7.11. A tracked change is a mark that shows where a deletion, insertion, or other editing change has been made in a document.

To quickly display or hide tracked changes or comments (known as mark-up) use the **View**, **Markup** menu command.

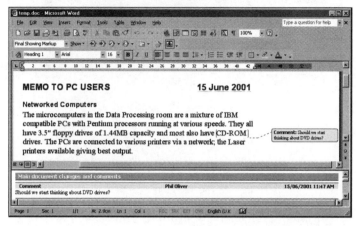

Fig. 7.11 A Comment in a Document with the Reviewing Pane Open.

To add a comment, place the pointer in the correct location, use the **Insert**, **Comment** command, and type the comment into the balloon that opens. If the Reviewing toolbar shown above is hidden, simply right-click any toolbar, and then click Reviewing on the shortcut menu. To open the reviewing pane, as shown above, use the **Show**, **Reviewing Pane** command from the Reviewing toolbar.

You can print a document with mark-up to keep a record of any changes made. If you want to see comments and tracked changes in balloons you must be in Print Layout or Web Layout view.

Formatting with Page Tabs

You can format text in columns by using tab stops. Word 2002 has default left tab stops every 3 ch from the left margin. We do not know what dimension the 'ch' is but the default tabs line up almost exactly at the old 1.27 cm intervals. By default the symbol for a left tab appears in the tab type button at left edge of the ruler as shown in Fig 5.12 on the next page.

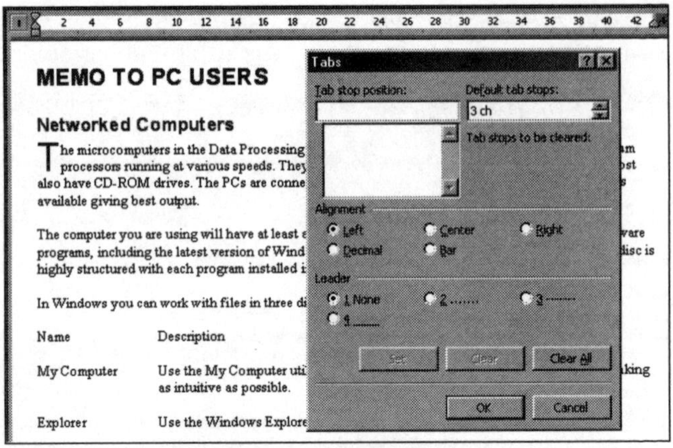

Fig. 7.12 The Tabs Dialogue Box.

To set tabs, use either the **Format**, **Tabs** command which opens the Tabs dialogue box shown above, or click on the tab type button (which cycles through the available tab stops) until the type you want is showing and then click the required position on the lower half of the ruler. To remove an added tab, just drag it off the ruler.

To clear the ruler of tab settings press the **Clear All** button in the Tabs dialogue box. When you set a tab stop on the ruler, all default tab stops to the left of the one you are setting are removed. Tab stops apply either to the paragraph containing the cursor, or to any selected paragraphs.

The tab stop types available have the following functions:

Button	*Name*	*Effect*
 **L**	**Left**	Left aligns text after the tab stop.
⊥	**Centre**	Centres text on tab stop.
⌐	**Right**	Right aligns text after the tab stop.
⊥·	**Decimal**	Aligns decimal point with tab stop.
I	**Bar**	Inserts a vertical line at the tab stop.

The tab type button actually cycles through two more types, first line indent and hanging indent. This gives you a quick way of adding these indents to the ruler.

If you want tabular text to be separated by characters instead of by spaces, select one of the three available characters from the **Leader** box in the Tabs dialogue box. The options are none (the default), dotted, dashed, or underline. The Contents pages of this book are set with right tabs and dotted leader characters.

Note: As all paragraph formatting, such as tab stops, is placed at the end of a paragraph, if you want to carry the formatting of the current paragraph to the next, press <Enter>. If you don't want formatting to carry on, press the down arrow key instead.

Formatting with Styles

We saw earlier on page 87, how you can format your work using Paragraph Styles, but we confined ourselves to using the default **Normal** styles only. In this section we will get to grips with how to create, modify, use, and manage styles.

As mentioned previously, a Paragraph Style is a set of formatting instructions which you save so that you can use it repeatedly within a document or in different documents. A collection of Paragraph Styles can be placed in a Template which could be appropriate for, say, all your memos, so it can be used to preserve uniformity. It maintains consistency and saves time by not having to format each paragraph individually.

Further, should you decide to change a style, all the paragraphs associated with that style reformat automatically. Finally, if you want to provide a pattern for shaping a final document, then you use what is known as a Template. All documents which have not been assigned a document template, use the **Normal.dot** global template, by default.

Paragraph Styles

Paragraph Styles contain paragraph and character formats and a name can be attached to these formatting instructions. From then on, applying the style name is the same as formatting that paragraph with the same instructions.

With Word 2002 you create your styles by example using the new **Styles and Formatting** Task Pane, as we show in Fig. 7.13 below.

***Creating a New Paragraph Style*:** Previously, we spent some time manually creating some hanging indents in the

last few paragraphs of the **PC Users3** document. Open that document and display the **Styles and Formatting** Task Pane by clicking its toolbar button, as shown here. Place the insertion pointer in one of the previously created hanging indent paragraphs, say, in the 'Name Description' line.

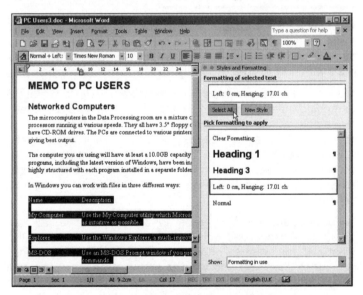

Fig. 7.13 Creating a New Style.

Notice that the selected item in the **Pick formatting to apply** list in the Task Pane has a rectangular selection marker around it. This in fact represents an unnamed style with the formatting we used to create the hanging indents. If you click the **Select All** button in the Task Pane all of our paragraphs with this formatting are highlighted in the main document.

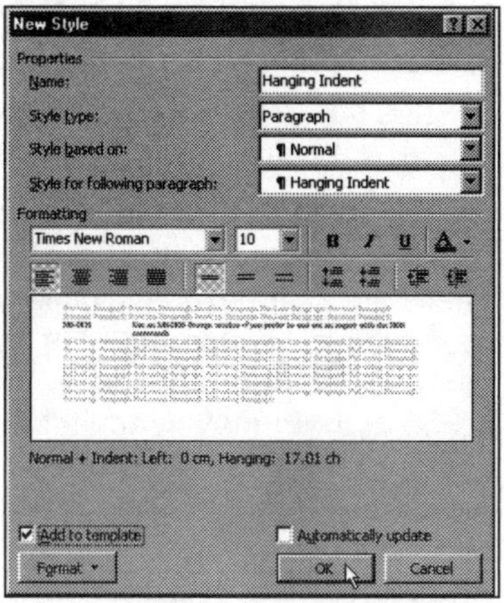

Next click the **New Style** button in the Task Pane to open the New Style box shown in Fig. 7.14. Type the new style name you want to create in the **Name** text box, say, 'Hanging Indent'. Lastly

Fig. 7.14 The New Style Box.

select the **Add to template** option at the bottom of the box and click **OK** to accept your changes.

Finally, one by one, highlight the other three paragraphs with hanging indents and change their style to the new 'Hanging Indent', by clicking the mouse in the **Style** box button on the Formatting Toolbar and selecting the new style from the displayed list, as shown in Fig. 7.15 below.

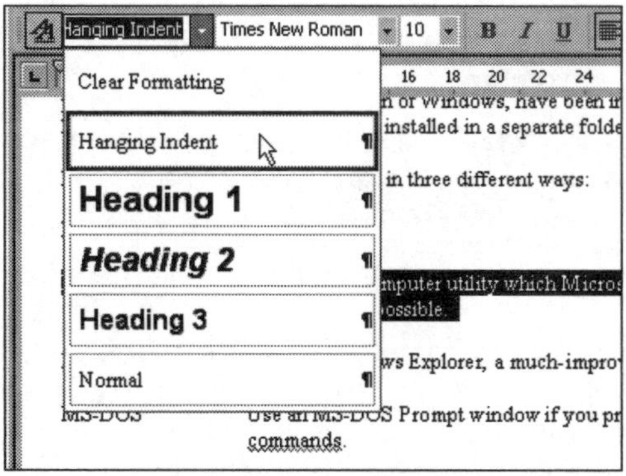

Fig. 7.15 Our New Style in Action.

It would have been nice if this last step could be carried out in the **Styles and Formatting** Task Pane, but the older Style box still seems to be necessary. Once this is done, however, our new style functions exactly the same in the Task Pane as the other ones.

Save the result as **PC Users4**, and make yourself a cup of coffee, or chocolate, or whatever turns you on.

You could also have a look at Word's built-in styles by selecting **S̲tyle Gallery** from the **F̲ormat, T̲heme** menu. There are over sixty available styles, one of which might suit your type of document. Try them with the **PC Users4** file open, as it reformats your document on a viewing pane. Some of them may need installing though, but it will carry this out for you without too much trouble.

Document Templates

A document template provides the overall pattern of your final document. It can contain:

- Styles to control your paragraph and formats.
- Page set-up options.
- Boilerplate text, which is text that remains the same in every document.
- AutoText, which is standard text and graphics that you could insert in a document by typing the name of the AutoText entry.
- Macros, which are programs that can change the menus and key assignments to comply with the type of document you are creating.
- Customised shortcuts, toolbars and menus.

If you don't assign a template to a document, then the default **Normal.dot** template is used by Word. To create a new document template, you either modify an existing one, create one from scratch, or create one based on the formatting of an existing document.

Creating a Document Template

To illustrate the last point above, we will create a simple document template, which we will call **PC User**, based on the formatting of the **PC Users4** document. But first, make sure you have defined the 'Hanging Indent' style as explained earlier.

To create a template based on an existing document do the following:

* Open the existing document.

* Select the **File, Save As** command which displays the Save As dialogue box, shown in Fig. 7.16 below.

* In the **Save as type** box, select Document Template.

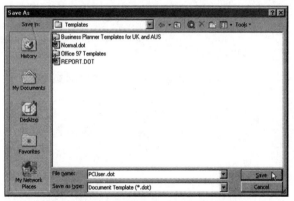

Fig. 7.16 Saving a Document as a Template.

* In the **Save in** box, use the Templates folder which should have opened for you.

* In the **File name** box, type the name of the new template (PC User in our example).

* Press the **Save** button, which opens the template file **PC User.dot** in the Word working area.

* Add the text and graphics you want to appear in all new documents that you base on this template, and *delete* any items (including text) you do not want to appear.

In our example, we deleted everything in the document, bar the heading, and added the words 'PC User Group' using **Insert**, **Picture**, **WordArt**, to obtain:

Fig. 7.17 Artwork and Text in our New Template.

* Click the **Save** button on the Toolbar, and close the document.

To use the new template, do the following:

* Use the **File**, **New** command which opens the **New Document** Task Pane. Select **General Templates** from the **New from template** section of the pane. The General tabbed sheet of the Templates box is opened, as shown in Fig. 7.18 below.

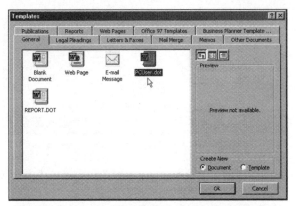

Fig. 7.18 The General Templates Including Our New One.

* Select the name of the template you want to use from the displayed list. This would be PCUsers.dot in our case.

* Make sure that the radio button **Document** is selected, and click the **OK** button.

The new document will be using the selected template.

Templates can also contain Macros as well as AutoText; macros allow you to automate Word keystroke actions only, while AutoText speeds up the addition of boilerplate text and graphics into your document. However, the design of these features is beyond the scope of this book.

Don't forget that Word has a series of built-in templates to suit 'every occasion' as we touched on in page 103.

The Default Character Format

As we have seen, for all new documents Word uses the Times New Roman type font with a 12 points size as the default for the Normal style, which is contained in the Normal template. If the majority of your work demands some different font style or size, then you can change these defaults.

To change the default character formatting, use the **Format**, **Font** command, select the new defaults you want to use, and press the **Default** button, as shown in Fig. 7.19.

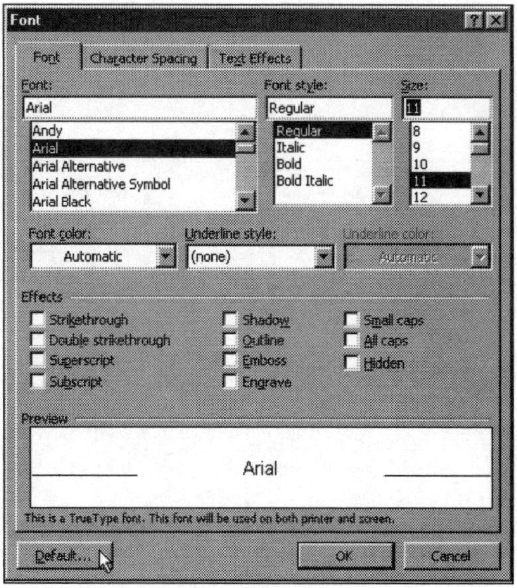

Fig. 7.19 Setting a New Default Font.

A warning box opens to make sure you really know what you are about to do. Pressing the **Yes** button, changes the default character settings for this and all subsequent new documents using the Normal template, but does not change already existing ones. Pressing **No** aborts the operation.

Special Characters and Symbols

Word 2002 has a redesigned Symbol dialogue box from which you can select characters and symbols and insert them into your document using the **Insert, Symbol** command. This is shown in Fig. 7.20 below.

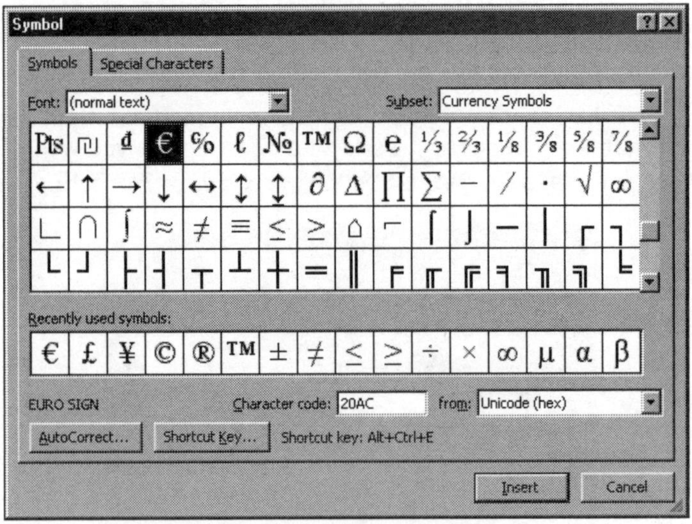

Fig. 7.20 The New Symbol Dialogue Box.

You should be able to find just about any symbol you require in the (normal text) font displayed. But if not, pressing the down-arrow button next to the **Font** box, will reveal the other available character sets. If you double-click the left mouse button on a character, it transfers it to your document at the insertion point.

Microsoft have made it easier to find symbols by grouping them into sets. Clicking the **Su̲bset** button opens a drop-down menu for you to quickly move between them.

The **A̲utoCorrect** button opens the box shown in Fig. 6.4 (page 107) so that you can insert any of the symbols in the **Replace t̲ext as you type** section.

Inserting Other Special Characters

You can include other special characters in a document, such as optional hyphens, which remain invisible until they are needed to hyphenate a word at the end of a line; non-breaking hyphens, which prevent unwanted hyphenation; non-breaking spaces, which prevent two words from splitting at the end of a line; or opening and closing single quotes.

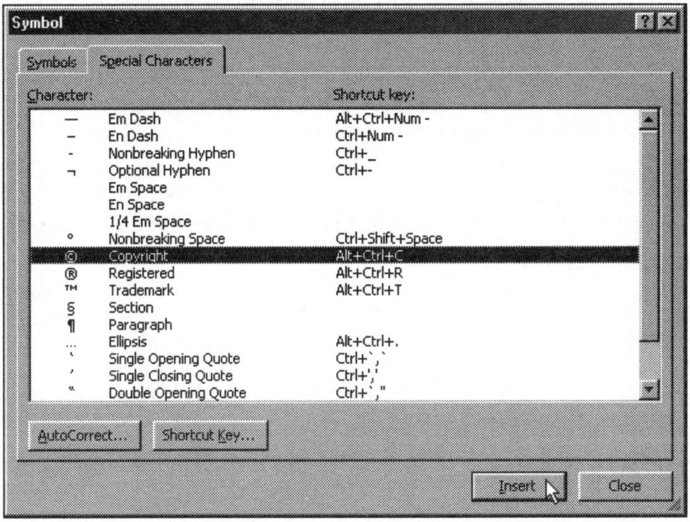

Fig. 7.21 The Special Characters Sheet.

There are two ways to insert these special characters in your document. One is to click the **Sp̲ecial Characters** tab of the Symbol dialogue box which reveals a long list of these special characters, as shown in Fig. 7.21 above. You then select one of them and click the **I̲nsert** button.

The other way is to use the shortcut key combinations listed in Fig. 7.21, which does not require you to open the dialogue box. But you do have to remember them though!

* * *

Word has many more features, far too numerous to mention in the space allocated to this book, although we will be discussing later on how you can use Word to share information with other Microsoft applications and how to use mail merge techniques. What we have tried to do so far, is give you enough basic information so that you can have the confidence to forge ahead and explore the rest of Word's capabilities by yourself.

Perhaps, you might consider exploring page numbering, headers and footers, tables, frames, drawing, and outlining, in that order. We leave it to you. However, if you would prefer to be guided through these topics, then may we suggest you look up the later chapters of the book *Microsoft Word 2002 explained* (BP510), also published by BERNARD BABANI (publishing) Ltd.

* * *

8

The Excel 2002 Spreadsheet

Microsoft Excel is a powerful and versatile software package which, over the years, has proved its usefulness, not only in the business world, but with scientific and engineering users as well.

The program's power lies in its ability to emulate everything that can be done by the use of pencil, paper and a calculator. Thus, it is an 'electronic spreadsheet' or simply a 'spreadsheet', a name which is also used to describe it and other similar products. Its power is derived from the power of the computer it is running on, and the flexibility and accuracy with which it can deal with the solution of the various applications it is programmed to manage. These can vary from budgeting and forecasting to the solution of complex scientific and engineering problems.

Excel 2002 has been designed to present the new look also found in the other Office XP applications, and includes several improvements over previous versions. These are:

- Adoption of the Task Pane - this eliminates the need to dig through menus and dialogue boxes to find the most common tasks, such as opening a New or existing Document, using the Clipboard, Search for other Office XP files, etc. For more details on these, please refer to the end of Chapter 4.

- Adoption of Smart Tags - these allow you to change AutoCorrect settings, give you formatting options when pasting data, Auto Fill options, Formula correction, etc.

- Adoption of the Watch Window - the evaluated values of specified cells are displayed in this window as you work so that you can keep an eye on results even if you are working on another, faraway part of the worksheet or workbook.

Starting the Excel Program

Excel is started in Windows either by clicking the **Start** button

then selecting <u>P</u>**rograms** and clicking on the Microsoft Excel icon on the cascade menu, clicking the Excel button on the Office Shortcut Bar, or the **Open Office Document** button on the Office

Shortcut Bar, or by double-clicking on an Excel workbook file. In the latter case the workbook will be loaded into Excel at the same time.

When you start Excel 2002 the program momentarily displays its opening screen, shown in Fig. 8.1, and then displays the first sheet of a new workbook (more about this shortly).

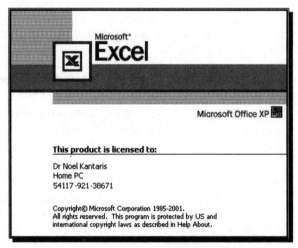

Fig. 8.1 Excel's Opening Screen.

Whether you have used a previous version of Excel or not,

the first time you use the program, it might be a good idea to click the **Microsoft Excel Help** button, shown here, and click the *What's new* link in the right pane of the Help screen.

This displays the Help screen shown in Fig. 8.2. Start by looking at the 'Key new features in Microsoft Excel' option, from which you can find out differences between this version of Excel and previous versions of the program. As you click each hypertext link, Excel displays several topics on the subject. After looking at these options, have a look at the other options displayed in the Help screen. We suggest you spend a little time here browsing through the various topics before going on.

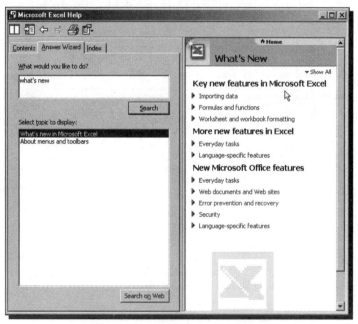

Fig. 8.2 The Microsoft Excel Help Screen.

For additional Help topics, click the Contents tab of the above screen, then double-click the displayed Microsoft Excel Help book to open a list of books covering various topics.

The Excel Screen

When Excel is loaded, a 'blank' spreadsheet screen displays with a similar Title bar, Menu bar, Toolbar and Formatting bar to those of Word. Obviously there are some differences, but that is to be expected as the two programs serve different purposes.

The opening screen of Excel is shown in Fig. 8.3. Do note the similarities with the opening Word screen. Excel follows the usual Microsoft Windows conventions with which you should be very familiar by now.

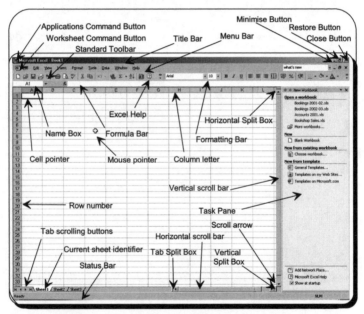

Fig. 8.3 The Opening Excel Workbook Screen.

The window as shown above takes up the full screen area. If you click on the application restore button, the top one of the two restore buttons at the top right of the screen, you can make Excel show in a smaller window. This can be useful when you are running several applications at the same time and you want to transfer between them with the mouse.

Note that the Excel window, which in this case displays an empty and untitled book (Book1), has some areas which have identical functions to those of Word (refer to 'The Word Screen' section in Chapter 4), and other areas which have different functions. Below, we describe only the areas that are exclusive to Excel.

Area	*Function*
Name box	Identifies the selected cell (by name or by cell co-ordinates), chart item, or drawing object.
Formula Bar	Can display a number, a label, or the formula behind a result.
Cell pointer	Marks the current cell.
Column letter	The letter that identifies each column.
Row number	The number that identifies each row.
Tab scrolling	Clicking on these buttons, scrolls sheet tabs right or left, when there are more tabs than can be displayed at once.
Current sheet	Shows the current sheet amongst a number of sheets in a file. These are named Sheet1, Sheet2, Sheet3, and so on, by default, but can be changed to, say, North, South, East, and West. Clicking on a sheet tab, moves you to that sheet.
Tab split box	The split box which you drag left to see more of the scroll bar, or right to see more tabs.

Finally, note the location of the horizontal and vertical split boxes. The first is located at the extreme right of the screen above the 'top vertical scroll arrow' button. The second is located at the extreme bottom-right corner of the screen, to the left of the 'right horizontal scroll arrow' button. Both of these split the screen and their use will be discussed later.

Workbook Navigation

When you first enter Excel, the program sets up a series of huge electronic pages, or worksheets, in your computer's memory, many times larger than the small part shown on the screen. Individual cells are identified by column and row location (in that order), with present size extending to 256 columns and 65,536 rows. The columns are labelled from A to Z, followed by AA to AZ, BA to BZ, and so on, to IV, while the rows are numbered from 1 to 65,536.

A worksheet can be thought of as a two-dimensional table made up of rows and columns. The point where a row and column intersect is called a cell, while the reference points of a cell are known as the cell address. The active cell (A1 when you first enter the program) is boxed.

Navigation around the worksheet is achieved by using one of the following keys or key combinations:

* Pressing one of the four arrow keys ($\rightarrow\downarrow\leftarrow\uparrow$) moves the active cell one position right, down, left or up, respectively.

* Pressing the <PgDn> or <PgUp> keys moves the active cell down or up one visible page.

* Pressing the <Ctrl+$\rightarrow$> or <Ctrl+$\downarrow$> key combinations moves the active cell to the extreme right of the worksheet (column IV) or extreme bottom of the worksheet (row 65,536).

* Pressing the <Home> key, moves the active cell to the beginning of a row.

* Pressing the <Ctrl+Home> key combination moves the active cell to the home position, A1.

* Pressing the <Ctrl+End> key combination moves the active cell to the lower right corner of the worksheet's currently used area.

* Pressing the **F5** function key will display the Go To dialogue box shown in Fig. 8.4.

Fig. 8.4 The Go To Dialogue Box.

In the **Go to** box a list of named ranges in the active worksheet (to be discussed shortly) is displayed, or one of the last four references from which you chose the **Go To** command.

In the **Reference** box you type the cell reference or a named range you want to move to.

To move the active cell with a mouse, do the following:

- Point to the cell you want to move to and click the left mouse button. If the cell is not visible, move the window by clicking on the scroll bar arrowhead that points in the direction you want to move,

- To move a page at a time, click in the scroll bar itself.

- For larger moves, drag the box in the scroll bar, but the distances moved will depend on the size of the worksheet.

When you have finished navigating around the worksheet, press the <Ctrl+Home> key combination which will move the active cell to the A1 position (provided you have not fixed titles in any rows or columns or have no hidden rows or columns - more about these later).

Note that the area within which you can move the active cell is referred to as the working area of the worksheet, while the letters and numbers in the border at the top and left of the working area give the 'co-ordinates' of the cells in a worksheet. The location of the active cell is constantly monitored by the 'selection indicator' which is to be found on the extreme left below the lower Toolbar of the application window. As the active cell is moved, this indicator displays its address, as shown in Fig. 8.5.

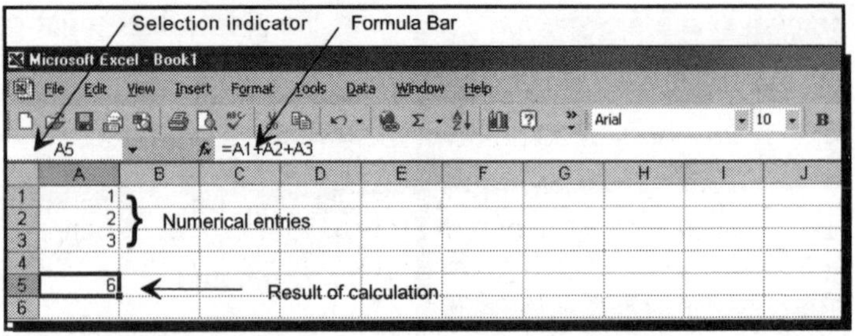

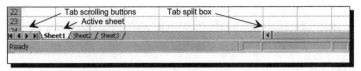

Fig. 8.5 The Selection Indicator and Formula Bar.

The contents of a cell are displayed above the column letters within what is known as the 'Formula Bar'. If you type text in the active cell, what you type appears in both the Formula Bar and the cell itself.

Typing a formula which is preceded by the equals sign (=) to, say, add the contents of three cells, causes the actual formula to appear in the Formula Bar, while the result of the actual calculation appears in the active cell when the <Enter> key is pressed.

Moving Between Sheets

You can scroll between sheets by clicking one of the arrows situated to the left of Sheet1, as shown below. We have labelled these as 'Tab scrolling buttons'. The inner arrows scroll sheets one at a time in the direction of the arrow, while the outer arrows scroll to the end, or beginning, of the group of available sheets. A sheet is then made current by clicking its tab.

Fig. 8.6 The Active Sheet and Tab Scrolling Buttons.

With the keyboard, you can scroll one sheet at a time, and make it active at the same time, by using the <Ctrl+PgDn> key combination. Using <Ctrl+PgUp> scrolls in the reverse direction.

To display more sheet tabs at a time, drag the split box to the right. The reverse action displays less sheet tabs. To rename sheets, double-click at their tab, then type a new name to replace the highlighted name of the particular sheet tab.

To insert a sheet in front of a certain sheet, make that sheet current, then use the **Insert, Worksheet** command sequence. To delete a sheet, make it current and use the **Edit, Delete Sheet** command.

Rearranging Sheet Order

If you need to rearrange the order in which sheets are being held in a workbook, you can do so by dragging a particular sheet to its new position, as shown in Fig. 8.7.

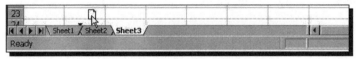

Fig. 8.7 Moving an Active Sheet.

While you are dragging the tab of the sheet you want to move, the mouse pointer changes to an arrow pointing to a sheet. The small solid arrowhead to the left of the mouse pointer indicates the place where the sheet you are moving will be placed.

Grouping Worksheets

You can select several sheets to group them together so that data entry, editing, or formatting can be made easier and more consistent.

To select adjacent sheets, click the first sheet tab, hold down the <Shift> key and then click the last sheet tab in the group. To select non-adjacent sheets, click the first sheet tab, hold down the <Ctrl> key and then click the other sheet tabs you want to group together.

Selecting sheets in the above manner, causes the word '[Group]' to appear in the Title bar of the active window, and the tabs of the selected sheets to be shown in white. To cancel the selection, click at the tab of any sheet which is not part of the selected group.

Selecting a Range of Cells

To select a range of cells, say, A3:C3, point to cell A3, then

- press the left mouse button, and while holding it pressed, drag the mouse to the right.

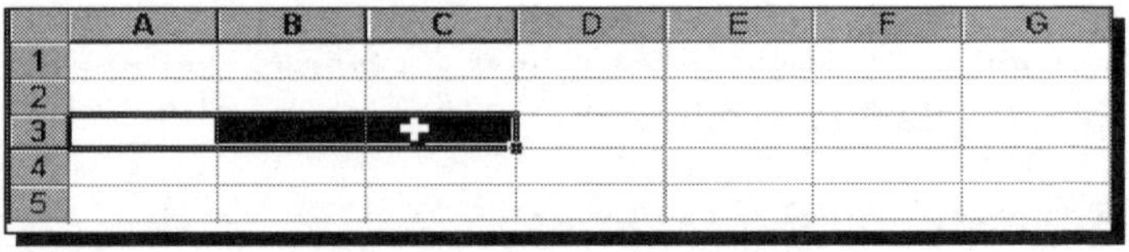

Fig. 8.8 Selecting a Range of Cells.

To select a range from the keyboard, first make active the first cell in the range, then

- hold down the <Shift> key and use the right arrow key (→) to highlight the required range.

To select a 3D range, across several sheets, select the range in the first sheet, then

- release the mouse button, hold down the <Shift> key, and click the Tab of the last sheet in the range.

Shortcut Menus

While a range of cells in a sheet is selected, or a group of sheets is active, you can access a shortcut menu of relevant commands by pressing the right mouse button. This produces a shortcut menu, as shown here, of the most common commands relevant to what you are doing at the time.

Fig. 8.9 A Shortcut Menu.

Viewing Multiple Workbook Sheets

To see more clearly what you are doing when working with multiple workbook sheets, type the text '1st' in location A1 of Sheet1, the text '2nd' in Sheet2, and so on (to add extra sheets in a workbook, use the **Insert, Worksheet** command). Then use the **Window, New Window** command to add three extra windows to your worksheet. Next, use the **Window, Arrange, Tiled** command to display the four sheets as shown in Fig. 8.10. What we have done below is to make active Sheet1 in Book1:1, Sheet2 in Book1:2, and so on, to demonstrate that each window contains all four sheets.

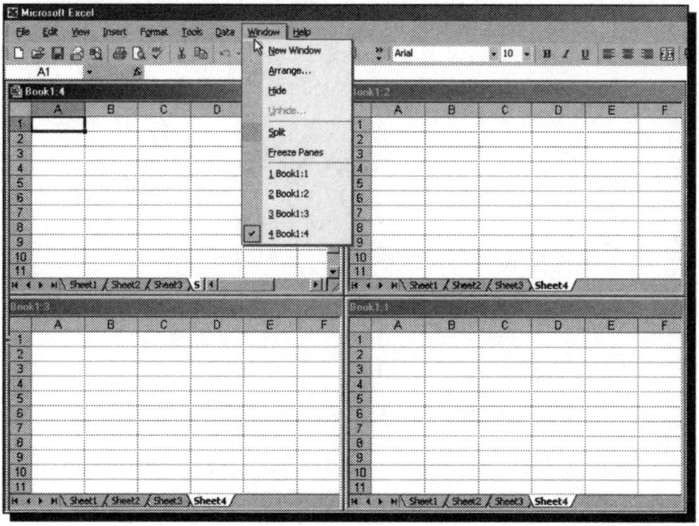

Fig. 8.10 Multiple Workbook Sheets in Tile View.

To move from one window to another, simply point with the mouse to the cell of the window you want to go to and click the left mouse button. To display a different sheet in each window, go to a window and click the sheet's tab.

To return to single-window view mode from a tiled or cascade mode, click the maximise button of the active window.

Entering Information

We will now investigate how information can be entered into a worksheet. But first, make sure you are in Sheet1, then return to the Home (A1) position, by pressing the <Ctrl+Home> key combination, then type the words:

    Project Analysis

As you type, the characters appear in both the 'Formula Bar' and the active cell. If you make a mistake, press the <BkSp> key to erase the previous letter or the <Esc> key to start again. When you have finished, press <Enter>.

Note that what you have just typed in has been entered in cell A1, even though the whole of the word ANALYSIS appears to be in cell B1. If you use the right arrow key to move the active cell to B1 you will see that the cell is indeed empty.

Typing any letter at the beginning of an entry into a cell results in a 'text' entry being formed automatically, otherwise known as a 'label'. If the length of the text is longer than the width of a cell, it will continue into the next cell to the right of the current active cell, provided that cell is empty, otherwise the displayed information will be truncated.

To edit information already in a cell, either

- double-click the cell in question, or

- make that cell the active cell and press the **F2** function key.

The cursor keys, the <Home> and <End> keys, as well as the <Ins> and <Del> keys can be used to move the cursor and/or edit information as required.

You can also 'undo' the last 16 actions carried out since the program was last in the **Ready** mode, by either using the **Edit, Undo Entry** command (<Ctrl+Z>), or clicking the **Undo** button.

Next, move the active cell to B3 and type

Jan

Pressing the right arrow key (→) will automatically enter the typed information into the cell and also move the active cell one cell to the right, in this case to C3. Now type

Feb

and press <Enter>.

The looks of a worksheet can be enhanced somewhat by using different types of borders around specific cells. To do

this, first select the range of cells, then click at the down arrow of the **Borders** button on the Formatting Toolbar, shown here, which displays twelve different types of borders (Fig. 8.11). In our example, we have selected the cell range A3:C3, then we chose the 8th border from the display table.

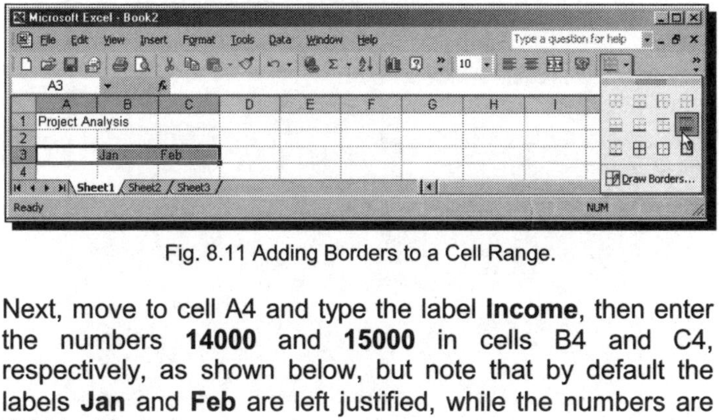

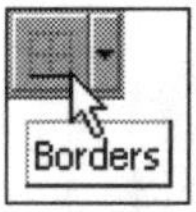

![Microsoft Excel - Book2 window showing Project Analysis with Jan, Feb labels]

Fig. 8.11 Adding Borders to a Cell Range.

Next, move to cell A4 and type the label **Income**, then enter the numbers **14000** and **15000** in cells B4 and C4, respectively, as shown below, but note that by default the labels **Jan** and **Feb** are left justified, while the numbers are right justified.

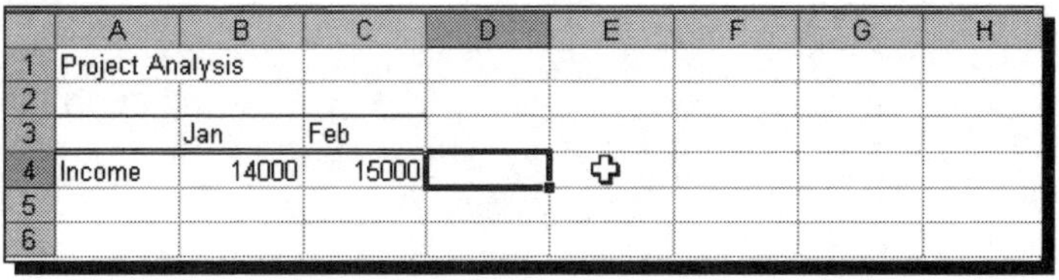

	A	B	C	D	E	F	G	H
1	Project Analysis							
2								
3		Jan	Feb					
4	Income	14000	15000		✿			
5								
6								

Fig. 8.12 Default Justification of Labels and Numbers.

Changing Text Alignment and Fonts

One way of improving the looks of this worksheet is to also right justify the text **Jan** and **Feb** within their respective cells. To do this, move the active cell to B3 and select the range B3 to C3 by dragging the mouse, then either click the **Align Right** button, shown here, or choose the **Format**, **Cells** command, then select the **Alignment** tab from the displayed Format Cells dialogue box, shown below, click the down-arrow against the **Horizontal** text box, highlight **Right** from the drop-down menu options, and press **OK**.

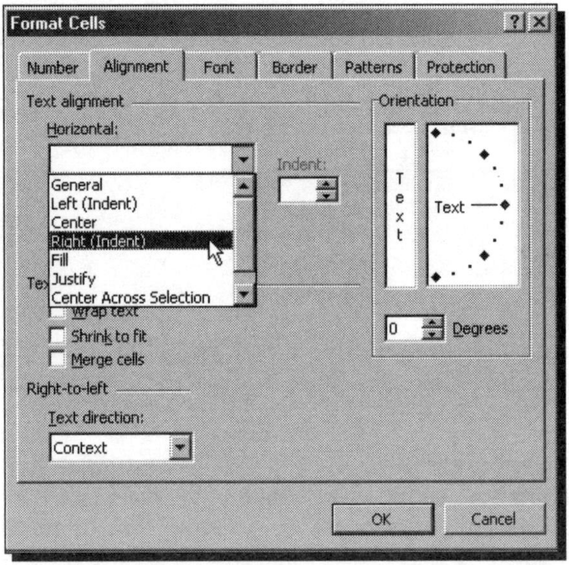

Fig. 8.13 Formatting Cells by Using the Alignment Tab Sheet.

No matter which method you choose, the text should now appear right justified within their cells. However, although the latter method is lengthier, it nevertheless provides you with greater flexibility in displaying text, both in terms of position and orientation.

We could further improve the looks of our worksheet by choosing a different font for the heading **Project Analysis**. To achieve this, select cell A1, then click on the down arrow against the **Font Size** button on the Formatting Bar, to reveal the band of available point sizes for the selected font, as shown overleaf. From this band, choose 14, then click in succession the **Bold** and **Italic** buttons.

Finally, since the numbers in cells B4 to C4 represent money, it would be better if these were prefixed with the £ sign. To do this, select the cell range B4:C4, then either click the **Currency** button on the Formatting Bar, shown here, or choose the **Format, Style** command and select **Currency** from the list under **Style name** in the displayed Style dialogue box.

The numbers within the chosen range will now be displayed in currency form, and the width of the cells will automatically adjust to accommodate them, if they are too long which is the case in our example.

To see the actual new width of, say column C4, place the mouse pointer, as shown, to the right of the column letter on the dividing line. When the mouse pointer changes to the shape shown in Fig. 8.14, press the left mouse button without moving the mouse. The current width will

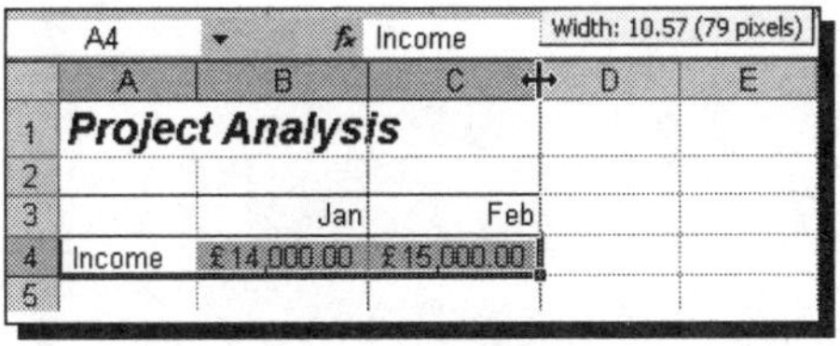

Fig. 8.14 Formatting Numbers in Currency Style.

then display within a pop-up text box as 79 pixels, increased from the default column width of 64 pixels.

This new width accommodates our numbers exactly, but we might like to increase it to, say, 82 pixels so that it looks better. To do this, place the mouse pointer in between the column letters, and drag the pointer to the right, until the width of the column displays as 82 pixels, which also happens to be 11 characters wide.

Saving a Workbook

Now, let us assume that we would like to stop at this point, but would also like to save the work entered so far before leaving the program. First, return to the Home position by pressing <Ctrl+Home>. This is good practice because the position of the cell pointer at the time of saving the file is preserved. For example, had you placed the cell pointer well beyond the data entry area of your worksheet at the time of saving, when you later opened this worksheet you might be confused to see empty cells surrounding the cell pointer - you might think that you have opened an empty worksheet.

Next, choose the **File, Save** command to reveal the Save As dialogue box. You could select to save your work in the default **My Documents** folder, or create a suitably named folder using the **Create New Folder** button on the Save As dialogue box, shown in Fig. 8.15.

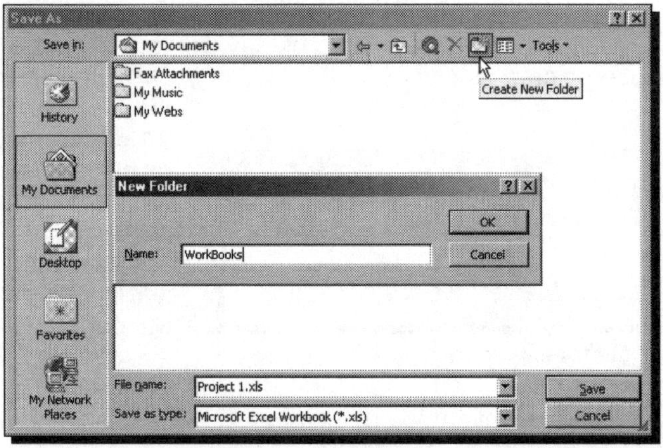

Fig. 8.15 Creating a New Folder in the Save As Dialogue Box.

We used this facility to create a folder called **WorkBooks** within the **My Documents** folder.

To save our work currently in memory, we selected the **WorkBooks** folder in the **Save in** field of the Save As dialogue box, then moved the cursor into the **File name** box, and typed **Project 1**. We suggest you do the same.

The file will be saved in the default file type *Microsoft Excel Workbook*, as displayed in the **Save as type** box. Excel adds the file extension **.xls** automatically and uses it to identify it.

By clicking the **Save as type** button at the bottom of the Save As dialogue box, you can save your work in a variety of other formats, including Web Page (HTML), Template, and earlier versions of Excel.

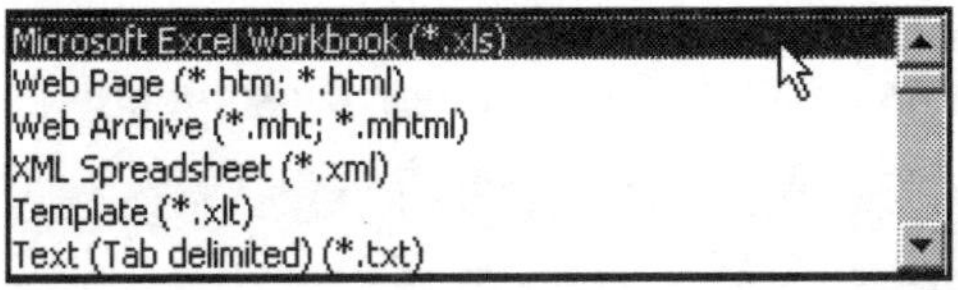

Fig. 8.16 Available Type Formats for Saving Work.

If you want to create backup files or provide password protection to your file, click the down-arrow against the **Tools** button at the top of the Save As dialogue box, and select **General Options** from the displayed drop down menu. This opens the Save Options dialogue box, shown in the middle of the composite screen dump in Fig. 8.17. Fill in this dialogue box appropriately and press the **OK** button.

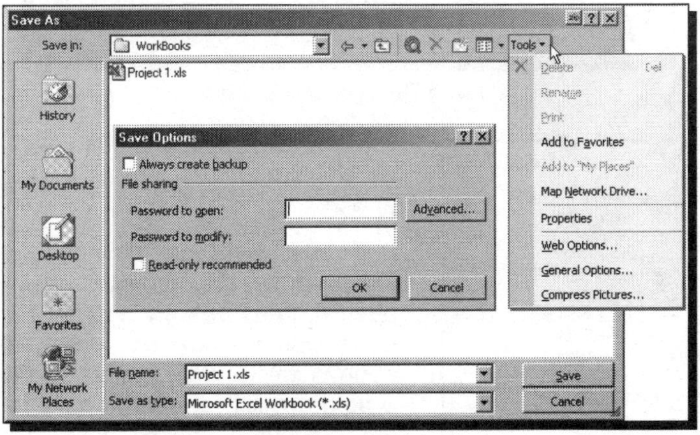

Fig. 8.17 The Save Options Dialogue Box.

Finally, pressing the **Save** button causes your work to be saved under the chosen filename.

Opening a Workbook

An already saved workbook, or file, can be opened by either clicking at the **Open** button, shown here, or selecting the **File, Open** command which displays the Open dialogue box. Excel asks for a filename to open, with the default *All Microsoft Excel Files* being displayed in the **Files of type** box, as shown in Fig. 8.18. If the file was saved, double-click the **WorkBooks** folder and select it by clicking its name in the list box, then click the **Open** button.

Fig. 8.18 The Open Dialogue Box.

Fig. 8.19 The Look In box of the Open Dialogue Box.

If you haven't saved it, don't worry as you could just as easily start afresh.

If you want to change the logged drive, click the down-arrow against the **Look in** box, of the Open dialogue box, and select the appropriate drive from the drop-down list, as shown here for our computer. In your case, this list will most certainly be different.

If you have been working recently with an Excel file and have saved it, and you have just launched Excel, the name of the file together with those of other files you have looked up or worked with recently, will appear in the **New Workbook** Task Pane as shown in Fig. 8.20.

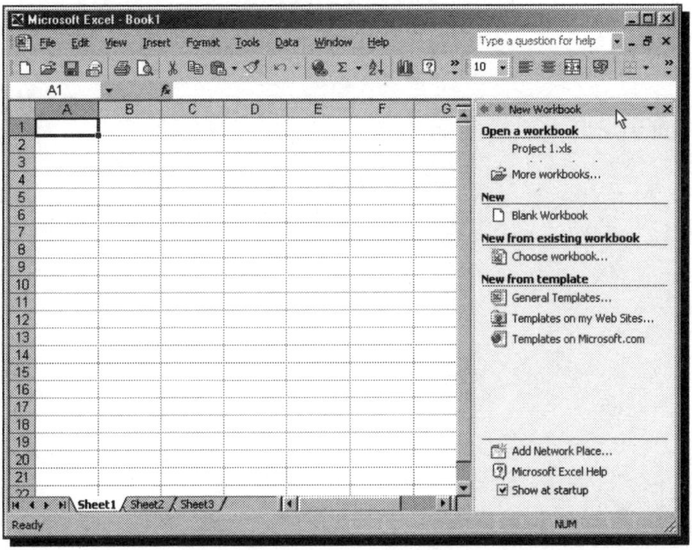

Fig. 8.20 The Task Pane List of Recently Used Files.

Exiting Excel

To exit Excel, close any displayed dialogue boxes by clicking the **Cancel** button, and make sure that the word **Ready** is displayed on the status bar (press the <Esc> key until it does), and either

- choose the **File, Exit** command,
- use the <Alt+**F4**> key combination, or
- click the **Close** button.

No matter which command you choose, if you have changed any opened worksheet, Excel will warn you and will ask for confirmation before exiting the program, as follows.

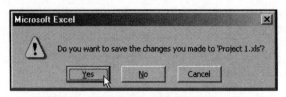

Fig. 8.21 Excel's File Save Warning Message.

If you do not want to save the changes, then press the **No** button, otherwise press **Yes**.

9

Filling in a Worksheet

We will use, as an example of how a worksheet can be built up, the few entries on 'Project Analysis' from the previous chapter. If you have saved **Project 1**, then either click its name in the Task Pane, click the **Open** button, or use the **File, Open** command, then highlight its filename in the Open dialogue box, and click the **OK** button. If you haven't saved it, don't worry as you could just as easily start afresh.

Next, either double-click on the contents of a cell to edit existing entries, or simply retype the contents of cells, so that your worksheet looks as near as possible to the one in Fig. 9.1. For formatting details, see below and the next page.

	A	B	C	D	E	F	G	H	I	J
1	*Project Analysis: Adept Consultants Ltd.*									
2										
3		Jan	Feb	Mar	1st Quarter					
4	Income	£ 14,000.00	£ 15,000.00	£ 16,000.00						
5	Costs:									
6	Wages	2000	3000	4000						
7	Travel	400	500	600						
8	Rent	300	300	300						
9	Heat/Light	150	200	130						
10	Phone/Fax	250	300	350						
11	Adverts	1100	1200	1300						
12	Total Costs									
13	Profit									
14	Cumulative									
15										

Fig. 9.1 Entering Data in Project 1 Worksheet.

The lines, like the double line stretching from A3 to E3 were entered by first selecting the cell range A3:E3, then clicking the down-arrow of the **Borders** button on the Formatting Bar, and selecting the appropriate border from the 12 displayed options.

Formatting Entries

The information in cell A1 (Project Analysis: Adept Consultants Ltd.) was entered left-justified and formatted by clicking on the **Font Size** button on the Formatting Bar, and

selecting 14 point font size from the band of available font sizes, then clicking in succession the **Bold** and **Italic** buttons, shown to the left.

The text in the cell block B3:E3 was formatted by first selecting the range and then clicking the **Centre alignment** button on the Formatting Bar, so the text within the range was displayed centre justified.

The numbers within the cell block B4:E4 were formatted by first selecting the range, then clicking the **Currency** button on the Formatting Bar, shown here, so the numbers appeared with two digits after the decimal point and prefixed with the £ sign.

All the text appearing in column A (apart from that in cell A1) was just typed in (left justified), as shown in the screen dump in Fig. 9.1. The width of all the columns A to E was adjusted to 11 characters; a quick way of doing this is to select one row of these columns, then use the **F<u>o</u>rmat, <u>C</u>olumn, <u>W</u>idth** command, and type 11 in the displayed box.

Filling a Range by Example

To fill a range by example, select the first cell of a range,

point at the bottom right corner of the cell and when the mouse pointer changes to a small cross, drag the mouse in the required direction to fill the range.

In the above case, we started with a cell containing the abbreviation 'Jan'. The next cell to the right will automatically fill with the text 'Feb' (Excel anticipates that you want to fill cells by example with the abbreviations for months, and does it for you). Not only that, but it also copies the format of the selected range forward.

The Auto Fill Smart Tag

When you release the mouse button, Excel places a Smart Tag next to the end of the filled-in range. Clicking the down-arrow of this Smart Tag displays a drop-down menu of options, as shown in Fig. 9.2.

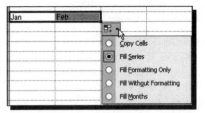

Fig. 9.2 The Auto Fill Smart Tag Options.

Entering Text, Numbers and Formulae

Excel allows you to format both text (labels) and numbers in any way you choose. For example, you can have numbers centre justified in their cells.

When text, a number, a formula, or an Excel function is entered into a cell, or reference is made to the contents of a cell by the cell address, then the content of the status bar changes from **Ready** to **Enter**. This status can be changed back to **Ready** by either completing an entry and pressing <Enter> or one of the arrow keys, or by pressing <Esc>.

We can find the 1st quarter total income from consultancy, by activating cell E4, typing

    =b4+c4+d4

and pressing <Enter>. The total first quarter income is added, using the above formula, and the result is placed in cell E4.

Now complete the insertion into the spreadsheet of the various amounts under 'costs' and then choose the **File, Save As** command to save the resultant worksheet under the filename **Project 2**, before going on any further. Remember that saving your work on disc often enough is a good thing to get used to, as even the shortest power cut can cause the loss of hours of hard work!

Using Functions

In our example, writing a formula that adds the contents of three columns is not too difficult or lengthy a task. But imagine having to add 20 columns! For this reason Excel has an inbuilt summation function which can be used to add any number of columns (or rows).

To illustrate how this and other functions can be used, activate cell E4 and first press <Del> to clear the cell of its formula, then click the **Insert Function** button, shown here, on the left of the Formula Bar. If the function you require appears on the displayed dialogue box under **Select a function**, choose it, otherwise type a brief description of what you want to do in the **Search for a function** text box and press **Go**, or select the appropriate class from the list under **Or select a category**.

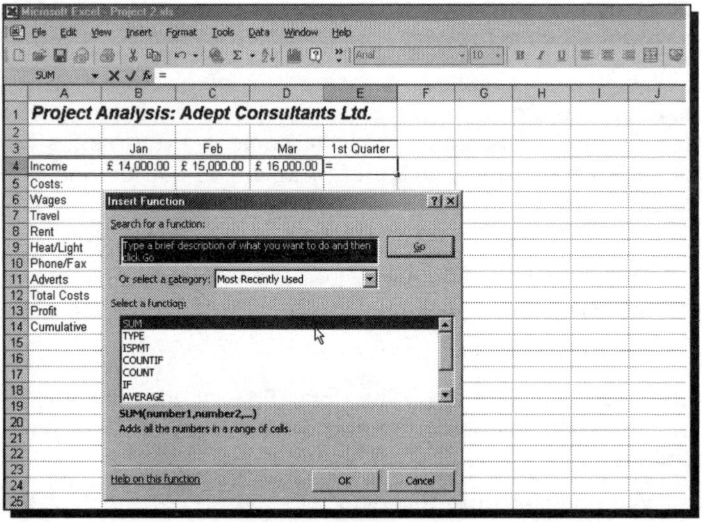

Fig. 9.3 Selecting a Function to Insert in a Cell.

Choosing the **SUM** function, inserts the entry SUM(B4:D4) in the Edit line, as shown below. Clicking the **OK** button, causes the Function Arguments dialogue box of the selected function to be displayed on the screen, as shown in Fig. 9.4.

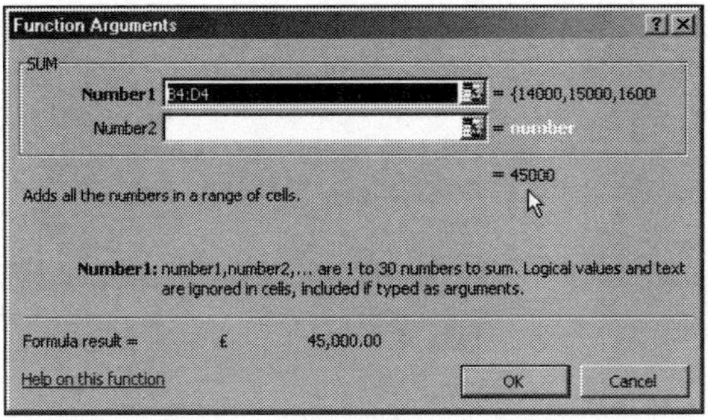

Fig. 9.4 The Function Arguments Dialogue Box.

Note that the arguments in the above case are given as B4:D4 in the **Number1** box and the actual result of the calculation is displayed next to it. Pressing the **OK** button, causes the function to be pasted into cell E4, but only the formula result is displayed in the cell. If you click in the **Number2** box you can select another cell range to be summed. The overall result appears at the bottom of the box.

Using the AutoSum Button

With addition, there is a better and quicker way of letting Excel work out the desired result. To illustrate this, select the cell range B6:E12, which contains the 'Costs' we would like to add up. To add these in both the horizontal and vertical direction, we include in the selected range an empty column to the right of the numbers and an empty row below the numbers, as shown in fig. 9.5.

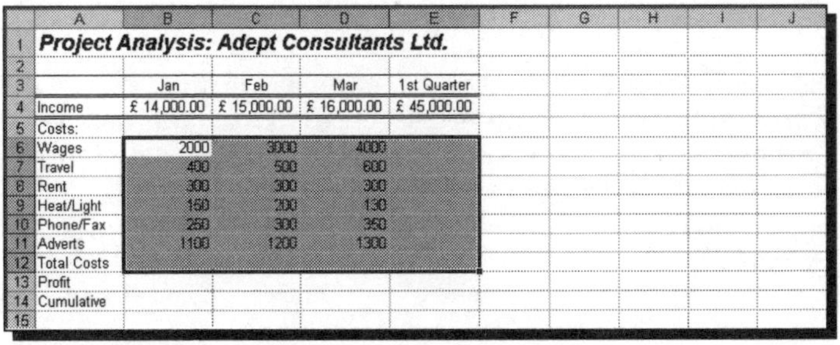

Fig. 9.5 Selecting a Range to be Summed.

Σ ▾   Pressing the **AutoSum** button, shown here, inserts the result of the summations in the empty column and row, as shown in Fig. 9.6. The selected range remains selected so that any other formatting can be applied by simply pressing the appropriate icon button.

	A	B	C	D	E	F	G	H	I
1	**Project Analysis: Adept Consultants Ltd.**								
2									
3		Jan	Feb	Mar	1st Quarter				
4	Income	£ 14,000.00	£ 15,000.00	£ 16,000.00	£ 45,000.00				
5	Costs:								
6	Wages	2000	3000	4000	9000				
7	Travel	400	500	600	1500				
8	Rent	300	300	300	900				
9	Heat/Light	150	200	130	480				
10	Phone/Fax	250	300	350	900				
11	Adverts	1100	1200	1300	3600				
12	Total Costs	4200	5500	6680	16380				
13	Profit								
14	Cumulative								
15									

Fig. 9.6 Using the AutoSum Toolbar Button on a Selected Range.

Note that the **AutoSum** button now has a down-arrow to the

right of it. Clicking this arrow, displays a list of alternative options, as shown here. From this list you can choose to calculate the **A**verage, **C**ount the entries, find the **Ma**x or **Mi**n values in a row or column, or indeed display the Insert Function dialogue box discussed earlier and shown in Fig. 9.3 by selecting the **More Functions** option.

Now complete the insertion of formulae in the rest of the worksheet, noting that 'Profit', in B13, is the difference between 'Income' and 'Total Cost', calculated by the formula **=b4-b12**. To complete the entry, this formula should be copied using the 'fill by example' method into the three cells to its right.

The 'Cumulative' entry in cell B14 should be a simple reference to cell B13, that is **=b13**, while in cell C14 it should be **=b14+b13**. Similarly, the latter formula is copied into cell D14 using the 'fill by example' method.

Next, format the entire range B6:E12 by selecting the range and clicking the **Currency** button.

If you make any mistakes and copy formats or information into cells you did not mean to, use the **Edit, Undo** command or click the **Undo** button which allows you to selectively undo what you were just doing. To blank the contents within a range of cells, first select the range, then press the <Del> key.

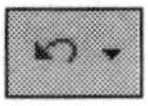

The worksheet, up to this point, should look as follows:

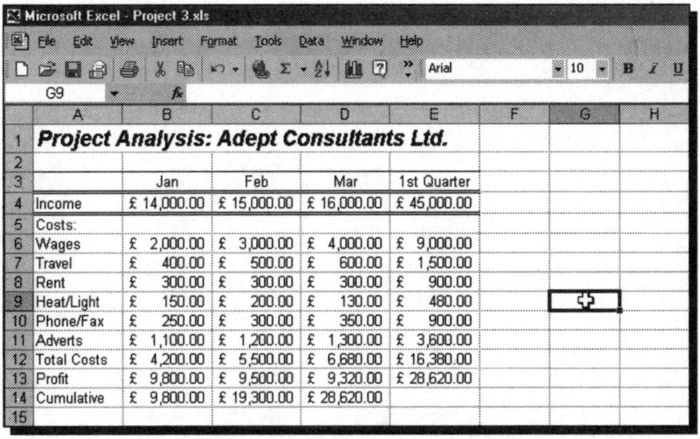

Fig. 9.7 The Completed 1st Quarter Worksheet.

Finally, use the **File, Save As** command to save your work under the filename **Project 3** in the **WorkBooks** folder.

Printing a Worksheet

To print a worksheet, make sure that the printer you propose to use was defined when you first installed Windows.

If you have named more than one printer in your original installation of Windows, and want to select a printer other than your original first choice, then select the **File, Print** (or <Ctrl+P> command, click the down-arrow against the **Name** box on the displayed Print dialogue box and select the required printer, as shown in Fig. 9.8.

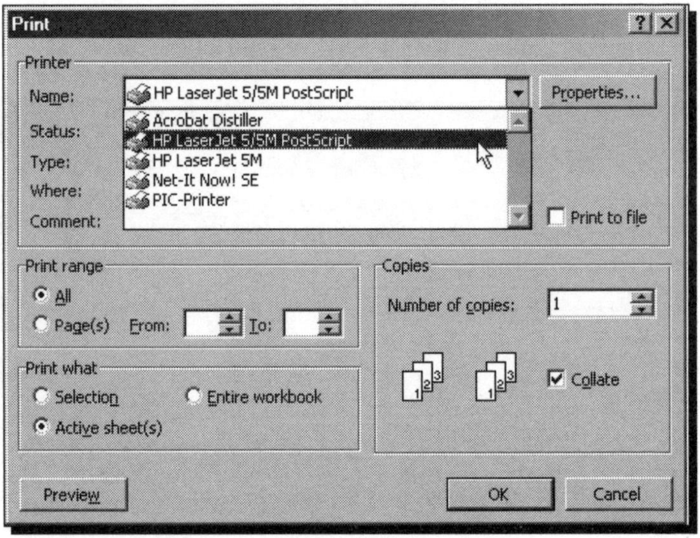

Fig. 9.8 The Print Dialogue Box.

If you want to change the paper size, print orientation or printer resolution, click the **Properties** button on the Print dialogue box. These and other changes to the appearance of the printout can also be made by choosing the **File, Page Setup** command which displays the Page Setup dialogue box, as shown in Fig. 9.9 on the next page.

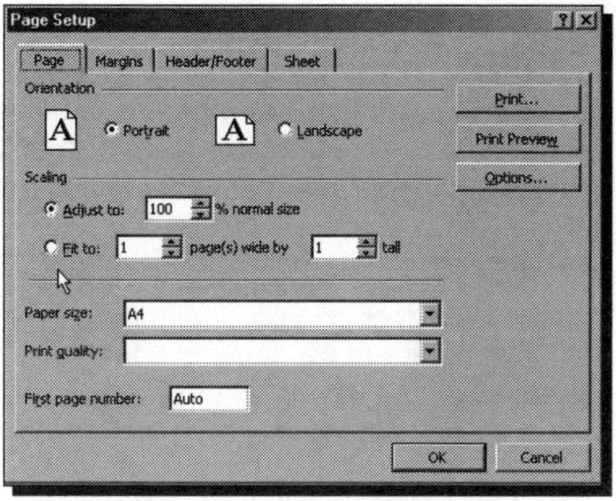

Fig. 9.9 The Page Setup Dialogue Box.

By selecting the appropriate Tab on this dialogue box, you can change your **Page** settings, page **Margins**, specify a **Header/Footer**, and control how a **Sheet** should be printed. Each Tab displays a different dialogue box, appropriate to the function at hand. In the **Header/Footer** dialogue box you can even click the down-arrow against the Header and Footer boxes to display a suggested list for these, appropriate to the work you are doing, the person responsible for it and even the date it is being carried out! Try it.

A very useful feature of Excel is the **Scaling** facility shown in the above dialogue box. You can print actual size or a percentage of it, or you can choose to fit your worksheet on to one page which allows Excel to scale your work automatically.

To preview a worksheet, click the **Print Preview** button on the extension of the Standard Toolbar, shown here - once this is done the button is transferred on to the Standard Toolbar next to the **Print** button, or click the **Print Preview** button on the Page Setup dialogue box, or the **Preview** button on the Print dialogue box. You can even use the **File, Print Preview** command!

The idea of all these preview choices is to make it easy for you to see your work on screen before committing it to paper, thus saving even a few more trees!

Enhancing a Worksheet

You can make your work look more professional by adopting various enhancements, such as single and double line cell borders, shading certain cells, and adding meaningful headers and footers.

However, with Excel you can easily select a predefined style to display your work on both the screen and on paper. To do this, place the active cell within the table (or range) you want to format, say C5, then select the **Format, AutoFormat** which will cause the following dialogue box to appear on the screen, displaying a sample of the chosen table format. In this way you can choose what best suits your needs. We selected 'Classic 2' and pressed **OK**.

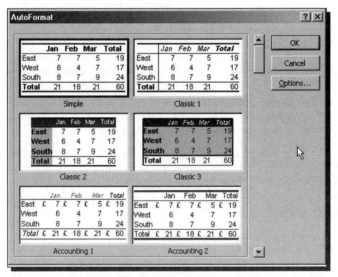

Fig. 9.10 The AutoFormat Dialogue Box.

Next, reduce the title of the worksheet to 'Project Analysis', then centre it within the range A1:E1, by first selecting the range, then clicking the **Merge and Centre** button, shown here, which centres the title within the specified range. Finally, save the worksheet as **Project 4**, before going on.

Header and Footer Icons and Codes

With the help of header and footer icons and their codes, shown below, you can position text or automatically insert information at the top or bottom of a report printout.

To add a header to our printed example, use the **File, Page Setup** command and click first the **Header/Footer** Tab, then the **Custom Header** button and type the information displayed below in the **Left section** and **Right section** of the Header box.

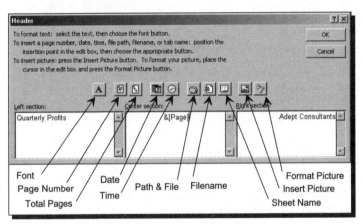

Fig. 9.11 The Header Dialogue Box.

While the insertion pointer is in, say, the **Center section** of the Header box, pointing and clicking on the **Sheet Name** button, inserts the &[Tab] code which has the effect of inserting the sheet name of the current active sheet at the time of printing. The first icon button displays the Font dialogue box, while the others display the following codes:

Code	Action
&[Page]	Inserts a page number.
&[Pages]	Inserts the total number of pages.
&[Date]	Inserts the current date.
&[Time]	Inserts the current time.
&[File]	Inserts the filename of the current workbook.

Setting a Print Area

To choose a smaller print area than the current worksheet, select the required area by highlighting the starting cell of the area and dragging the mouse, or using the **<Shift+Arrows>**, to highlight the block, and use the **File**, **Print** command which displays the dialogue box in Fig. 9.12.

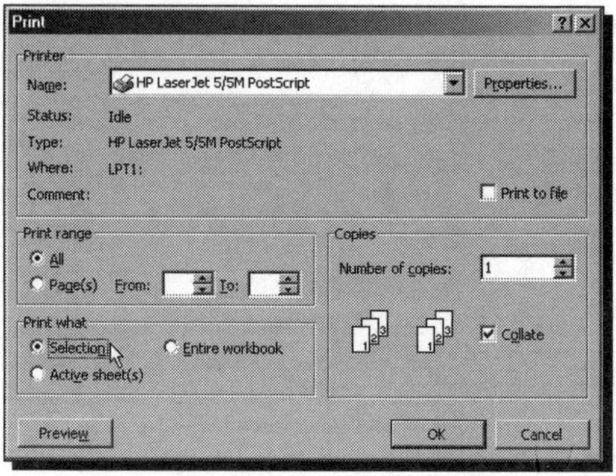

Fig. 9.12 Printing a Selection Area.

Choose the **Selection** button in the **Print what** box, and either click the **Preview** or the **OK** button to preview your report on screen or print it on paper. When in preview mode, the following buttons are available to you.

The first two allow you to change sheets, while the next one allows you to review your print output magnified or at full page size - when in full page size, the mouse pointer looks like a magnifying glass. The next four buttons can be used to print, change page settings, display and change the margins, or adjust the page size by dragging the page breaks to a new position. To return to normal view, click the **Close** button.

Another way to set the area to print is to select it first, then use the **File, Print Area, Set Print Area** menu command. To print selected sheets or the entire workbook, click the appropriate button in the **Print what** box of the Print dialogue box.

The default selection in the **Print what** box is **Active sheet(s)** which is also what will be printed out if you click the

Print button, shown here. If you have included headers and footers, these will be printed out irrespective of whether you choose to print a selected range or a selected worksheet. To centre the page horizontally on the paper, use the **File, Page Setup** command, click the Margins tab and select the option. Finally, previewing our worksheet, produced the screen in Fig, 9.13 in which we show how you can fine-tune the margins so that the worksheet is centred on the page:

| Setup... | Margins | Page Break Preview | Close | Help |

| Quarterly Profits | 1 | Adept Consultants |

Project Analysis

	Jan	Feb	Mar	1st Quarter
Income	£ 14,000.00	£ 15,000.00	£ 16,000.00	£ 45,000.00
Costs:				
Wages	£ 2,000.00	£ 3,000.00	£ 4,000.00	£ 9,000.00
Travel	£ 400.00	£ 500.00	£ 600.00	£ 1,500.00
Rent	£ 300.00	£ 300.00	£ 300.00	£ 900.00
Heat/Light	£ 150.00	£ 200.00	£ 130.00	£ 480.00
Phone/Fax	£ 250.00	£ 300.00	£ 350.00	£ 900.00
Adverts	£ 1,100.00	£ 1,200.00	£ 1,300.00	£ 3,600.00
Total Costs	£ 4,200.00	£ 5,500.00	£ 6,680.00	£ 16,380.00
Profit	£ 9,800.00	£ 9,500.00	£ 9,320.00	£ 28,620.00
Cumulative	£ 9,800.00	£ 19,300.00	£ 28,620.00	

Fig. 9.13 Changing the Margins of a Report Page Preview.

3-Dimensional Worksheets

In Excel, a Workbook is a 3-dimensional file made up with a series of flat 2-dimensional sheets stacked 'on top of each other'. Each sheet is the same size, and in itself, behaves the same as the more ordinary worksheets. As mentioned previously, each separate sheet in a file has its own Tab identifier at the bottom of the screen. Ranges can be set to span several different sheets to build up 3-dimensional blocks of data. These blocks can then be manipulated, copied, or moved to other locations in the file. A cell can reference any other cell in the file, no matter what sheet it is on, and an extended range of functions can be used to process these 3-dimensional ranges.

Manipulating Ranges

The best way to demonstrate a new idea is to work through an example - we will use the worksheet saved under **Project 4**. Next, start Excel, use the **File, Open** command, or click the **File Open** button, and select **Project 4**. Pressing <Enter>, displays a worksheet similar to the one shown in Fig. 9.13.

Copying Sheets in a Workbook

We will now fill another three sheets behind the present one, in order to include information about ADEPT Consultants' trading during the other three quarters of the year. The easiest way of doing this is by copying the information in Sheet1, including the formatting and the entered formulae, onto the other three sheets, then edit the numerical information in these appropriately.

To simplify this operation, Excel has a facility which allows you to copy a sheet into a workbook. There are two ways of doing this: (a) with the mouse, or (b) using the menus.

With the mouse, make the sheet you want to copy the current sheet, then press the <Ctrl> key, and while keeping it pressed, point with the mouse on the Tab of Sheet1 and drag it to the right, as shown in Fig. 9.14.

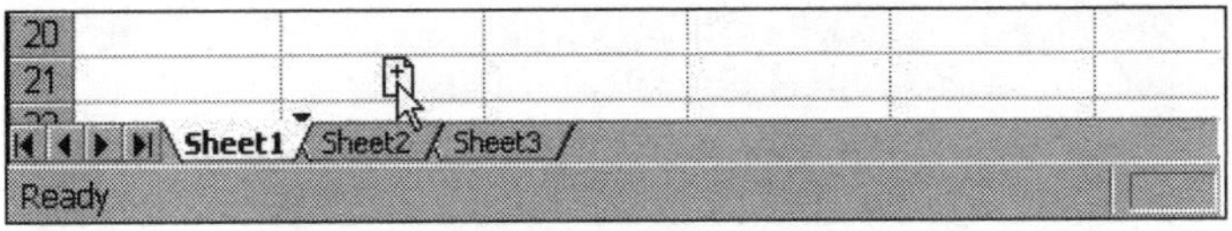

Fig. 9.14 Copying a Sheet into a Workbook.

A small black triangle indicates the place where the copy will be inserted, as shown above. If you insert a copy, say before Sheet2, when you release the mouse button the inserted sheet will be given the name Sheet1(2), while inserting a second copy before Sheet2 will be given the name Sheet1(3). To delete a worksheet, right-click its tab and select **Delete** from the pop-up menu.

To copy a sheet with the menus, right-click the sheet, then select the **Move or Copy** command to display the dialogue box in Fig. 9.15. Next, highlight Sheet2 in the **Before sheet** list, check the **Create a copy** option at the bottom of the box, and click **OK**. Sheet1(2) will be inserted in the Workbook, in the above case.

When you have three copies placed, double-click the Tabs of Sheet1 and the three new sheets and change their names to 'Quarter 1', 'Quarter 2', 'Quarter 3' and 'Quarter 4', respectively, as shown in Fig. 9.16.

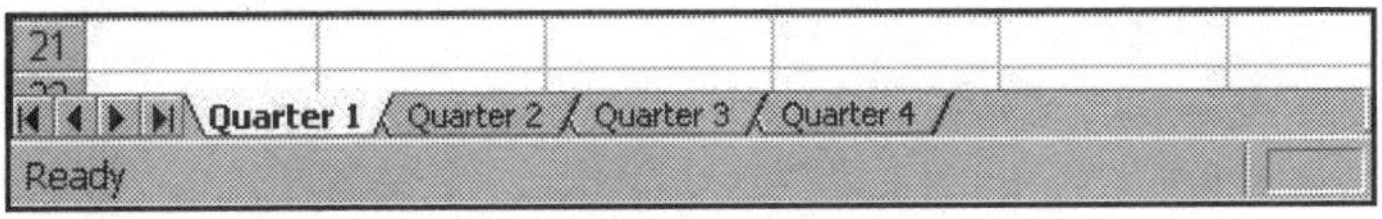

Fig. 9.15 Copying a Sheet.

Fig. 9.16 Renaming the Tabs of Worksheets.

The correct contents of the second sheet should be as shown in Fig. 9.17 on the next page.

	A	B	C	D	E	F
1	Project Analysis 2nd Quarter					
2						
3		Apr	May	Jun	2nd Quarter	
4	Income	£ 15,500.00	£ 16,000.00	£ 16,500.00	£ 48,000.00	
5	Costs:					
6	Wages	£ 3,500.00	£ 4,000.00	£ 4,500.00	£ 12,000.00	
7	Travel	£ 500.00	£ 550.00	£ 580.00	£ 1,630.00	
8	Rent	£ 300.00	£ 300.00	£ 300.00	£ 900.00	
9	Heat/Light	£ 150.00	£ 120.00	£ 100.00	£ 370.00	
10	Phone/Fax	£ 300.00	£ 350.00	£ 400.00	£ 1,050.00	
11	Adverts	£ 1,250.00	£ 1,300.00	£ 1,350.00	£ 3,900.00	
12	Total Costs	£ 6,000.00	£ 6,620.00	£ 7,230.00	£ 19,850.00	
13	Profit	£ 9,500.00	£ 9,380.00	£ 9,270.00	£ 28,150.00	
14	Cumulative	£ 9,500.00	£ 18,880.00	£ 28,150.00		
15						
16						
17						
18						
19						

Quarter 1 \ Quarter 2 / Quarter 3 / Quarter 4 /

Fig. 9.17 The Data for the Second Quarter.

The easiest way to enter these 2nd Quarter results is to edit the copied data (from Quarter 1) by either using the EDIT key (**F2**), or double-clicking the cell you want to edit. You should now be in a position to complete editing this sheet. Be extra careful, from now on, to check the identification Tab at the bottom of the screen, so as not to get the sheets mixed up. You do not want to spend time editing the wrong worksheet!

After building up the four worksheets (one for each quarter - see below for details on the 3rd and 4th quarters) save the file as **Project 5**.

	Jul	Aug	Sep	Oct	Nov	Dec
Income	17,000	17,500	18,000	18,500	19,000	19,500
Costs:						
Wages	4,000	4,500	5,000	4,500	5,000	5,500
Travel	600	650	680	630	670	700
Rent	300	300	300	300	300	300
Heat/Light	50	80	120	160	200	250
Phone/Fax	350	380	420	400	420	450
Adverts	1,400	1,450	1,500	1,480	1,500	1,530

Linking Sheets

A consolidation sheet could be placed in front of our 'stack' of data sheets to show a full year's results, by making a copy of the 1st Quarter sheet and placing it in front of it. Next, delete the entries in columns B to E, and name it 'Consolidation'.

We are now in a position to link the consolidation sheet to the other quarterly data sheets so that the information contained on them is automatically summarised and updated on it. The quarter totals in columns E of sheets Quarter 1, Quarter 2, Quarter 3, and Quarter 4, can be copied in turn to the clipboard using the **Edit, Copy** command, and then pasted to the appropriate column of the Consolidation sheet using the **Edit, Paste Special** command and clicking the **Paste Link** button on the displayed dialogue box.

Note: Empty cells linked with this method, like those in cells E5 of each quarter, appear as 0 (zero) in the Consolidation sheet. These can be removed by highlighting them and pressing the <Delete> key. Do not check the **Skip blanks** box in the Paste Special dialogue box, as this greys out the **Paste Link** button and clicking **OK** gives the wrong result!

Next, insert appropriate formulae in row 14 to correctly calculate the cumulative values in the Consolidation sheet. The result should be as follows:

	A	B	C	D	E	F	G	H
1	*Project Analysis - Year Summary*							
2								
3		1st Quarter	2nd Quarter	3rd Quarter	4th Quarter			
4	Income	£ 45,000.00	£ 48,000.00	£ 52,500.00	£ 57,000.00			
5	Costs:							
6	Wages	£ 9,000.00	£ 12,000.00	£ 13,500.00	£ 15,000.00			
7	Travel	£ 1,500.00	£ 1,630.00	£ 1,930.00	£ 2,000.00			
8	Rent	£ 900.00	£ 900.00	£ 900.00	£ 900.00			
9	Heat/Light	£ 480.00	£ 370.00	£ 250.00	£ 610.00			
10	Phone/Fax	£ 900.00	£ 1,050.00	£ 1,150.00	£ 1,270.00			
11	Adverts	£ 3,600.00	£ 3,900.00	£ 4,350.00	£ 4,510.00			
12	Total Costs	£ 16,380.00	£ 19,850.00	£ 22,080.00	£ 24,290.00			
13	*Profit*	£ 28,620.00	£ 28,150.00	£ 30,420.00	£ 32,710.00			
14	*Cumulative*	£ 28,620.00	£ 56,770.00	£ 87,190.00	£ 119,900.00			
15								

Fig. 9.18 The Linked Data in a Consolidation Sheet.

Finally, save the resultant workbook as **Project 6**.

Relative and Absolute Cell Addresses

Entering a mathematical expression into Excel, such as the formula in cell C14 which was

   =B14+C13

causes Excel to interpret it as 'add the contents of cell one column to the left of the current position, to the contents of cell one row above the current position'. In this way, when the formula was later copied into cell address D14, the contents of the cell relative to the left position of D14 (i.e. C14) and the contents of the cell one row above it (i.e. D13) were used, instead of the original cell addresses entered in C14. This is relative addressing.

   To see the effect of relative versus absolute addressing, copy the formula in cell C14 into C17, as shown in Fig. 9.19.

	C17	▼	*fx*	=B17+C16		
	A	B	C	D	E	F
1	**Project Analysis - Year Summary**					
2						
3		1st Quarter	2nd Quarter	3rd Quarter	4th Quarter	
4	Income	£ 45,000.00	£ 48,000.00	£ 52,500.00	£ 57,000.00	
5	Costs:					
6	Wages	£ 9,000.00	£ 12,000.00	£ 13,500.00	£ 15,000.00	
7	Travel	£ 1,500.00	£ 1,630.00	£ 1,930.00	£ 2,000.00	
8	Rent	£ 900.00	£ 900.00	£ 900.00	£ 900.00	
9	Heat/Light	£ 480.00	£ 370.00	£ 250.00	£ 610.00	
10	Phone/Fax	£ 900.00	£ 1,050.00	£ 1,150.00	£ 1,270.00	
11	Adverts	£ 3,600.00	£ 3,900.00	£ 4,350.00	£ 4,510.00	
12	Total Costs	£ 16,380.00	£ 19,850.00	£ 22,080.00	£ 24,290.00	
13	*Profit*	£ 28,620.00	£ 28,150.00	£ 30,420.00	£ 32,710.00	
14	*Cumulative*	£ 28,620.00	£ 56,770.00	£ 87,190.00	£ 119,900.00	
15						
16						
17			£ -			
18						
19						
20				Paste Options		
21						

Fig. 9.19 Demonstrating Relative and Absolute Cell Addressing.

Note that in cell C14 the formula was =B14+C13. However, when copied into cell C17 the formula appears as

    =B17+C16

This is because it has been interpreted as relative addressing. In this case, no value appears in cell C17 because we are attempting to add two blank cells.

Now change the formula in C14 by editing it to

    =$B$14+$C$13

which is interpreted as absolute addressing. Copying this formula into cell C17 calculates the correct result. Highlight cell C17 and observe the cell references in its formula; they have not changed from those of cell C14.

The $ sign must prefix both the column reference and the row reference. Mixed cell addressing is permitted; as for example when a column address reference is needed to be taken as absolute, while a row address reference is needed to be taken as relative. In such a case, the column letter is prefixed by the $ sign.

When building an absolute cell reference in a formula, it is easier to select each cell address within a formula by double-clicking on it with the left mouse button then, when selected, keep on pressing the **F4** key until the correct $ prefix is set.

Freezing Panes on Screen

Sometimes there might be too much information on screen and attempting to see a certain part of a sheet might cause the labels associated with that information to scroll off the screen.

To freeze column (or row) labels of a worksheet on screen, move the cell pointer to the right (or below) the column (or row) which you want to freeze, and use the **Window, Freeze Panes** command. Everything to the left of (or above) the cell pointer will freeze on the screen.

To unfreeze panes, use the **Window, Unfreeze Panes** command.

The Paste Smart Tag

Note that in Fig. 9.19, when you try to **Paste** the contents of a cell (or range of cells), Excel now displays a Smart tag at the bottom right corner of the cell in which you are about to paste data. When the mouse pointer is placed on this tag, a down-arrow appears next to it which when clicked opens up

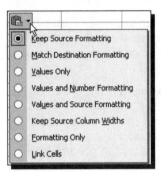

a menu of the most useful paste features you can use with that type of data, as shown in Fig. 9.20. In our case, the default selection is what we need.

Fig. 9.20 The Paste Smart Tag Menu Options.

10

Spreadsheet Charts

Excel allows information within a worksheet to be represented in graphical form, which makes data more accessible to non-expert users who might not be familiar with the spreadsheet format. The saying 'a picture is worth a thousand words', applies equally well to charts and figures.

The package allows the use of several chart and graph types, including area, bar, column, line, doughnut, radar, XY, pie, combination, and several 3-D options of these charts. In all, Excel allows fourteen different types of charts, with almost 100 predefined formats, which can be selected by using the appropriate icon. These are made available to you once you have selected the data you want to chart and clicked on the **Chart Wizard** button on the toolbar.

Charts (you can have several per worksheet) can be displayed on screen at the same time as the worksheet from which they were derived, since they appear in their own 'chart' frame and can be embedded anywhere on a worksheet. Furthermore, they can be sent to an appropriate output device, such as a plotter or printer. Although this charting module rivals a standalone graphics package, and one could write a separate book on it, an attempt will be made to present its basics, in the space available within this book.

Preparing for a Column Chart

In order to illustrate some of the graphing capabilities of Excel, we will now plot the income of the consulting company we discussed in the **Project 6** file. However, before we can go on, you will need to complete the entries for the last two quarters of trading of the Adept Consultants' example, if you haven't already done so - see end of previous chapter.

Next, link the quarterly totals to the consolidation sheet, calculate the year's total, as shown in Figure 10.1, and save the resultant workbook as **Project 7**, before going on.

	F4		f_x =SUM(B4:E4)				
	A	B	C	D	E	F	G
1	*Project Analysis - Year Summary*						
2							
3		**1st Quarter**	2nd Quarter	3rd Quarter	**4th Quarter**	**Total**	
4	Income	£ 45,000.00	£ 48,000.00	£ 52,500.00	£ 57,000.00	£ 202,500.00	
5	Costs:						
6	Wages	£ 9,000.00	£ 12,000.00	£ 13,500.00	£ 15,000.00	£ 49,500.00	
7	Travel	£ 1,500.00	£ 1,630.00	£ 1,930.00	£ 2,000.00	£ 7,060.00	
8	Rent	£ 900.00	£ 900.00	£ 900.00	£ 900.00	£ 3,600.00	
9	Heat/Light	£ 480.00	£ 370.00	£ 250.00	£ 610.00	£ 1,710.00	
10	Phone/Fax	£ 900.00	£ 1,050.00	£ 1,150.00	£ 1,270.00	£ 4,370.00	
11	Adverts	£ 3,600.00	£ 3,900.00	£ 4,350.00	£ 4,510.00	£ 16,360.00	
12	**Total Costs**	£ 16,380.00	£ 19,850.00	£ 22,080.00	£ 24,290.00	£ 82,600.00	
13	*Profit*	£ 28,620.00	£ 28,150.00	£ 30,420.00	£ 32,710.00	£ 119,900.00	
14	*Cumulative*	£ 28,620.00	£ 56,770.00	£ 87,190.00	£ 119,900.00		

Fig. 10.1 The Year's Consolidated Worksheet of Adept Consultants.

Now we need to select the range of the data we want to graph. The range of data to be graphed in Excel does not have to be contiguous for each graph, as with some other spreadsheets. With Excel, you select your data from different parts of a sheet with the <Ctrl> key pressed down. This method has the advantage of automatic recalculation should any changes be made to the original data. You could also collect data from different sheets to one 'graphing' sheet by linking them as we did with the consolidation sheet.

If you don't want the chart to be recalculated when you do this, then you must use the **Edit, Copy** and **Edit, Paste Special** commands and choose the **Values** option from the displayed dialogue box, which copies a selected range to a specified target area of the worksheet and converts formulae to values. This is necessary, as cells containing formulae cannot be pasted directly since it would cause the relative cell addresses to adjust to the new locations; each formula would then recalculate a new value for each cell and give wrong results.

The Chart Wizard

To obtain a chart of 'Income' versus 'Quarters', select the data in cell range A3..E4, then either click the **Chart Wizard** button, shown here, or use the **Insert, Chart** command. The Chart Wizard then opens the first of four dialogue boxes, as shown below, which guide you through the process.

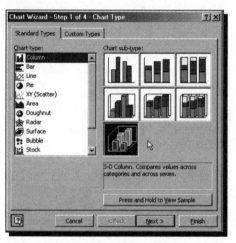

Fig. 10.2 The First Chart Wizard Dialogue Box.

Now select the 3-D Column type and click the **Next >** button at the bottom of the displayed Chart Wizard dialogue box. The second dialogue box is then displayed as shown on the next page, after clicking the **Columns** radio button pointed to in Fig. 10.3.

The third Chart Wizard dialogue box allows you to give a title to your chart and annotate the x- and y-axes, while the fourth dialogue box allows you to place the chart either on a separate sheet or on the sheet that was active when you first started the charting process. On pressing the **Finish** button the chart shown in Fig. 10.4 should appear on your worksheet.

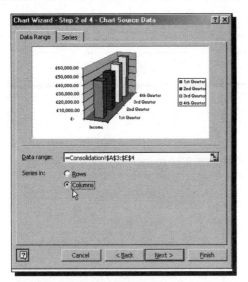

Fig. 10.3 A 3-D Columnar Income Chart.

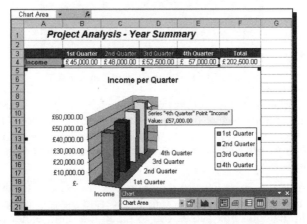

Fig. 10.4 The Income per Quarter Columnar Chart.

Note that to find out the exact details of a given column on a chart, you need only place the mouse pointer on it to open a banner with the desired information.

While the frame containing a chart is selected (you can tell from the presence of the small black squares around it), you can change its size by dragging the small two-headed arrow pointer (which appears when the mouse pointer is placed on the small black squares of the frame). You can also move the frame and its contents to another position on the worksheet by pointing to the chart area, pressing and keeping depressed the left mouse button until the pointer changes to a small four-headed arrow shape, then dragging the changed mouse pointer to a new position.

Note that in Fig. 10.4 a Chart Toolbar appeared when we finished with the Chart Wizard. As you can see in Fig. 10.5 below, you can use this toolbar to change to a different chart object, format the selected chart object, change the chart type, turn on/off the chart legend, turn on/off the selected data table for the chart, redraw the chart by row or column, and angle selected chart objects clockwise or anticlockwise. In fact, everything that you need to do to a chart is available right there on this Chart Toolbar which is displayed by default every time you start working with a chart.

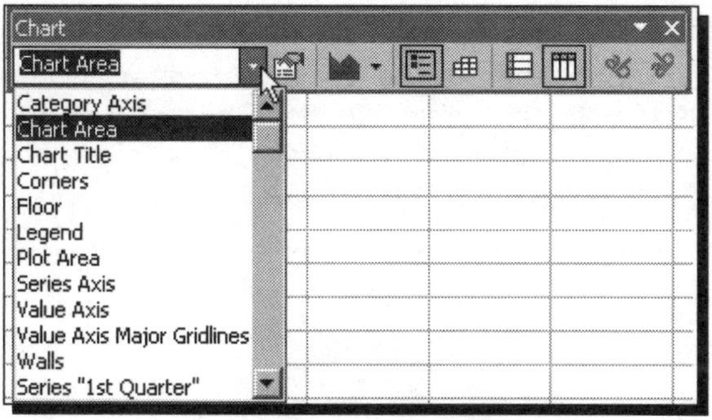

Fig. 10.5 The Chart Toolbar.

As an example of what you can do with a chart, first select the object 'Chart Area', then either click the **Format Chart Area** button on the Chart Toolbar, double-click within the chart area or use the **Format, Selected Chart Area** command. Using any one of these three procedures displays the dialogue box in Fig. 10.6 shown on the next page.

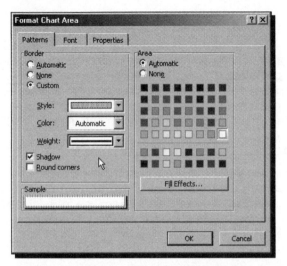

Fig. 10.6 The Format Chart Area Dialogue Box.

From this dialogue box you can choose a pattern to be used as a frame, by selecting **Custom** under the Patterns tab and choose the 8th **Style**, the 4th **Weight** line, check the **Sha<u>d</u>ow** box and press **OK**.

Try it, then change the second quarter income from £48,000 to £58,000 (on the Quarter 2 sheet), and watch how the change is reflected on the redrawn graph on the Consolidation sheet displayed below.

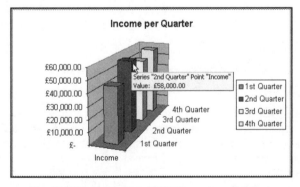

Fig. 10.7 The Formatted and Redrawn Income Chart.

Finally, revert to the original entry for the first quarter's income, change your chart back to a simple column type, and then save your work again under the filename **Project 7** by simply pressing the **Save** button shown here. Your current work will be saved to disc replacing the previous version under the same filename.

When Excel creates a chart, it plots each row or column of data in the selected range as a 'data series', such as a group of bars, lines, etc. A chart can contain many data series, but Excel charts data according to the following rules:

1.   If the selected range contains more rows than columns of data, Excel plots the data series by columns.

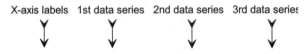

2.   If the selected range contains more columns than rows of data, or the same number of columns and rows, Excel plots the data series by rows.

Legend   X-axis labels
labels   1st data series
          2nd data series

If you select a range to chart which includes column and row headings, and text above or to the left of the numeric data, Excel uses the text to create the axis labels, legends, and title.

If your data selection does not obey these rules, you must tell Excel how your data series is structured in the 2nd Chart Wizard dialogue box.

Editing a Chart

The easiest way to edit a chart is to right-click it within the chart area, but near its outer rim. This displays the shortcut menu shown in Fig. 10.8 on the next page.

As a chart is made up of several objects, for example, data series, plot area, the various axis data areas, legends, and chart area, you will get a different shortcut menu if you were pointing to these different areas. Try it. As you right-click different areas, their name will appear in the 'Name box' which is situated below the 'Font' box. The shortcut menu shown in Fig. 10.8 is the one you will get when you right-click the 'Chart Area'.

We have already used the first menu option to format our chart. The second menu option allows you to quickly change the chart type, while the third option can be used to change the source data. The fourth menu option allows you to add Titles, change axes, add grid lines and data labels, while the fifth option lets you specify whether you want your chart to be located in a new sheet or where you created it.

Fig. 10.8 The Chart Area Shortcut Menu.

Saving Charts

When you save a workbook, the chart or charts you have created are saved with it. It is, therefore, a good idea not only to give each chart a title (by using **Chart Options** in the above shortcut menu - Fig. 10.8), but to also locate it on a differently named sheet.

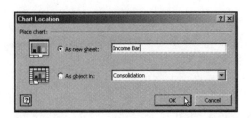

To put the chart on a separate sheet, use the **Location** option in Fig. 10.8 and give it the name **Income Column**, as shown here.

Finally, save the workbook under the filename **Project 8**.

Predefined Chart Types

To select a different type of chart, click the **Chart Wizard** button shown here, or select the **Insert, Chart** command. The 1st Chart Wizard dialogue box displayed previously, lists 14 different chart options. These chart-types are normally used to describe the following relationships between data:

Area: for showing a volume relationship between two series, such as production or sales, over a given length of time.

Bar: for comparing differences in data (noncontinuous data that are not related over time) by depicting changes in horizontal bars to show positive and negative variations from a given position.

Bubble: for showing a type of XY (scatter) chart. The size of the data (radius of the bubble) indicates the value of a third variable.

Column: for comparing separate items (noncontinuous data which are related over time) by depicting changes in vertical bars to show positive and negative variations from a given position.

Cone: for showing 3-D column and bar charts in a more dramatic way.

Cylinder: similar to Cone.

Doughnut: for comparing parts with the whole. Similar to pie charts, but can depict more than one series of data.

	Line:	for showing continuous changes in data with time.
	**Pie:**	for comparing parts with the whole. You can use this type of chart when you want to compare the percentage of an item from a single series of data with the whole series.
	**Pyramid:**	similar to Cone.
	**Radar:**	for plotting one series of data as angle values defined in radians, against one or more series defined in terms of a radius.
	**Surface:**	for showing optimum combinations between two sets of data, as in a topographic map. Colours and patterns indicate areas that are in the same range of values.
	**Stock:**	for showing high-low-close type of data variation to illustrate stock market prices or temperature changes.
	**XY (Scatter):**	for showing scatter relationships between X and Y. Scatter charts are used to depict items which are not related over time.

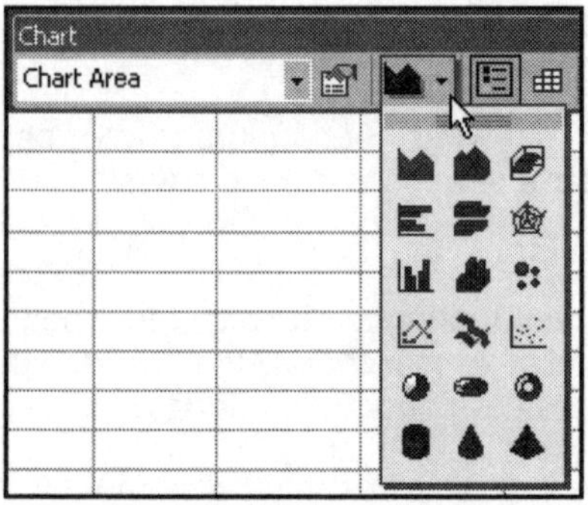

You can change the type of chart by selecting one of the fourteen offered when the **Chart Type** button is clicked on the Chart Toolbar, as shown in Fig. 10.9.

Fig. 10.9 Changing the Chart Type.

Customising a Chart

In order to customise a chart, you need to know how to add legends, titles, text labels, arrows, and how to change the colour and pattern of the chart background, plot areas and chart markers, and how to select, move and size chart objects.

Drawing a Multiple Column Chart

As an exercise, we will consider a new column chart which deals with the quarterly 'Costs' of Adept Consultants. To achieve this, first select the Consolidation sheet of workbook **Project 8**, then highlight the cell range A3:E3, press the <Ctrl> key, and while holding it down, use the mouse to select the costs range A6:E11.

Next, click the **Chart Wizard** button (or use the **Insert, Chart** command), select Column from the **Chart type** list, click the fourth **Chart sub-type** option, and press the **Next** button. The 6 different quarterly costs will be drawn automatically, as displayed in the composite screen dump in Fig. 10.10.

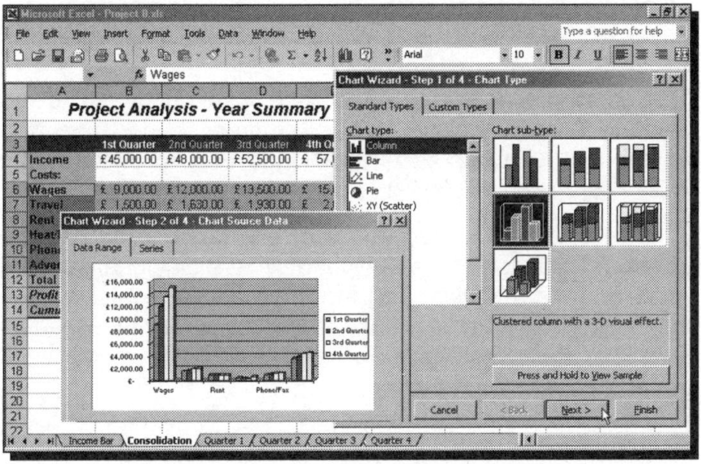

Fig. 10.10 Creating the Costs Column Chart of Adept Consultants.

Because the selected range contains more rows than columns of data, Excel follows the 1st rule of data series selection which, however, might not be what you want.

To have the 'quarters' appearing on the x-axis and the 'costs' as the legends, we need to tell Excel that our data series is in rows by clicking the **Rows** button on the 2nd Chart Wizard dialogue box. Immediately this is done the column chart changes to:

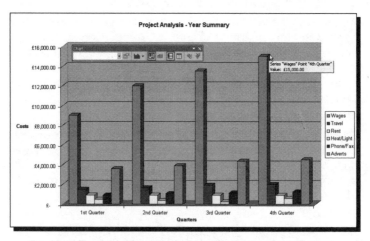

Fig. 10.11 The Adept Consultants Costs Shown in a Column Chart.

The chart title and axes titles were inserted by typing the heading 'Project Analysis - Year Summary' in the **Chart title** box of the 3rd Chart Wizard dialogue box, followed by the **Axis Titles** shown above.

Once you are satisfied with your efforts, click the **As new sheet** radio button of the 4th Chart Wizard dialogue box, and name your chart **Costs Column**. If you make a mistake and you want to try again, make sure the unwanted chart is selected, then press the <Del> key. Finally, save your work under the filename **Project 9**.

Changing a Title and an Axis Label

To change a title, an axis label, or a legend within a chart, click the appropriate area on the chart. This reveals that these are individual objects (they are surrounded by small black squares called 'handles') and you can edit, reposition, or change their font and point size. You can even rotate text within such areas in any direction you like. You could, of course, use the Chart Toolbar to achieve these changes.

To demonstrate these options, we will use the **Costs Column** chart saved in **Project 9**, so get it on screen if you are to follow our suggestions.

To change the font size of a chart title, click the Chart Title area to select it and double-click on the border that is displayed when you select it. Doing this, displays the Format dialogue box for the selected object, and clicking the Font tab reveals the contents of Fig. 10.12.

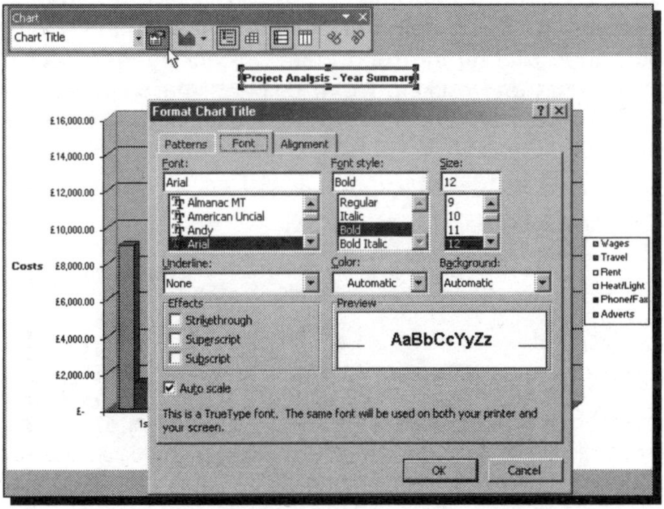

Fig. 10.12 Changing the Font Size of a Selected Object.

From here, we changed the font size of the chart title from 12 to 16 points. We also selected the Costs label and changed its size from 10 to 14 points, then clicked the Alignment tab to change its orientation to 90°, as shown on the next page.

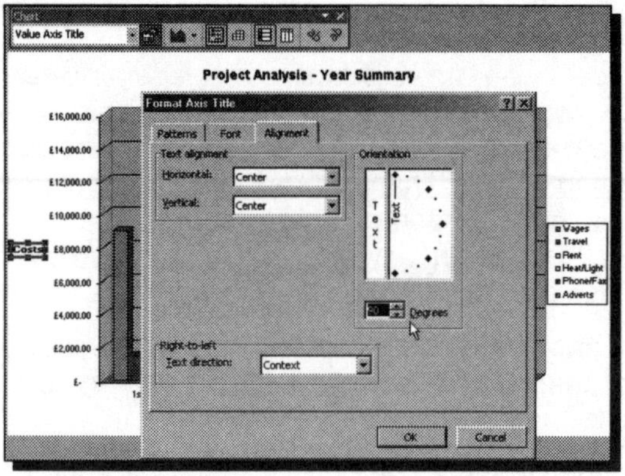

Fig. 10.13 Changing the Orientation of a Selected Object.

Drawing a Pie Chart

To change the chart type, simply select the chart, then click the Chart Wizard and choose the 3-D Pie chart from the displayed list. If the selected chart was the 'quarterly costs' chart, then clicking the **Next** button, checking the **Co_lumns** radio button and clicking **Next**, displays the chart type that would be redrawn for the specified data series, as shown below.

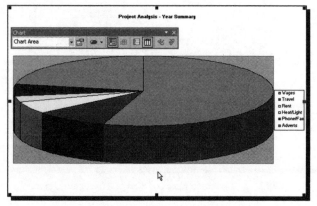

Fig. 10.14 Displaying Costs as a 3-D Pie Chart.

However, so as not to spoil your **Costs Column** chart, click the **Cancel** button at this stage.

To obtain a pie chart without spoiling the chart it is based on, you must select the data range again, then click the Chart Wizard, choose the pie chart from the displayed chart types, then select the specific pie chart that best fits your data, specify the type of series, and give the chart a title.

As a last example in chart drawing, we will use the data range A6:A11 and F6:F11 of the Consolidation worksheet to plot a 3-D pie chart. The steps are the same as before, but for the 3-D option and specifying the type of series data as 'columns'. Note that the chart title should now reflect the Year Totals, rather than the Quarter summaries. The result should be as shown in Fig. 10.15.

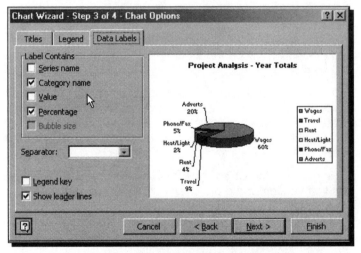

Fig. 10.15 Selecting Label Contents for a Pie Chart.

To display the above chart, we clicked the Data Labels tab and checked both the **Category name** and the **Percentage** check boxes in the 3rd dialogue box of the Chart Wizard.

This chart tells us, for example, that Wages for the whole year amount to 60% of the total yearly costs. Other cost categories are also displayed with their appropriate percentages. Clicking the **Finish** button displays the pie chart in its finished form, as shown overleaf in Fig. 10.16.

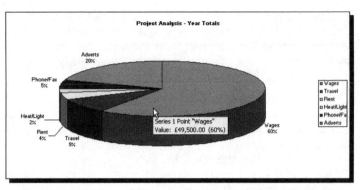

Fig. 10.16 A Pie Chart of the Yearly Total Costs of Adept Consultants.

Pointing to any pie slice, causes the pop-up poster to be displayed, informing you of the actual data series, its value and its percentage of the whole. It is now obvious that the information contained in this chart is much more than in the 2-D version.

If you want to explode an individual pie slice, you can do so by simply dragging it. This is possible as each slice is treated as a separate object, but you must increase the size of your chart before you can accurately pinpoint the required slice.

Finally, use the **Chart, Location** menu command to name this last version of the pie chart as **Costs Pie** and save your workbook.

* * *

Excel has many more features than the ones we have introduced in this book. For example, you could use Excel's database and macro capabilities, and also explore its various tools, such as the Goal Seek, Scenarios, Auditing, and Solver. We hope we have given you sufficient basic knowledge to be able to explore these topics by yourself.

However, if you would prefer to be guided through these topics, then may we suggest you look up the later chapters of the book *Microsoft Excel 2002 explained* (BP511), also published by BERNARD BABANI (publishing) Ltd.

11

The PowerPoint Environment

Microsoft PowerPoint 2002 is a powerful and versatile Graphics Presentation package which deserves more attention than it gets from most users of Microsoft Office.

The key element of PowerPoint is the Slide Show and the production of ancillary material, such as scripted notes to accompany each slide, laser copies of slides, and an outline view of all the information in the presentation. However, Microsoft uses the word slide to refer to each individual page of a presentation and you can format the output for overhead projector acetates, or for electronic presentation on screen.

In addition, you can apply the skills you have already gained in using Word and Excel and use material created in these applications within PowerPoint.

Starting the PowerPoint Program

PowerPoint is started in Windows either by clicking the **Start** button then selecting **Programs** and clicking on the Microsoft

PowerPoint icon on the cascade menu, clicking the **PowerPoint** button on the Office Shortcut Bar, or by clicking the **Open a Document** button on the Office Shortcut Bar and double-clicking on a PowerPoint presentation file. In the latter case the presentation will be loaded into PowerPoint at the same time.

When you start PowerPoint 2002 the program momentarily displays its opening screen, shown in Fig. 11.1, before displaying its first presentation document as shown in Fig. 11.2.

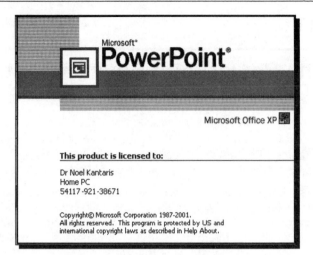

Fig. 11.1 PowerPoint's Opening Screen.

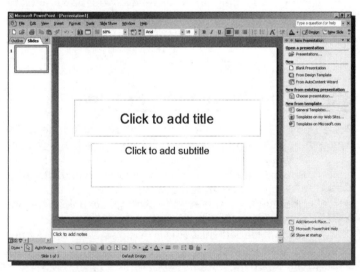

Fig. 11.2 The Microsoft PowerPoint Opening Presentation Document.

Whether you have used a previous version of PowerPoint or not, the first time you use the program, it might be a good idea to click the Microsoft PowerPoint Help link, shown here, and to be found at the bottom right-hand corner of the program's screen. This opens the Help screen shown in Fig. 11.3 below.

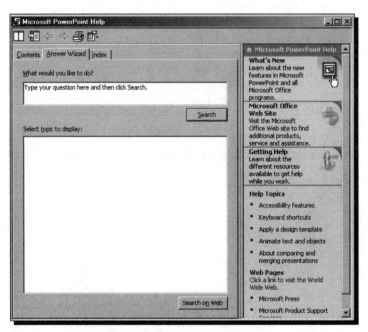

Fig. 11.3 The PowerPoint Help Screen.

Clicking the **What's New** link, pointed to in Fig. 11.3, displays a list of topics relating to the subject.

For additional Help topics, click the Contents tab of the above screen, then double-click the displayed Microsoft PowerPoint Help book to open a list of books covering various topics. As you can see, the Help System is similar to the other Office XP applications.

The PowerPoint Screen

When PowerPoint is loaded, a screen displays with similar Title bar, Menu bar, Toolbar and Formatting bar to those of Word and Excel. Obviously there are differences, but that is to be expected as PowerPoint serves a different purpose to the other programs.

The opening presentation screen of PowerPoint is shown in Fig. 11.4 below. The program follows the usual Microsoft Windows conventions with which you should be very familiar by now. Scroll bars and scroll buttons only appear within the window in which you load a presentation.

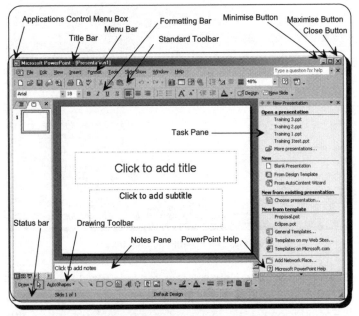

Fig. 11.4 The PowerPoint Opening Presentation Screen.

On the right of the opening presentation screen the Task Pane is displayed with listed options that make it easy for you to open an existing presentation, to start creating your presentation, or get presentation templates from the Web.

The first option, at the top of the **New Presentation** Task

Pane, allows you to open an existing presentation.
Clicking this option, displays the Open dialogue box
which also displays when you click the **Open** button
on the Standard Toolbar.

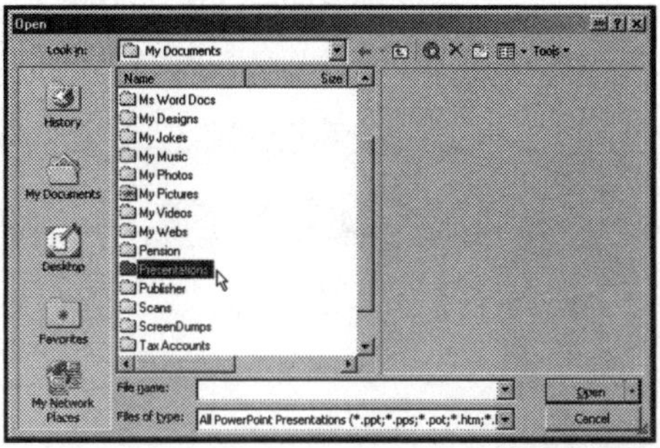

Fig. 11.5 The Open Presentation Dialogue Box.

The three options that allow you to create a new
presentation, are as follows:

Blank Presentation 	Allows you to start with a blank presentation with all values for colour scheme, fonts, and other design features set to default values. The same dialogue box also displays when you click the **New** button on the Standard Toolbar.
From Design Template	Allows you to select a presentation template that determines the colour scheme, fonts, and other design features of the presentation.
From AutoContent Wizard	Activates a Wizard that helps you determine the content and organisation of your presentation.

The penultimate option on the Task Pane allows you to create a presentation based on an existing one, while the last option allows you to use templates, either built-in or down-loaded from the Internet.

We will now use the AutoContent Wizard from the Task Pane to look for an existing presentation. Click this link to display the first of five Wizard screens, as shown in Fig. 11.6.

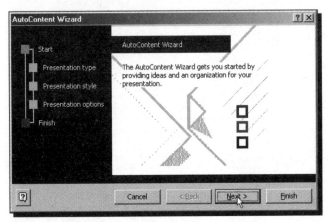

Fig. 11.6 Starting the AutoContent Wizard.

Clicking **Next**, displays the second Wizard screen (Fig. 11.7).

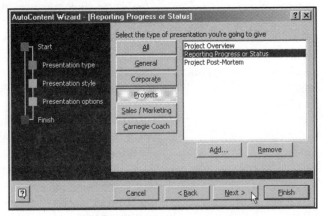

Fig. 11.7 Selecting the Type of Presentation.

For the type of presentation we selected **Projects**, then chose the second of the three projects displayed. Clicking **Next** displays the third Wizard screen, as shown in Fig. 11.8.

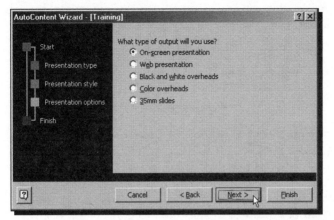

Fig. 11.8 Selecting Presentation Options.

Clicking the **Next** button displays the fourth Wizard screen which asks you to type in a title for the presentation - we typed   *Project Status*. Finally, clicking the **Finish** button displays the completed presentation shown in Fig. 11.9.

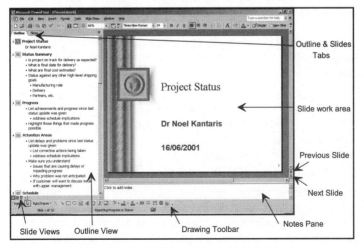

Fig. 11.9 The First of Ten Slides on Project Status.

PowerPoint Views

The Slide Views bar at the bottom left corner of the Presentation window together with the two tabs at the top of the left pane (see Fig. 11.9) are shown enlarged below.

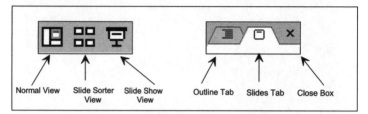

Normal View   Slide Sorter   Slide Show   Outline Tab   Slides Tab   Close Box
                    View   View

Fig. 11.10 The Slide Views Bar and Controlling Tabs.

The three **Slide View** buttons are the key to the editing power of PowerPoint, while the two tabs control what you see in the left pane.

Normal View

The Normal view is the main editing view, which is used to write and design a presentation. The view has three working areas (see Fig. 11.9): on the left, two tabs alternate between an outline view of your slide text and a thumbnails display of your slides; on the right, the slide pane, which displays a large view of the current slide; and on the bottom, the notes pane.

You can use these panes to work on all aspects of your presentation, and you can adjust their size by dragging their borders. The Outline and Slides tabs change to display an icon when the pane becomes narrow, and if you only want to see the current slide in the window as you edit, you can close the tabs with the Close box shown in Fig. 11.10.

The notes pane is used to add speaker notes or information you want to share with the audience. You can even have graphics in your notes, in which case you must add the notes in Notes Page View - use the **View, Notes Page** menu command.

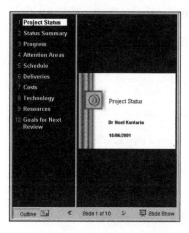

The Outline and Slide panes are also displayed when you save your presentation as a Web page. The only difference is that the outline pane displays a table of contents so that you can navigate through your presentation, as shown here. Try it!

Outline View

In this view (Fig. 11.11), the Outline View pane is enlarged making it easier for you to organise and edit your presentation text.

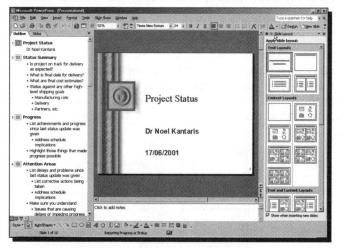

Fig. 11.11 The Outline View of Project Status.

Slide View

The Slide View allows you to see an enlarged slide area of a selected slide. To select another slide, click on the column of numbered slides making up your presentation, as shown in Fig. 11.12 on the next page.

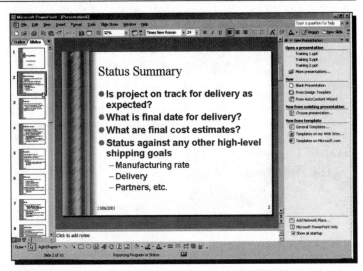

Fig. 11.12 Slide View of Project Status.

Slide Sorter View

In this view (Fig. 11.13), you can see the whole presentation at once. You can reorder slides, add transitions, and set timing for electronic presentations. You can also select animated transitions for moving from slide to slide.

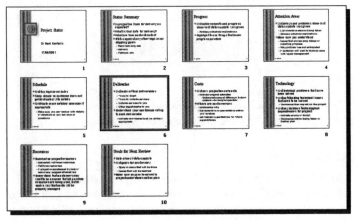

Fig. 11.13 Slide Sorter View of Project Status.

Notes Pages View

This is where you create speaker's notes which contain graphics for any or all of your presentation slides. To open up this view, use the **View, Notes Page** menu command.

Fig. 11.14 The Speaker's Notes.

As an example, we have used the 10th slide from our demonstration set, and imported a graphic in the speaker's notes area, as shown in Fig. 11.14. To do this, first type a line of text, similar to 'This is a test to see if a picture could be included', then use the **Insert, Picture, Clip Art** menu command (or click the **Insert Clip Art** button on the Draw Toolbar instead), and select an appropriate graphic (we will discuss this procedure in the next chapter).

Drawing objects and pictures are not displayed in the notes pane (try it for yourself by using the **View, Normal** command), but appear when you work in Notes Page View or when you print slides with notes.

Slide Show View

In this view you see your work as an electronic presentation, with each slide filling the screen. You can also see the effect of the transitions and timing that you set in the Slide Sorter View.

To see the next slide in full-screen view either click the left mouse button or press the right cursor key. To return to a previous slide in full-screen view press the left cursor key. To return to a previous PowerPoint view from a full-screen Slide Show View, press <Esc>, or click the right mouse button to display the quick menu, shown here, and click the **End Show** menu option.

The fourth and fifth menu options can be used in the following way:

While you are showing a slide show, you can take minutes, record action items, and add to your notes pages by right-clicking a slide while in full-view and selecting the **Meeting Minder** menu option which opens the dialogue box shown in Fig. 11.15.

Fig. 11.15 The Meeting Minder Screen.

Such notes only appear on your screen - other participants see only the slide show. Action items appear on a new slide at the end of your slide show and can be posted to Microsoft Outlook, or can be transferred to a new Word document and then printed with that document.

While preparing a presentation, you can make notes relating to each slide by right-clicking a slide while in full-screen view and selecting the **Speaker Notes** menu option. This displays the dialogue box shown in Fig. 11.16.

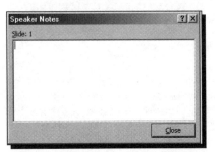

Fig. 11.16 The Speaker Notes Screen.

These notes can be printed and then used either to remember key points during a presentation, or to help the audience follow the presentation. Both the notes and handout pages have masters, where you can add items you want to appear on each page.

Setting Transitions, Animation and Timings

Your presentation will appear more professional if you set timings, transitions and animation. To do this, activate the Slide Sorter View and observe the extra Toolbar that appears below the Standard and Formatting Bars.

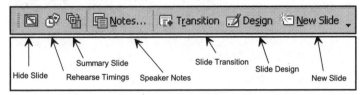

Fig. 11.17 The Slide Sorter Toolbar.

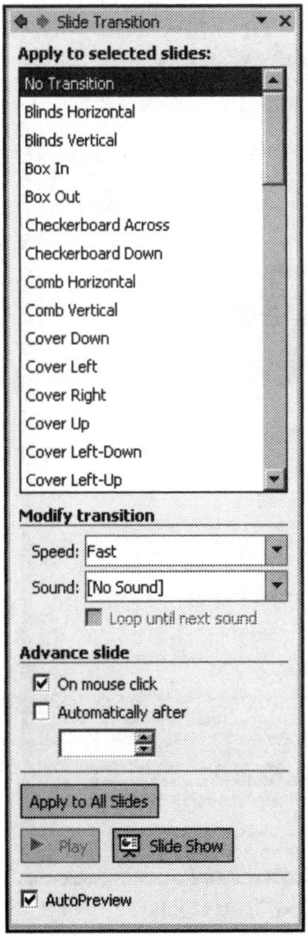

Clicking the fifth button on Slide Sorter Toolbar, displays the **Slide Transition** Task Pane, shown in Fig. 11.18. You can select a Transition Effect by choosing one from the list under **Apply to selected slides**. The effect will be seen on the slide which was selected at the time.

Now try the various options for yourself by, say, selecting *Shape circle* from the displayed list, then choosing *Camera* for sound under the **Modify transition**, check the 'Automatically after' box under **Advance slide** and select *00:03* for the timing, then click the **Apply to All Slides** button. The current effective timings will be displayed below each slide when in Slide Sorter View. Finally, click the **Slide Show** button to see all these options come to life. We hope you enjoy the show!

Fig. 11.18 The Slide Transition Pane.

The Slide Master

While a slide is selected, you can get a lot of help if you do the following:

- Click on the **Microsoft PowerPoint Help** button on the Toolbar to open its Help screen. In the 'What would you like to do?' help box of the Answer Wizard tab, type the string 'slide master', and click the **Search** button.

- From the displayed list, select the second option 'About the slide master' which opens up an extremely useful help screen, shown in Fig. 11.19, from which you can learn a lot.

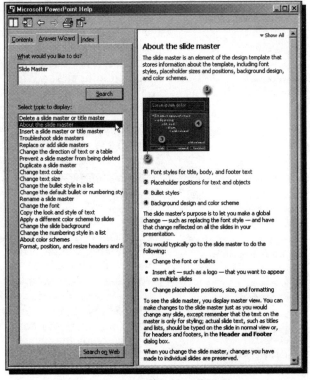

Fig. 11.19 The Help Screen on Slide Master.

In essence, each design template comes with its own slide master. The elements on the slide master control the design of the template, many of which have a separate title master.

When you apply a design template to a presentation, PowerPoint automatically updates the text styles and graphics on the slide master (use the **View, Master, Slide Master** command to see the one in Fig. 11.20), and changes the colour scheme to the one in the new design template.

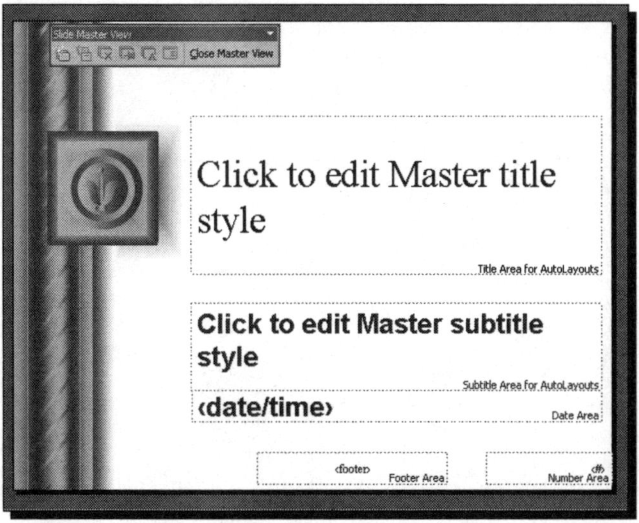

Fig. 11.20 Example of a Slide Master.

Any object you have added to the slide master, such as a text box or graphic, will not be deleted when you apply a new design template.

12

Designing a Presentation

In this chapter we will use PowerPoint's Wizards to design a simple presentation quickly and effectively. Below, we show the first page of the finished presentation in overhead format, so that you can have an idea of the overall design.

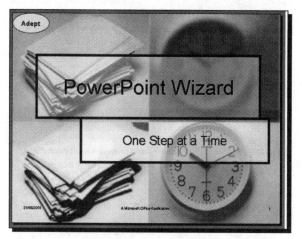

Fig. 12.1 The First Page of a Finished Presentation.

The AutoContent Wizard

When you first start PowerPoint, you are offered the opportunity to design a presentation using the AutoContent Wizard, select a template on which to base your work, begin with a blank presentation, or open an existing presentation.

Most users would, without question, like to produce a presentation in no time at all. The **AutoContent Wizard** is an excellent starting point, even if you know what you want to do and how to do it.

Later you can customise your presentation using PowerPoint's editing tools. But for now, click the **From AutoContent Wizard** link on the **New Presentation** Task Pane to start the display of five dialogue boxes in which you are:

- Provided with ideas and an organisation for your presentation.

- Asked to select the type of presentation you are going to give (we selected *Training*).

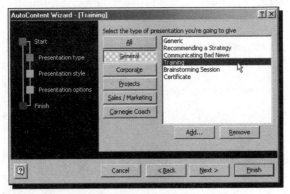

Fig. 12.2 Selecting the Type of Presentation.

Asked to specify what type of output you require (we selected *Black and white overheads*).

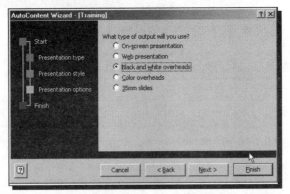

Fig. 12.3 Selecting Type of Output.

- Asked to type in the title of your presentation (we typed *PowerPoint Wizard*, and *A Microsoft Office Application* for the footer.

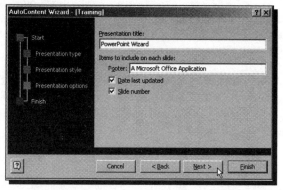

Fig. 12.4 Typing a Title and a Footer for the Presentation.

- Told that this is the only information required to create your presentation.

Clicking the **Finish** button on the last dialogue box, creates your presentation and displays it in Outline view complete with suggested topics, as shown in Fig. 12.5, where the 4th slide is displayed.

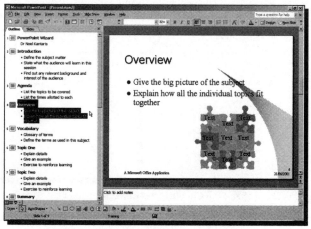

Fig. 12.5 Outline View of Selected Presentation.

The suggested topics of each slide can be changed to suit your needs, as shown below in Fig. 12.6. In this slide, we have added some extra demoted (more indented) topics by using the <Tab> key, and deleted topics (including objects) that were of no relevance to our presentation. To return to the original bullet level from a demoted level, use the <Shift+Tab> key.

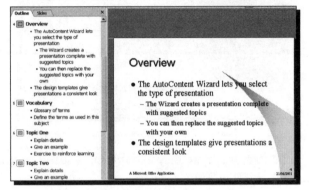

Fig. 12.6 The Changed Contents of a Slide.

The actual name of the person designing these slides that appears below the title of the 1st slide, is taken by PowerPoint automatically from information held on the *user* of the program. You could replace this by editing the relevant line when in Outline View (we typed here the text *One Step at a Time*).

Fig. 12.7 Changing the Contents of the First Slide.

Save the result of your work so far under the filename **Training 1**.

Clicking the **Slide Sorter View** button at the bottom of the screen, displays all the slides in your presentation, as follows:

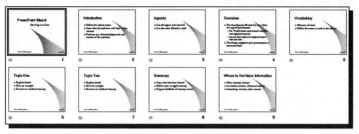

Fig. 12.8 Our Presentation in Slide Sorter View.

To move a slide to a different position in the set, simply left-click it and drag the modified pointer to the new position.

Selecting a Template

Fig. 12.9 Selecting a Template.

Our presentation might not look exactly what we had in mind, but we can select a different template to change the overall design. To change the default design of slides, first click the **Slide Sorter View** button, then do the following:

- Double-click the area at the bottom of the screen on the Status bar that holds the name of the current template (in our example this should read **Training**), or click the **Slide Design** button. This opens the **Slide Design** Task Pane, shown in Fig. 12.9, for you to select a presentation.

- Select the **proposal.pot** template, click the down-arrow to the right of it, and choose **Apply to All Slides** option from the drop-down menu shown here.

What appears on your screen next, is the display of all your slides in the chosen template. Clicking the Slides tab, then the 1st slide changes your display to that of Fig. 12.10 below. Clicking other slides, displays them in full size.

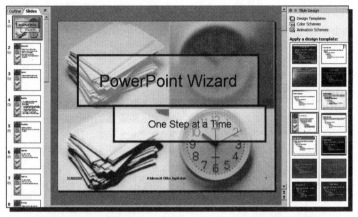

Fig. 12.10 Our Presentation Using the Proposal.pot Template.

Adding a Drawing to a Presentation

You can use the various buttons on the Drawing Toolbar at the bottom of the screen (if not activated use the **View, Toolbars, Drawing** command) to add to your presentation. The function of each Drawing tool will be described shortly.

To use the various Drawing tools, you must have a Presentation window open (we chose the 1st slide of our Training example for the display of our drawing). If you want your drawing to occur in all subsequent slides, you should use the **View, Master, Slide Master** menu command and start your drawing on the displayed Master slide.

Below, we used the Oval tool, the Text Box tool, and the Fill Colour tool to produce the logo shown here, which we placed at the top left corner of the 1st slide of our presentation, as shown in Fig. 12.11.

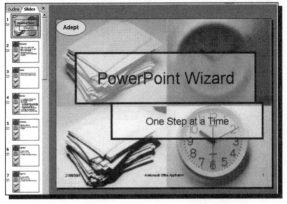

Fig. 12.11 Adding a Drawing to our Presentation.

You, of course, can use your drawing skills to produce your own logo. Save your creation under **Training 2**.

The Drawing Toolbar

The various functions offered by the Drawing Toolbar (see Fig. 12.12) are shared by all Office XP applications and give PowerPoint a superior graphics capability. Amongst the many features available are:

AutoShapes – the additional AutoShape categories, such as connectors, block arrows, flowchart symbols, stars and banners, callouts, and action buttons make drawing diagrams much easier.

Bezier curves – used to easily create exact curves with pinpoint precision.

3-D effects – allow you to transform 2-D shapes into realistic 3-D objects with new 3-D effects, such as changing the lighting perspective of a 3-D object.

Draw ▾	
▹	Group objects, change their order, rotate, etc.
	Select Objects
AutoShapes ▾	
	Select from various shapes
\	
↘	Line
	Arrow
☐	Rectangle
○	Oval
🔲	Text Box
🔷	Insert WordArt
♻	Insert Diagram or Organization Chart
🔳	Insert Clip Art
🖼	Insert Picture
🪣 ▾	Fill Color
🖌 ▾	Line Color
🅰 ▾	Font Color
≡	Line Style
⋮⋮⋮	Dash Style
⇄	Arrow Style
◼	Shadow Style
⬛	3-D Style
◂	More Buttons

Fig. 12.12 The Drawing Toolbar Buttons.

Perspective shadows – allow you to select from a wide range of shadows with perspective, and you can adjust the depth and angle of each shadow to make pictures more realistic.

Connectors – used to create diagrams and flowcharts with new straight, angled, and curved connectors between the shapes; when shapes are moved, the connectors remain attached and automatically reposition themselves.

Arrowhead styles – allow you to change the width and height of arrowheads for maximum effect.

Object alignment – allow you to distribute and space objects evenly, both horizontally and vertically.

Precise line-width control – allows you increased control over the width of lines by selecting pre-set options or customised line widths.

Image editing – lets you easily adjust the brightness or contrast of a picture.

Transparent background – allows you to insert a bit map on your slides or Web pages that appears to be part of the design by turning background colours into transparent areas.

Inserting WordArt

The title and subtitle in Fig. 12.11 look rather severe in their heavy frames, so we will use WordArt to make them a bit more jazzy. To do this, first click each object (title and subtitle and press the <Delete> key - you will have to do this twice for each object, once to remove the typed words and a second time to remove the text box.

 Next, click the **Insert WordArt** button, shown here, on the Drawing Toolbar. This opens the Microsoft WordArt Gallery, shown in Fig. 12.13 from which you can choose how you would like your title to be represented (we chose the one pointed to). Pressing the **OK** button opens the Edit WordArt Text box shown in Fig. 12.14 in which you type the title of your presentation. You will have to repeat this procedure for the subtitle, but choose a different WordArt image.

The final result, after scaling and moving the two text objects, is shown in Fig. 12.15 in which we also show the choices available when the **Character Spacing** button on the WordArt Toolbar is clicked. It is worthwhile spending some time here to familiarise yourself with the various options available on this Toolbar.

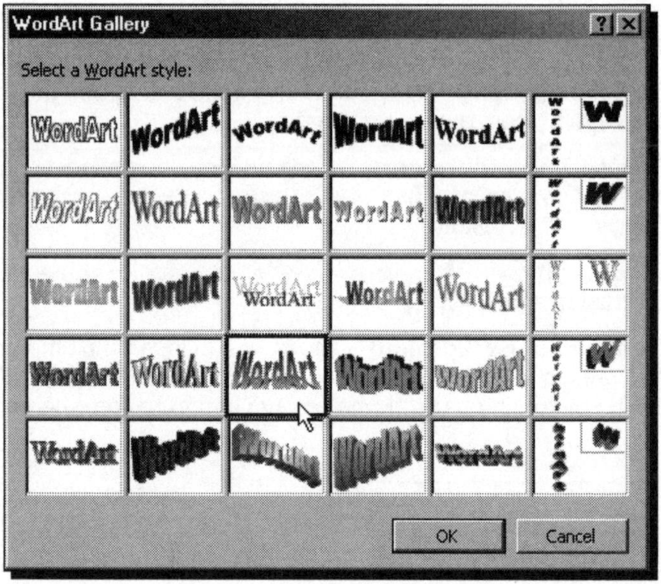

Fig. 12.13 The WordArt Gallery.

Fig. 12.14 The Edit WordArt Text Box.

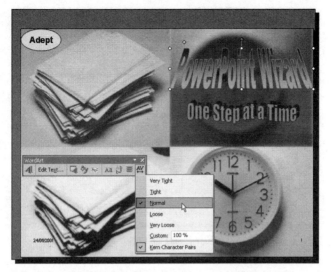

Fig. 12.15 Using the Options Available on the WordArt Toolbar.

Save the final presentation as **Training 3**. PowerPoint inserts the three letter extension **.ppt**, to distinguish such files from others in the Office suite. In the future, double-clicking on this file in a My Computer or Explorer window, will open PowerPoint with the file active.

Inserting a Picture or a Clip Art Image

A Picture or a Clip Art image can be inserted in a slide by using the appropriate buttons on the Drawing Toolbar. For example, in our case clicking the **Insert Picture** button shown here, opens the dialogue box in Fig. 12.16. In your case this might be different, particularly if you are not running under Windows Me. Nevertheless, selecting a picture and pressing the **Insert** button inserts the picture on your chosen slide.

To insert a Clip Art image, click the button shown here, then click the Clip Organizer option under the **See also** section at the bottom of the Task Pane, to open the Microsoft Clip Organizer window. Under the Collection List, choose Office Collections.

Fig. 12.16 The Insert Clip Art Dialogue Box.

This opens a further list of Clip Art sub-topics, as shown in Fig. 12.17, from which you can choose one to suit your needs.

Fig. 12.17 The Academic Sub-Option Clip Art Images.

The Picture Bar

Should you want to change a picture or a Clip Art image you have inserted into your presentation, click it to open the Picture Toolbar shown in Fig. 12.18. The tools on this bar can be used to manipulate pictures to suit your needs. Their functions are as follows:

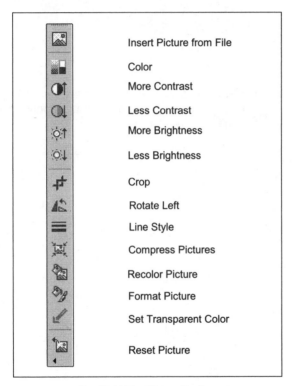

Insert Picture from File

Color

More Contrast

Less Contrast

More Brightness

Less Brightness

Crop

Rotate Left

Line Style

Compress Pictures

Recolor Picture

Format Picture

Set Transparent Color

Reset Picture

Fig. 12.18 The Picture Toolbar.

Try using these tools on an imported image to see how you can enhance or utterly destroy it! If, at the end of the day, you don't save it, it doesn't matter what you do to it. Just experiment.

* * *

PowerPoint is obviously capable of a lot more than we have introduced here, but you should now have the confidence to explore more of the package by yourself.

* * *

13

The Access 2002 Database

Microsoft Access 2002 is a database management system (DBMS) designed to allow users to store, manipulate and retrieve information easily and quickly. A database is a collection of data that exists and is organised around a specific theme or requirement. It can be of the 'flat-file' type, or it can have relational capabilities, as in the case of Access, which is known as a relational database management system (RDBMS).

The main difference between flat-file and relational database systems is that the latter can store and manipulate data in multiple 'tables', while the former systems can only manipulate a single table at any given time. To make accessing the data easier, each row (or **record**) of data within a database table is structured in the same fashion, i.e., each record will have the same number of columns (or **fields**).

We define a database and its various elements as:

Database	A collection of data organised for a specific theme in one or more tables.
Table	A two-dimensional structure in which data is stored, like in a spreadsheet
Record	A row of information in a table relating to a single entry and comprising one or more fields.
Field	A single column of information of the same type, such as people's names.

In Access 2002 the maximum size of a database is 2 gigabytes and in addition it can include linked tables in other files. The number of objects in a database is limited to 32,768, while the maximum number of fields in a table is 255.

A good example of a flat-file database is the invoicing details kept on clients by a company. These details could include name of client, description of work done, invoice number, and amount charged, as shown in Fig. 13.1:

NAME	Consultancy	Invoice	Value
VORTEX Co. Ltd	Wind Tunnel Tests	9901	120.84
AVON Construction	Adhesive Tests	9902	103.52
BARROWS Associates	Tunnel Design Tests	9903	99.32
STONEAGE Ltd	Carbon Dating Tests	9904	55.98
PARKWAY Gravel	Material Size Tests	9905	180.22
WESTWOOD Ltd	Load Bearing Tests	9906	68.52

Fig. 13.1 An Example of a Flat-File Database.

Such a flat-file DBMS is too limited for the type of information normally held by most companies. If the same client asks for work to be carried out regularly, then the details for that client (which could include address, telephone and fax numbers, contact name, date of invoice, etc.), will have to be entered several times. This can lead to errors, but above all to redundant information being kept on a client - each entry will have to have the name of the client, their address, telephone and fax numbers.

The relational facilities offered by Access, overcome the problems of entry errors and duplication of information. The ability to handle multiple tables at any one time allows for the grouping of data into sensible subsets. For example, one table, called client, could hold the names of the clients, their addresses, telephone and fax numbers, while another table, called invoice, could hold information on the work done, invoice number, date of issue, and amount charged. The two tables must have one unique common field, such as a client reference number. The advantage is that details of each client are entered and stored only once, thus reducing the time and effort wasted on entering duplicate information, and also reducing the space required for data storage.

Starting the Access Program

Access is started in Windows either by clicking the **Start** button then selecting **Programs** and clicking on the 'Microsoft Access' icon on the cascade menu, clicking the **Access** button, or the **Open Office Document** button on the Office Shortcut Bar, or by double-clicking on an Access document file. In the latter case the document will be loaded into Access at the same time.

When you start Access 2002 the program momentarily displays its opening screen, shown in Fig. 13.2, and then displays the first page of a new document (more about this shortly).

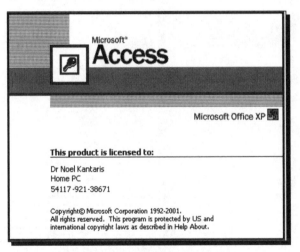

Fig. 13.2 Access' Opening Screen.

Whether you have used a previous version of Access or not, the first time you use the program, it might be a good idea to click the **Microsoft Access Help** button, shown here, and click the *What's new* link in the right pane of the Help screen.

This displays the Help screen shown in Fig. 13.3. Start by looking at the 'Key new features in Microsoft Access' option, from which you can find out differences between this version of Access and previous versions of the program. As you click each hypertext link, Access displays several topics on the subject. After looking at these options, have a look at the others displayed in the Help screen. We suggest you spend a little time here browsing through the various topics before going on.

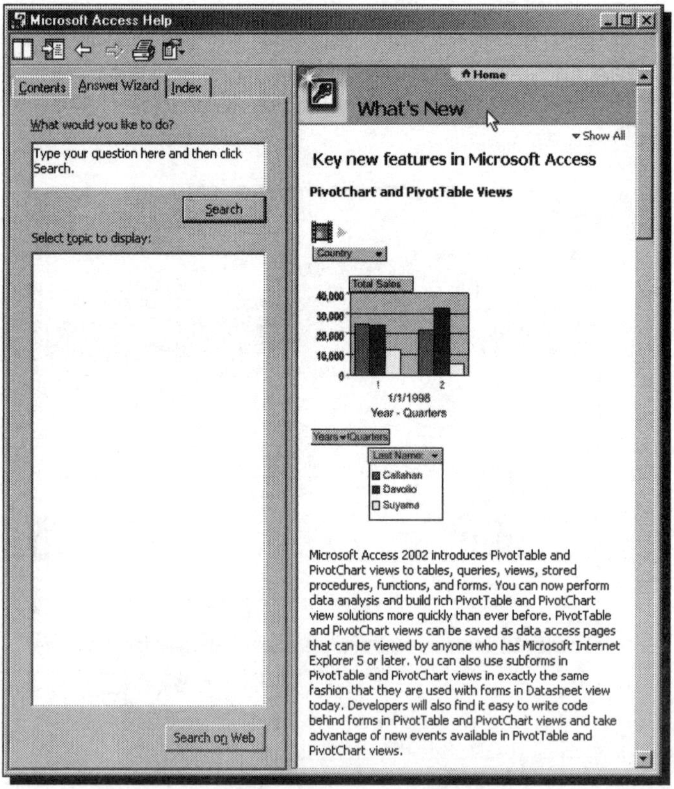

Fig. 13.3 The Microsoft Access Help Screen.

For additional Help topics, click the Contents tab of the above screen, then double-click the displayed Microsoft Access Help book to open a list of books covering various topics.

Parts of the Access Screen

Before we start designing a database, let us take a look at the Access opening screen. In Fig. 13.4, we also show what displays if you select the **General Templates** option under the **New from templates** list in the Task Pane.

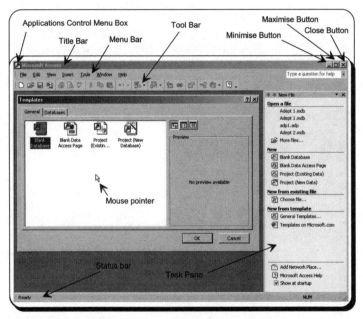

Fig. 13.4 The Access 2002 Opening Screen.

As you can see, these windows have common screen elements with those of other Microsoft Office applications. As usual, depending on what you are doing with Access, the items on the menu bar can be different from those of the opening screen.

Clicking the Databases tab of the Templates box shown in Fig. 13.4 above, displays a list of ready made database templates to suit various tasks, such as 'Asset Tracking', 'Contact Management', 'Event Management', 'Expenses', etc. It is worth having a look at these.

Database Elements

Before we start designing a database using Microsoft Access, it would be a good idea to look at the various elements that make up a database. To do so, start Access, which opens the **New File** Task Pane.

Next, and if this is being done immediately after starting Access, select the **General Templates** from the list under the **New from template** option on the Task Pane. If Access is already up and running but the Task Pane is not visible, use the **View, Toolbars, Task Pane** command to open it. The Templates dialogue box is opened. If necessary, click the General tab to display what is shown in Fig. 13.5 below.

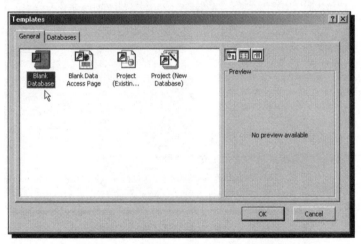

Fig. 13.5 The Access General Templates Dialogue Box.

To create a new database, select the **Blank Database** icon, and press the **OK** button. This opens the File New Database dialogue box shown in Fig. 13.6 on the next page.

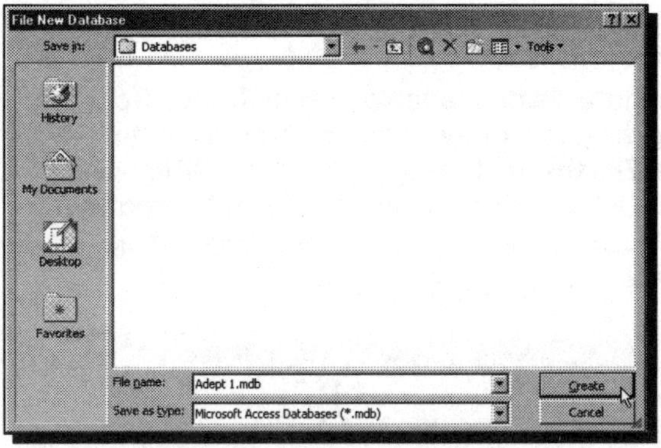

Fig. 13.6 The File New Database Dialogue Box.

In the **File name** box, type the database name, say **Adept 1**, which replaces the default name **db1**. Access adds the extension **.mdb** automatically. We also decided to save this example in a folder called **Databases** which was created inside the **My Documents** folder. Finally, pressing the **Create** button displays the Database dialogue box as follows:

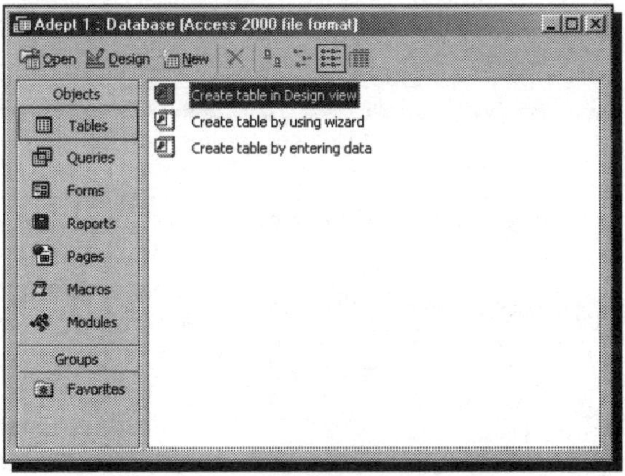

Fig. 13.7 The Database Dialogue Box.

It is from here that you can design the various elements that make up a database, such as Tables, Queries, Forms, and Reports, all of which we will examine in some detail in this and the next chapter.

Creating a Table

To design a database table, select Tables from the **Objects** list and click one of the three table-creation buttons displayed on the Database dialogue box. We will choose to use the second button, which opens the Table Wizard with the option of selecting one of two predefined table applications, Business or Personal, as shown in Fig. 13.8.

Table Wizard

Which of the sample tables listed below do you want to use to create your table?

After selecting a table category, choose the sample table and sample fields you want to include in your new table. Your table can include fields from more than one sample table. If you're not sure about a field, go ahead and include it. It's easy to delete a field later.

○ Business
○ Personal

Sample Tables:

Mailing List
Contacts
Customers
Employees
Products
Orders

Sample Fields:

MailingListID
Prefix
FirstName
MiddleName
LastName
Suffix
Nickname
Title
OrganizationName
Address

Fields in my new table:

>
>>
<
<<

Rename Field...

Cancel   < Back   Next >   Finish

Fig. 13.8 The Table Wizard Box.

The same dialogue box can be opened by clicking the **New** button on the Database dialogue box which opens the New Table dialogue box shown to the left. The third option starts the Table Wizard, while the penultimate option allows you to import tables and objects from an external file into the current database, and the last option allows you to link a table in the current database to external tables.

New Table

Datasheet View
Design View
Table Wizard
Import Table
Link Table

This wizard creates a new table to store data.

OK   Cancel

The database we are going to create holds the invoicing details which the firm Adept Consultants keep on their clients. One table will hold the details of the clients, while another will hold the actual invoice details. Therefore, to start, choose 'Customers' from the **Sample Tables** list of the Table Wizard dialogue box, to reveal a list of appropriate fields for that table, as shown in Fig. 13.9.

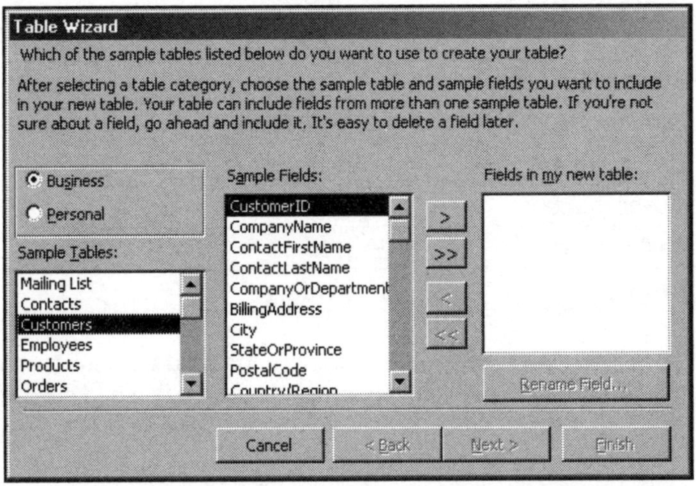

Fig. 13.9 Selecting a Table Category from the Table Wizard.

You can either select all the fields or you can select a few. For our example, we selected the following fields: CustomerID, CompanyName, BillingAddress, City, StateOrProvince, PostalCode, ContactTitle, PhoneNumber, FaxNumber and Notes, by highlighting each in turn and pressing the ▸ button.

Don't worry if these field names are not exactly what you want, as they can be easily changed. To change field names, highlight them in turn in the 'Fields in my new table' list and click the **Rename Field** button to reveal the Rename field dialogue box shown here.

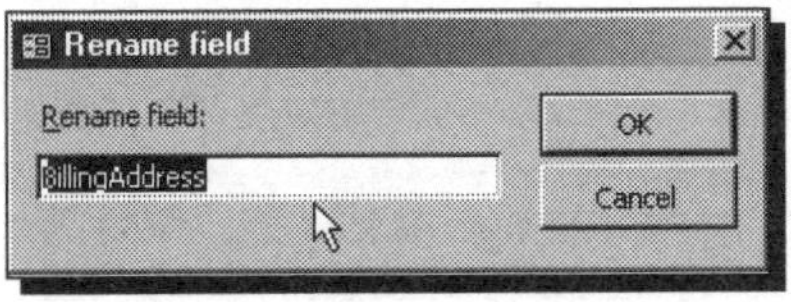

We suggest you change the selected field names to those listed below.

CustomerID	CustomerID
CompanyName	Name
BillingAddress	Address
City	Town
StateOrProvince	County
PostalCode	PostCode
ContactTitle	Contact
PhoneNumber	Phone
FaxNumber	Fax
Notes	Order

When you have completed renaming the field names, press the **Next** button, which displays the first of two dialogue boxes. In each of these, do the following:

- In answer to the question 'What do you want to name your table?', accept the suggested name **Customers** and press **Next**.

- In answer to the question 'After the wizard creates the table, what do you want to do?', click the **Enter data directly into the table** radio button, and press **Finish**.

This displays the Customers table, as shown in Fig. 13.10 below, ready for you to enter data.

Fig. 13.10 The Customers Table Data Entry Screen.

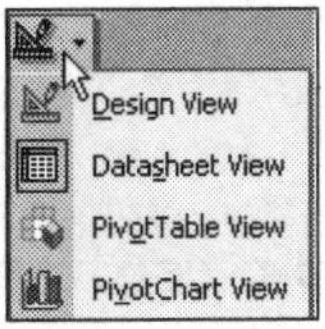

To redesign the table, including changing its field names, click the **Design View** button shown here, and select the **Design View** option from the drop-down menu, or use the **View, Design View** command. This displays the Customers Table as shown in Fig. 13.11 below.

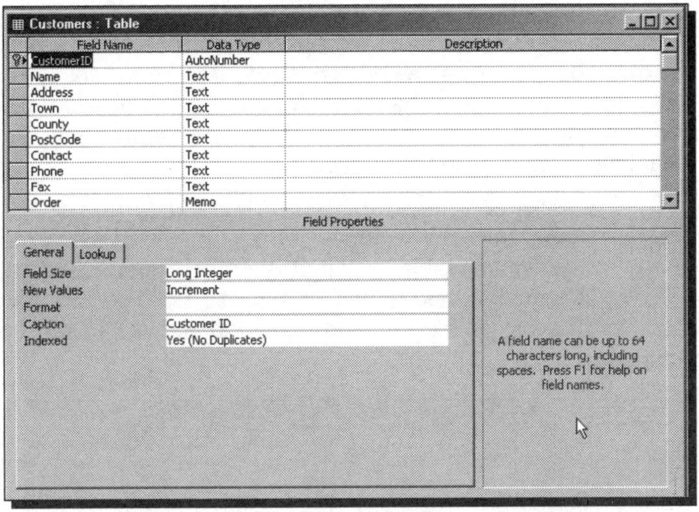

Fig. 13.11 The Customers Table in Design View.

As each field name is highlighted, a Field Properties box appears at the bottom of the screen. If you were using this Table View to rename fields, then you should also edit the name appearing against the Caption property, or remove it altogether.

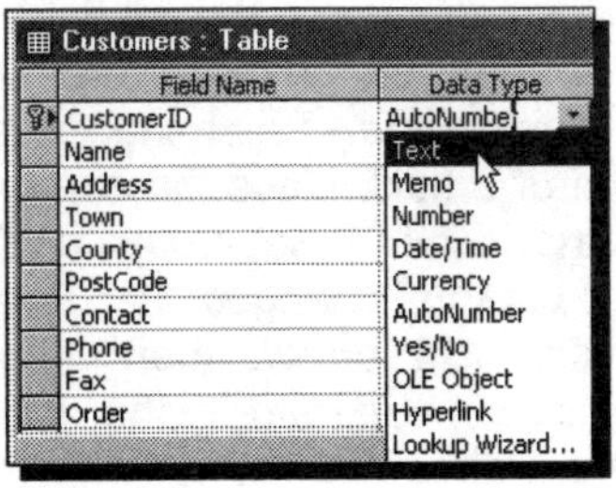

Next, place the cursor at the end of the Data Type descriptor of the CustomerID field which causes a down-arrow button to be displayed. Clicking this, displays a list of data types, as shown here.

As we will be using text to give our customers a unique ID, change the data type of this field from AutoNumber to Text.

Having done so, click the **Save** button (or use the **File, Save** command) to save your design changes up to this point. Next, as the Order field was renamed from one called Notes, Access expects entries in this field to be of Memo type by default. However, we intend to use this field as an auto-numbering field, keeping track of the order in which records were added to the database. Hence, we must change the current data type to AutoNumber and re-save our changes. It is important to do the intermediate save, because Access does not allow the removal of an AutoNumber field at the same time as changing another field to this type.

Finally, click the **Datasheet View** button (or use the **View, Datasheet View** command) to revert to the Customers table so that you can start entering information, as shown in Fig. 13.12. The required data for the rest of the fields is shown in Fig. 13.13 on the next page.

Customer ID	Name	Address	Town	County	Post Code	Contact
VORT	VORTEX Co. Ltd	Windy House	St. Austell	Cornwall	TR18 1FX	Brian Storm
AVON	AVON Construction	Riverside House	Stratford-on-Avon	Warwickshire	AV15 2QW	John Waters
BARR	BARROWS Associates	Barrows House	Bodmin	Cornwall	PL22 1XE	Mandy Brown
STON	STONEAGE Ltd	Data House	Salisbury	Wiltshire	SB44 1BN	Mike Irons
PARK	PARKWAY Gravel	Aggregate House	Bristol	Avon	BS55 2ZX	James Stone
WEST	WESTWOOD Ltd	Weight House	Plymouth	Devon	PL22 1AA	Mary Slim
GLOW	GLOWORM Ltd	Light House	Brighton	Sussex	BR87 4DD	Peter Summers
SILV	SILVERSMITH Co	Radiation House	Exeter	Devon	EX28 1PL	Adam Smith
WORM	WORMGLAZE Ltd	Glass House	Winchester	Hampshire	WN23 5TR	Richard Glazer
EALI	EALING Engines Design	Engine House	Taunton	Somerset	TN17 3RT	Trevor Miles
HIRE	HIRE Service Equipment	Network House	Bath	Avon	BA76 3WE	Nicole Webb
EURO	EUROBASE Co. Ltd	Control House	Penzance	Cornwall	TR15 8LK	Sarah Star

Fig. 13.12 Data Entered in Customers Table of Database.

The widths of the above fields were changed so that all fields could be visible on the screen at the same time. To change the

Customer ID	Name
VORT	VORTEX Co. Ltd
AVON	AVON Construction
BARR	BARROWS Associates
STON	STONEAGE Ltd

width of a field, place the cursor on the column separator until the cursor changes to the vertical split arrow, then drag the column separator to the right or left, to increase or decrease the width of the field.

Sorting a Database Table

As you enter information into a database table, you might elect to change the field headings by clicking the **Design View** button and editing a field name, say from Name to CompanyName. If you do this, on return to the Customers table you will find that the records have sorted automatically in ascending order of the entries of the field in which you left the cursor while in the Design Table.

Contact	Phone	Fax	Order
⊞ Brian Storm	01776-223344	01776-224466	1
⊞ John Waters	01657-113355	01657-221133	2
⊞ Mandy Brown	01554-664422	01554-663311	3
⊞ Mike Irons	01765-234567	01765-232332	4
⊞ James Stone	01534-987654	01534-984567	5
⊞ Mary Slim	01234-667755	01234-669988	6
⊞ Peter Summers	01432-746523	01432-742266	7
⊞ Adam Smith	01336-997755	01336-996644	8
⊞ Richard Glazer	01123-654321	01123-651234	9
⊞ Trevor Miles	01336-010107	01336-010109	10
⊞ Nicole Webb	01875-558822	01875-552288	11
⊞ Sarah Star	01736-098765	01736-098567	12
*			(AutoNumber)

Fig. 13.13 Additional Data for Customers Table.

If you want to preserve the order in which you entered your data, then sort by the last field (Order) with its type as AutoNumber. This can be done at any time, even after you have finished entering all other information in your table.

Sorting a database table in ascending order of an AutoNumber type field, results in the database table displaying in the order in which the data was originally entered in that table. Above, we show the Contact field, so that you can cross-check the original order of your Customer table, as well as the rest of the information in that table not shown in the screen dump of the previous page.

To sort a database table in ascending or descending order of the entries of any field, place the cursor in the required field and click the **Sort Ascending** or **Sort Descending** button, shown here.

With the keyboard, select the **Records, Sort** command, then choose either the **Sort Ascending** or the **Sort Descending** option.

Applying a Filter to a Sort

If you would like to sort and display only records that fit selected criteria, use the **Records, Filter, Advanced Filter/Sort** command, which opens the Filter dialogue box, shown in Fig. 13.14.

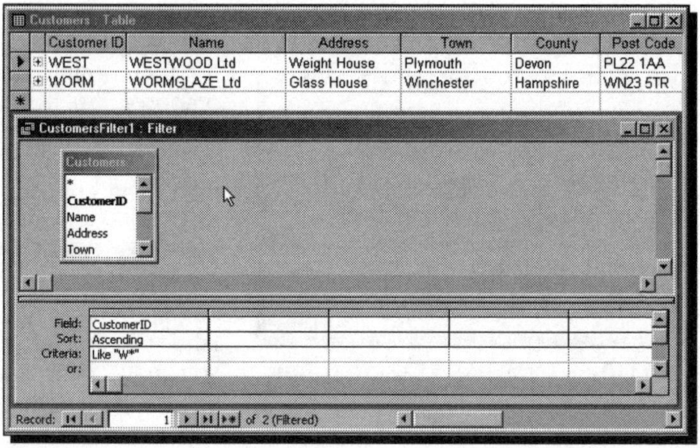

Fig. 13.14 Applying a Filter to a Sort.

The upper portion of the dialogue box displays all the fields in the Customers table, while the lower portion is where you enter your filter restrictions. In the above example, we chose to view, in ascending order, the records within the CustomerID field that start with W - we typed W* and Access displayed *Like "W*"*.

On pressing the **Apply Filter** button on the Standard Toolbar, the Customers table displays with only two entries, as seen in the above composite screen dump in which the

 filter restrictions as well as the result arising from such a filter are displayed. To revert to the display of all the records, click the same button again, which now appears on the Toolbar depressed, and bears the name **Remove Filter**.

Using a Database Form

Once a table has been selected from the Database window,

clicking the down-arrow against the **New Object** button and selecting **AutoForm**, automatically displays each record of that table in form view. The created form for the Customers table is shown in Fig. 13.15.

Forms can be used to enter, change or view data. They are mainly used to improve the way in which data is displayed on the screen.

Forms can also be used to sort records in a database table in descending or ascending order of a selected field.

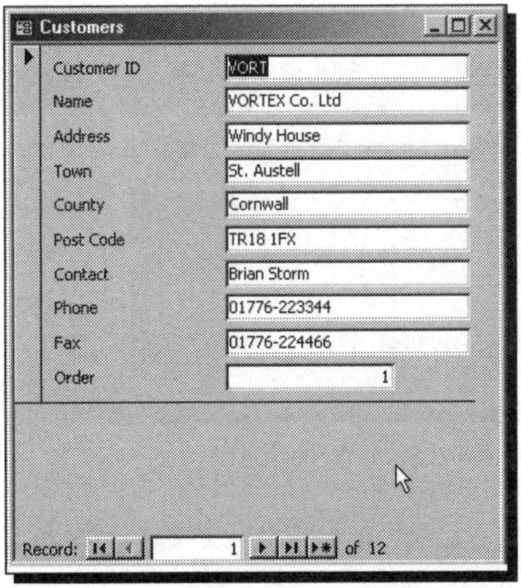

When you attempt to close a new **Form** window, you will be asked if you would like to save it. An Access database can have lots of different forms, each designed with a different purpose in mind. Saved forms are displayed in the Database window when you click the **Forms** button in the Objects menu. In the above example, we chose the default name suggested by Access, which was Customers.

Fig. 13.15 An AutoForm for Customers Table.

In the next chapter we will discuss Form design in some detail, including their customisation.

Working with Data

Adding Records to a Table: Whether you are in Table view or Form view, to add a record, click the **New Record** button, shown here.

When in Table view, the cursor jumps to the first empty record in the table (the one with the asterisk in the box to the left of the first field). When in Form view, Access displays an empty form which can be used to add a new record.

Finding Records in a Table: Whether you are in Table or Form view, to find a record click the **Find** button, or use **Edit, Find** to open the dialogue box shown in Fig 13.16

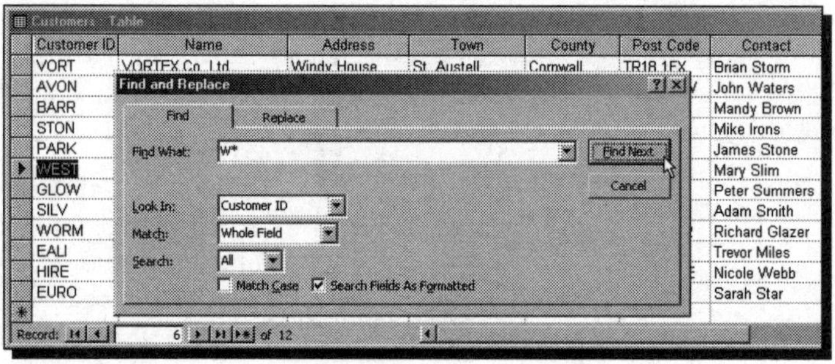

Fig. 13.16 Finding Records in a Table.

Note the field name in the **Look In** box of the dialogue box, which is CustomerID, indicating that we are only interested in finding a match within the CustomerID field.

To find all the records starting with **w**, we type **w*** in the **Find What** box of the dialogue box. Pressing the **Find Next** button, highlights the first record with the CustomerID 'WEST'. Pressing the **Find Next** button again, highlights the next record that matches our selected criteria, which in this case will be 'WORM'.

Deleting Records from a Table: To delete a record when in Table view, point to the box to the left of the record to highlight the entire record, as shown in Fig. 13.17 below, then press the <Del> key.

Fig. 13.17 Selecting a Record for Deletion.

To delete a record when in Form view, first display the record you want to delete, then use the **Edit, Select Record** command to select the whole record, and press the <Del> key.

In both cases you will be given a warning and you will be asked to confirm your decision.

Delete, Insert, and Move Fields in a Table: To delete a

field from a table, close any forms that might be open, load the table from the Database window, then click the **Design View** button, click the row selector to highlight the field you want to remove, as shown in Fig. 13.18 below, and click the **Delete Rows** button, shown here, or use the **Edit, Delete** command.

Customers : Table		
Field Name	Data Type	
CustomerID	Text	
Name	Text	
Address	Text	
Town	Text	
County	Text	

Fig. 13.18 Selecting a Field for Deletion.

To insert a field in a table, display the table in Design View,

and highlight the field above which you want to insert the new field, and click the **Insert Rows** button, shown here, or use the **Insert, Rows** command.

To move a field from its current to a new position in a table, select the field you want to move in Design View, then point to the row selector so that the mouse pointer is inclined as shown in Fig. 13.19, and drag the row to its new position.

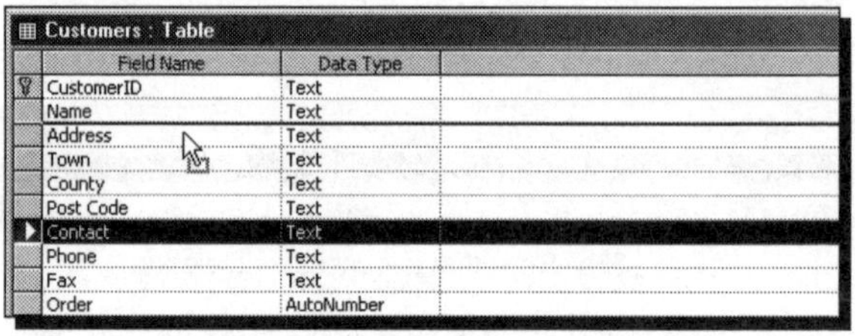

Field Name	Data Type	
CustomerID	Text	
Name	Text	
Address	Text	
Town	Text	
County	Text	
Post Code	Text	
Contact	Text	
Phone	Text	
Fax	Text	
Order	AutoNumber	

Fig. 13.19 Moving a Field in a Table.

Note that while you are dragging the field, the mouse pointer changes to the one pointing at the Name field in the above composite. Releasing the mouse button, moves the Contact field to the position of the thin horizontal line and pushes all other fields below it one row down.

Printing a Table View

You can print a database table by clicking the **Print** button, or by using the **File, Print** command which displays the Print dialogue box shown in Fig. 13.20. Alternatively, you can preview a database on screen by clicking the **Preview** button.

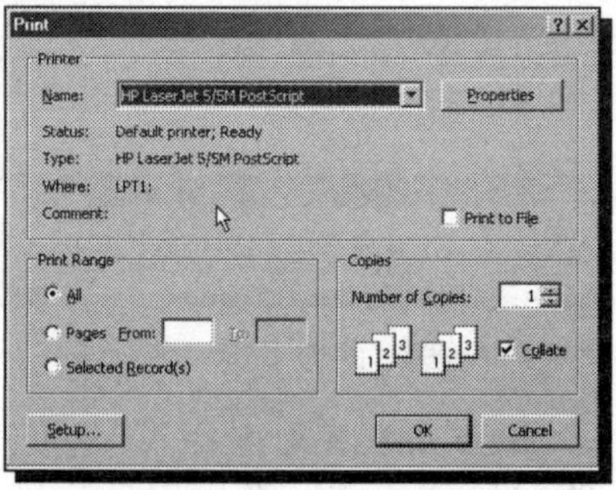

Fig. 13.20 The Print Dialogue Box.

However, printing directly from here, produces a predefined printout, the format of which you cannot control, apart from the margins and print orientation. To control these, click the **Setup** or **Properties** button.

For a better method of producing a printed output, see the Report Design section in the next chapter.

Relational Database Design

In order to be able to discuss relational databases, we will add an Orders table to our database by doing the following:

- Open the **Adept 1** database and with the Tables Object active, click the **New** Toolbar button.

- Use the Table Wizard and select Orders from the displayed **Sample Tables** list. Next, select the five fields displayed below under **Fields in my new table** from the **Sample Fields** list, and press **Next**.

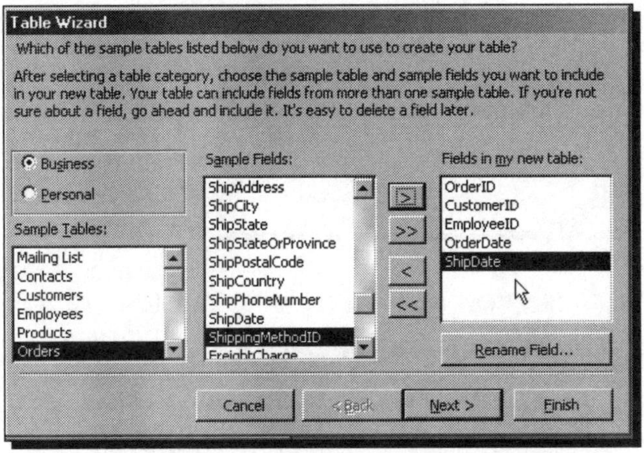

Fig. 13.21 Creating an Orders Table for Adept 1 Database.

In the next four dialogue boxes, do the following:

- Accept the default name (Orders), click the **No, I'll set the primary key** radio button, and press **Next**.

- Accept the default field (OrderID) as the field which holds data that is unique to each record, click the **Numbers and/or letters I enter when I add new records** radio button and press **Next**.

- On the next dialogue box you specify whether the new table is related to any other tables in the database. Accept the default which is, that it is not related, and press **Next**.

Although the two tables are actually related, we chose at this stage to tell the Wizard that they are not. This might appear to you as odd, but the Wizard makes certain assumptions about unique fields (for example, that ID fields are numbers), which is not what we want them to be. We choose to remain in control of the design of our database and, therefore, we will define the relationship between the two tables later.

• In the final dialogue box, click the **Enter data directly into the table** radio button, and press **Finish**.

The Wizard displays the newly created table ready for you to enter your data. However, before doing so, use the Design Table facility, as discussed previously, to change the Data Types of the selected Field Names to those displayed here.

⊞ Orders : Table		
Field Name	Data Type
🔑 OrderID	Text
CustomerID	Text
▶ EmployeeID	Text
OrderDate	Date/Time
ShipDate	Date/Time

The information you need to enter in the Orders table is shown in Fig. 13.22 below.

Order ID	Customer ID	Employee ID	Order Date	Ship Date
01002STO	STON	C.H. Wills	20/04/2001	25/05/2001
01006PAR	PARK	A.D. Smith	13/05/2001	16/06/2001
01010WES	WEST	W.A. Brown	15/05/2001	26/06/2001
01018GLO	GLOW	L.S. Stevens	25/06/2001	19/07/2001
01025SIL	SILV	S.F. Adams	28/06/2001	22/07/2001
01029WOR	WORM	C.H. Wills	20/07/2001	13/08/2001
01039EAL	EALI	A.D. Smith	30/07/2001	25/08/2001
01045HIR	HIRE	W.A. Brown	18/08/2001	08/09/2001
01051EUR	EURO	L.S. Stevens	25/08/2001	19/09/2001
01064AVO	AVON	S.F. Adams	20/09/2001	15/10/2001
01085VOR	VORT	A.D. Smith	20/03/2001	10/04/2001
01097AVO	AVON	W.A. Brown	25/03/2001	14/04/2001
01099BAR	BARR	S.F. Adams	01/04/2001	02/05/2001

Record: ◄◄ ◄ 1 ► ►► ►* of 13

Fig. 13.22 Data for the Orders Table.

Relationships

Information held in two or more tables of a database is normally related in some way. In our case, the two tables, Customers and Orders, are related by the CustomerID field.

To build up relationships between tables, return to the Database window and click the **Relationships** button on the Tool bar, shown here. This opens the following window in which the index field in each table is emboldened.

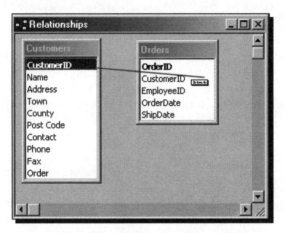

Fig. 13.23 Building Relationships Between Tables.

You can build relationships between tables by dragging a field name from one table into another. In our example below, we have dragged CustomerID from the Customers table (by pointing to it, pressing the left mouse button, and while keeping the mouse button pressed, dragging the pointer) to the required field in the other table, in this case CustomerID in the Orders table.

Releasing the mouse button opens the dialogue boxes shown in Fig. 13.24 on the next page (the **Join Properties** dialogue box is displayed by pressing the **Join Type** button on the **Edit Relationships** dialogue box).

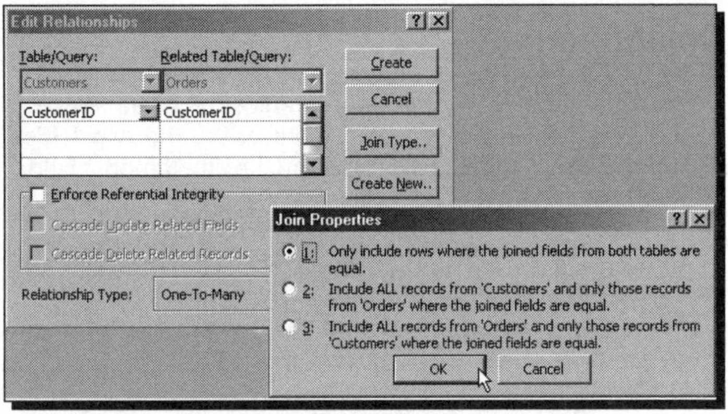

Fig. 13.24 Specifying the Type of Join in New Queries.

In the Join Properties dialogue box you can specify the type of join Access should create in new queries - more about this later. For the present, press the **OK** button on the Join Properties dialogue box, to close it, then check the **Enforce Referential Integrity** box in the Relationships dialogue box, and press the **Create** button.

Access creates and displays graphically the chosen type of

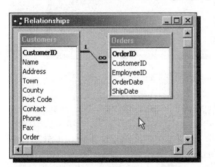

relationship in the Relationships window shown here. Note the relationship '1 customer to many (∞) orders' symbolism in the Relationships window.

Because Access is a relational database, data can be used in queries from more than one table at a time. As

Fig. 13.25 The Relationships Screen.

we have seen, if the database contains tables with related data, the relationships can be defined easily.

Usually, the matching fields have the same name, as in our example of Customers and Orders tables. In the Customers table, the CustomerID field is the primary field and relates to the CustomerID field in the Orders table - there can be several orders in the Orders table from one customer in the Customers table.

The various types of relationships are as follows:

- Inherited - for attaching tables from another Access database. The original relationships of the attached database can be used in the current database.

- Referential - for enforcing relationships between records according to certain rules, when you add or delete records in related tables within the same database. For example, you can only add records to a related table, if a matching record already exists in the primary table, and you cannot delete a record from the primary table if matching records exist in a related table.

Viewing and Editing Relationships

To view the current relationships between tables, activate the Database window and press the **Relationships** button. This displays the following:

To edit a relationship, double-click the left mouse button at the pointer position shown here. The tip of the mouse pointer must be on the inclined line joining the two tables in the Relationships window, as shown, before Access will respond. If you have difficulty with this action, first point to the relationship line and click once to embolden it, then use the **Relationships, Edit Relationship** command. Either of these two actions will open the Relationships dialogue box in which you can change the various options already discussed.

To remove a relationship, activate it (point and click to embolden it), then press the <Del> key. To delete a table, you must first detach it from other tables, then select it in the Database Window and press the <Del> key.

Creating an Additional Table

As an exercise, create a third table using the Table Wizard and select Invoices from the displayed **Sample Tables** list. Then choose the five fields displayed below - the names and their data types have been changed using the Design Table facility.

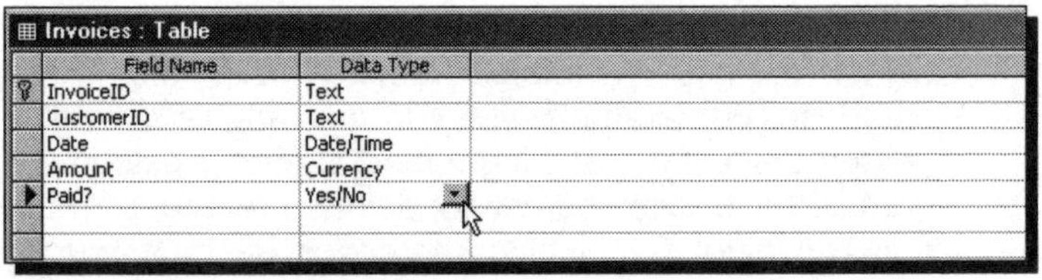

Invoices : Table

Field Name	Data Type
InvoiceID	Text
CustomerID	Text
Date	Date/Time
Amount	Currency
Paid?	Yes/No

Fig. 13.26 Creating an Invoices Table.

Next, enter the data given below and build up appropriate relationships between the Invoices table, the Customers table and the Orders table, as shown on the next page.

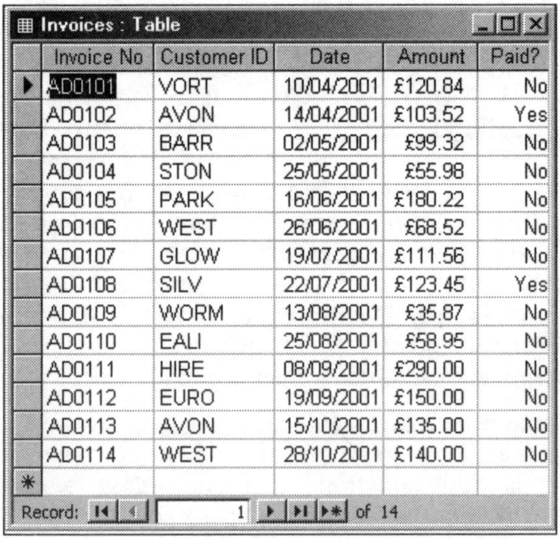

Invoices : Table

Invoice No	Customer ID	Date	Amount	Paid?
AD0101	VORT	10/04/2001	£120.84	No
AD0102	AVON	14/04/2001	£103.52	Yes
AD0103	BARR	02/05/2001	£99.32	No
AD0104	STON	25/05/2001	£55.98	No
AD0105	PARK	16/06/2001	£180.22	No
AD0106	WEST	26/06/2001	£68.52	No
AD0107	GLOW	19/07/2001	£111.56	No
AD0108	SILV	22/07/2001	£123.45	Yes
AD0109	WORM	13/08/2001	£35.87	No
AD0110	EALI	25/08/2001	£58.95	No
AD0111	HIRE	08/09/2001	£290.00	No
AD0112	EURO	19/09/2001	£150.00	No
AD0113	AVON	15/10/2001	£135.00	No
AD0114	WEST	28/10/2001	£140.00	No

Record: 1 of 14

Fig. 13.27 Data for Invoices Table of Adept 1 Database.

The relationships between the three tables should be arranged as follows:

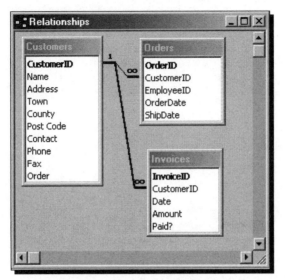

Fig. 13.28 The Relationships Between Tables.

It is important that you should complete this exercise, as it consolidates what we have done so far and, in any case, we will be using all three tables in what comes next. So go ahead and try it, then save the resultant database under its original filename **Adept 1**.

14

Forms, Reports & Queries

In this chapter, we introduce the subject of Forms, Reports, and Queries. We will show you how to use the various Wizards to create:

- Forms to find, edit, and add data in a convenient manner. Access provides you with an easy way of designing various types of forms, some of which are discussed here. Forms look good on screen, but do not produce very good output on paper.

- Reports to produce good looking output on paper. However, reports do not necessarily look good on screen.

- Queries so that you can ask questions about the data in your database tables. For example, we could find out whether we have more than one order from the same customer in our Adept database.

Creating Forms

We saw in the previous chapter how easy it was to create a single column form to view our Customers table. To see this again, open **Adept 1** and in the Database window click the **Forms** button in the **Objects** list, as shown in Fig. 14.1, then double-click the Customers entry.

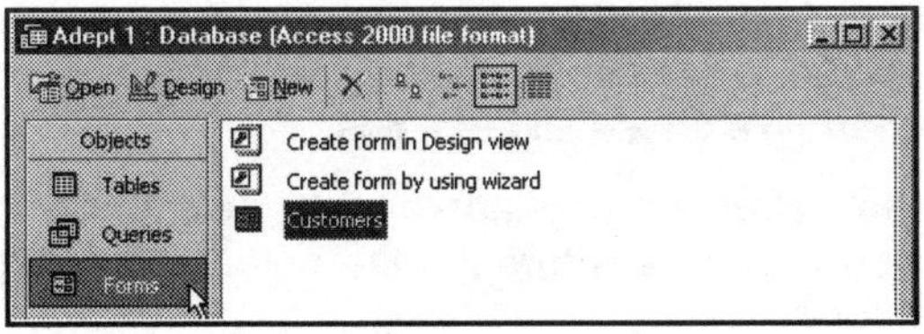

Fig. 14.1 Creating a Single Column Form.

Using the Form Wizard

You can use the Form Wizard to easily display data from either a table or a query in form view.

In the Database window, first click the **Forms** button in the Objects list, then the **New** button on the Toolbar, which opens the New Form dialogue box, shown below. As you can see from this screen dump, there are different types of forms available for you to choose from. Their function will be discussed shortly.

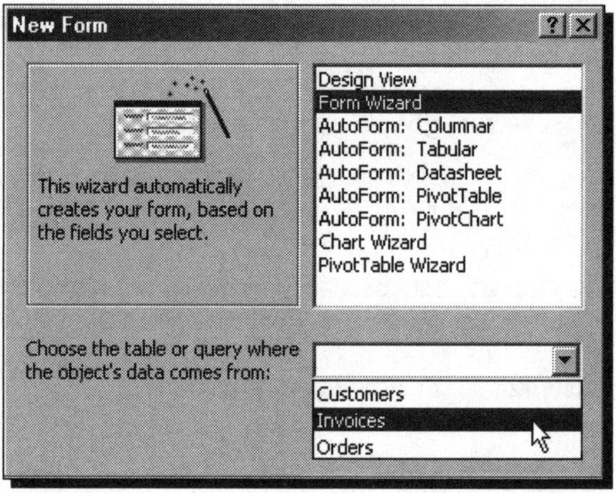

Fig. 14.2 Creating a New Form Using the Form Wizard.

To continue with our example, we first selected the Form Wizard, then chose the Invoices table on which to base the new form, and pressed the **OK** button (which is obscured in the above screen dump by the drop-down list of database tables). This causes the Wizard to display the first of four additional dialogue boxes, shown on the next page, in which you are asked to specify the fields that contain the data you want to chart. We chose all the fields.

As usual, after making appropriate selections, click the **Next** button to progress through the automatic design of the particular form.

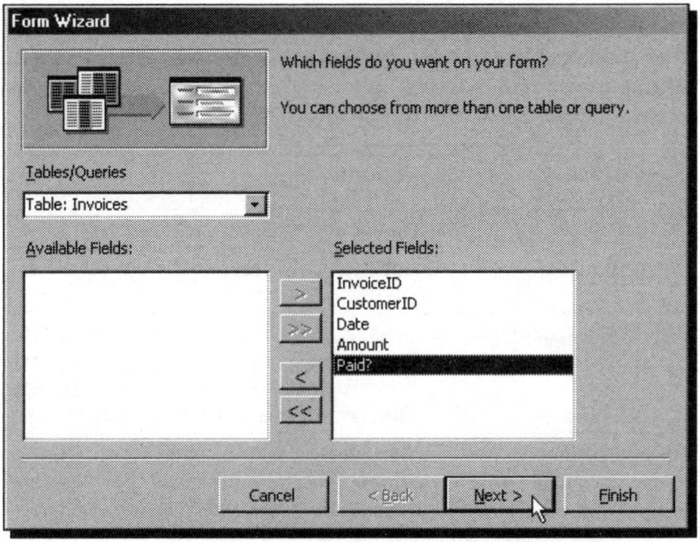

Fig. 14.3 Selecting the Fields for the New Form.

In the next three dialogue boxes that are displayed by the Wizard, make the following selections in order of appearance:

- **Columnar** for the layout of your form.

- **Standard** as the style for your Labels and Data.

- **Open the form to view or enter information**.

Pressing the **Finish** button, displays the following form.

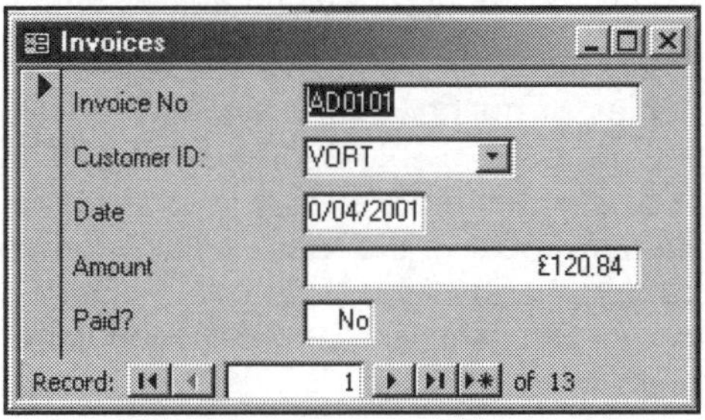

Fig. 14.4 The New Invoices Form.

Types of Forms

The available choice of Form designs have the following function:

Type of Form	Function
Design View	Design a form from scratch.
Form Wizard	Automatically creates a form based on the fields you select.
AutoForm: Columnar	Creates a columnar form with all the field labels appearing in the first column and the data in the second. The form displays one record at a time.
AutoForm: Tabular	Tabulates a screen full of records in tabular form with the field labels appearing at the head of each column.
AutoForm: Datasheet	Similar to the Tabular form, but in worksheet display format.
Chart Wizard	Displays data graphically.
PivotTable Wizard	Creates a form with an Excel PivotTable - an interactive table that can summarise a large number of data using the format and calculation methods specified by the user.

Access also allows you to design a form that contains another form. This type of form, called main/subform, allows data from related tables to be viewed at the same time.

Subforms are especially effective when you want to show data from tables or queries with a one-to-many relationship. For example, you could create a form with a subform to show data from a Customers table and an Invoices table. The data in the Customers table is the 'one' side of the relationship, while the data in the invoices table is the 'many' side of the relationship - each customer can be issued with more than one invoice.

Customising a Form

You can customise a form by changing the appearance of text, data, and any other attributes. To have a look at some of these options, double-click on Customers to display the Customers form, then click the **Design View** button on the Toolbar.

What appears on your screen when the Toolbox button is activated is shown in Fig. 14.5 .

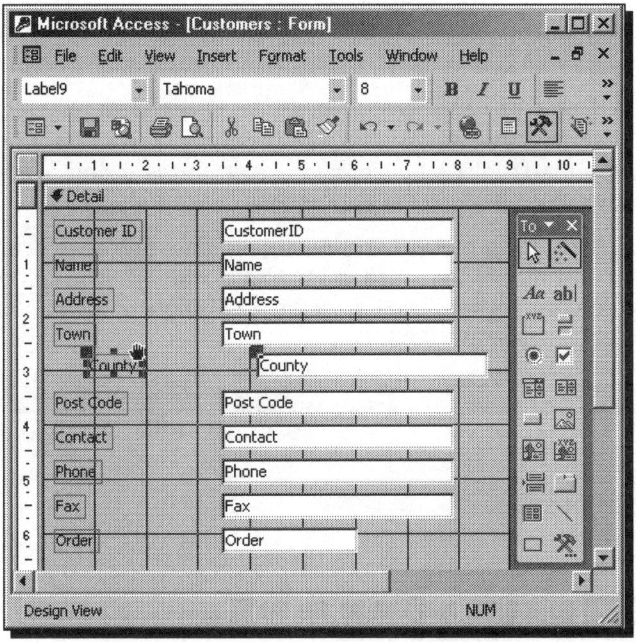

Fig. 14.5 The Customers Form in Design View.

As you can see, a form in Design View is made up of label and data boxes. Clicking at the County box, for example, causes markers to appear around it as shown above. When the mouse pointer is then placed within either the label box or data box, it changes to a hand (as shown), which indicates that you can drag the box to a new position, as we have done above. This method moves both label and data boxes together.

If you look more closely at the markers around the label and data boxes, you will see that they are of different size, as shown below.

Fig. 14.6 Label and Data Markers.

The larger ones are 'move' handles, while the smaller ones are 'size' handles. In the above example you can use the 'move' handles on either the label or the data box (as shown) to move one independently of the other. Note the shape of the hand in this case which is different to our previous screen dump.

The label box can also be sized. To size the data box, click on it so that the markers appear around it. Boxes on a form can be made larger by simply pointing to the sizing handles and dragging them in the appropriate direction.

In addition to moving and enlarging label and data boxes, you can further customise a form using the various buttons that appear on the Toolbar when in Design or Form View, shown below in two tiers.

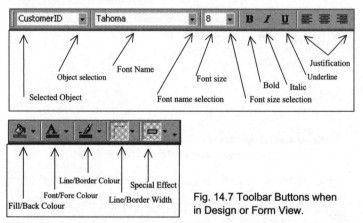

Fig. 14.7 Toolbar Buttons when in Design or Form View.

Do try and experiment with moving and sizing label and data boxes and also increasing their font size. If you don't like the result, simply don't save it. Skills gained here will be used in the Report design section.

The Toolbox

The Toolbox can be used either to design a Form or Report from scratch (a task beyond the scope of this book), or to add controls to them, such as a Combo (drop-down) box. The function of each tool on the Toolbox is listed below.

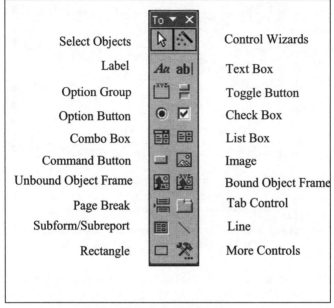

Select Objects	Control Wizards
Label	Text Box
Option Group	Toggle Button
Option Button	Check Box
Combo Box	List Box
Command Button	Image
Unbound Object Frame	Bound Object Frame
Page Break	Tab Control
Subform/Subreport	Line
Rectangle	More Controls

Fig. 14.8 The Toolbox Buttons.

As an example of using the Toolbox, let us assume that we would like to use a form to enter new data into our Invoices table, but with the ability of selecting the CustomerID field from a drop-down menu - a Combo box.

To achieve this, execute the following steps:

• On the Database window first click the **Forms** button in the **Objects** list, then double-click on Invoices. If you have not created the Invoice form, you must do so as explained in the 'Using the Form Wizard' section at the beginning of this chapter, before going on.

- When the Invoice form appears on the screen, click the **Design View** button on the Toolbar, and enlarge the Invoices form so that both the Header and Footer sections are visible on the form, as shown in Fig. 14.9.

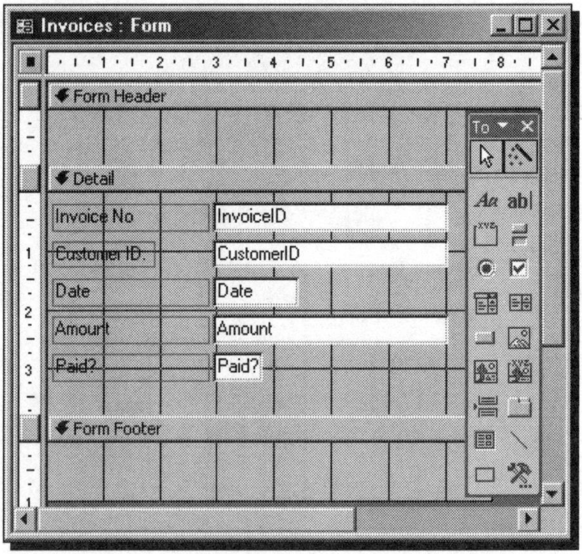

Fig. 14.9 The Invoices Form in Design View.

- Click the CustomerID field on the form, and delete both its Label and Data boxes by clicking each individually and pressing the <Del> key.

- Click the Combo Box on the Toolbox, and point and click at the area where the CustomerID field used to be on the form.

- In the subsequent dialogue boxes, select options which will cause the Combo Box to look up the values from the Customers table, and from the CustomerID field and store a selected value in the CustomerID field. Specify that the Combo Box should have the label Customer ID:.

- Move and size both the Label and Data boxes of the Combo box into the position shown in Fig. 14.10.

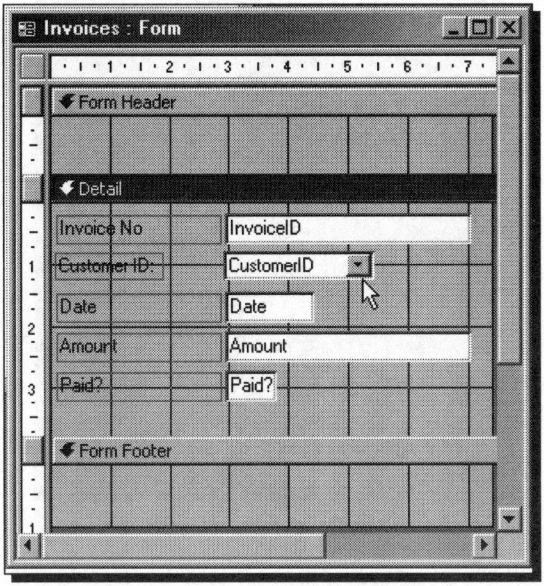

Fig. 14.10 Creating a Combo Box.

- Click the **Form View** button on the Toolbar, followed by the **New Record** button at the bottom of the Invoices form, both of which are shown below.

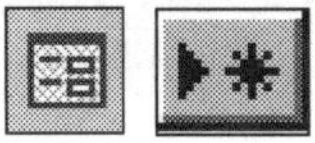

The entry form should now look as shown in Fig. 14.11 on the next page.

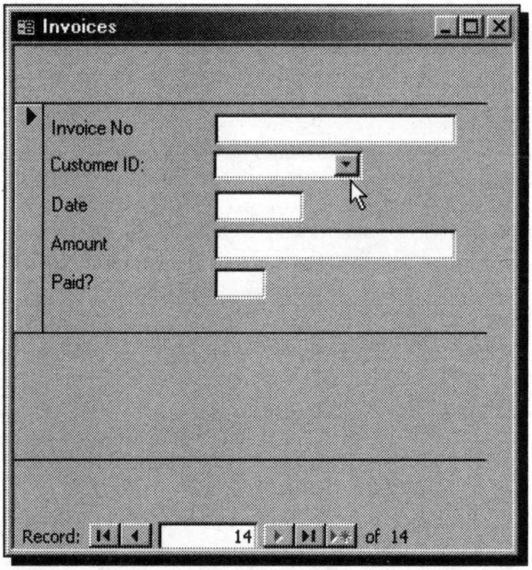

Fig. 14.11 The Invoices Form with a Combo Box.

From now on, whenever you want to add a new invoice to the Invoices table, use the Invoices form from the Database window, then click the **New Record** button on either the Toolbar or the Invoices form itself to display an empty form.

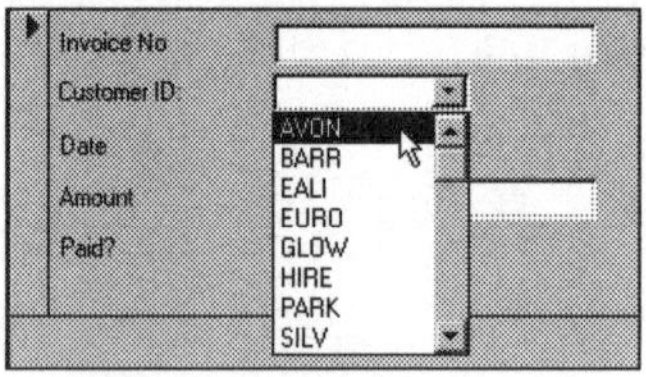

Fig. 14.12 The Customer ID Combo Box.

Next, type in the relevant information in the appropriate data boxes on the form, but when you come to fill in the Customer ID field, click instead the down arrow against its data box to display the drop-down menu shown here. Select one of the existing customers on the list, and click the **Next Record** button 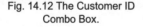 at the bottom of the Invoices form.

Try the above procedure with the following details:

```
AD0114     WEST     28/10/01     £140
```

then verify that indeed the information has been recorded by double-clicking the Invoices table on the Database window. Don't forget to save the changes to the Invoices form.

Using the Report Wizard

We will use the skills gained in manipulating Forms in Design View to produce an acceptable report created by the Report Wizard. To produce a report of the Invoices table, do the following:

- Click the **Reports** button in the **Objects** list on the Database window and then press the **New** button.

- In the New Report dialogue box, select the **Report Wizard** option, and choose 'Invoices' as the table where the object's data will come from, and press **OK**.

- Select all the fields (except for the Paid? field) which are to appear on your report and click the **Next** button.

- Select the InvoiceID field as the sort field, and accept all subsequent default settings. Call the report 'Invoices'. The report is created for you, the top portion of which is shown in Fig. 14.13 below in its raw state.

Invoices			
CustomerID	**Invoice No**	**Date**	**Amount**
AVON			
	AD0102	14/04/2001	£103.52
	AD0113	15/10/2001	£135.00
BARR			
	AD0103	02/05/2001	£99.32
BALI			
	AD0110	25/08/2001	£58.95
EURO			
	AD0112	19/09/2001	£150.00
GLOW			
	AD0107	19/07/2001	£111.56
HIRE			
	AD0111	08/09/2001	£290.00
PARK			
	AD0105	16/06/2001	£180.22
SILV			
	AD0108	22/07/2001	£123.45

Fig. 14.13 Part of the Invoices Report.

Creating a Query

You create a query so that you can ask questions about the data in your database tables. For example, we could find out whether we have more than one order from the same customer in our Adept database.

To do this, start Access, open **Adept 1**, and in the Database window click the **Queries** button in the **Objects** list, followed by the **New** button which opens the New Query dialogue box. Selecting the **Find Duplicates Query Wizard**, displays the screen in Fig. 14.14.

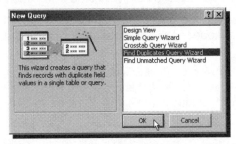

Fig. 14.14 Using the Find Duplicate Query Wizard.

On clicking **OK**, the Find Duplicates Query Wizard dialogue box is displayed, as shown in Fig. 14.15. Next, select the Orders table from the displayed database tables and press the **Next** button.

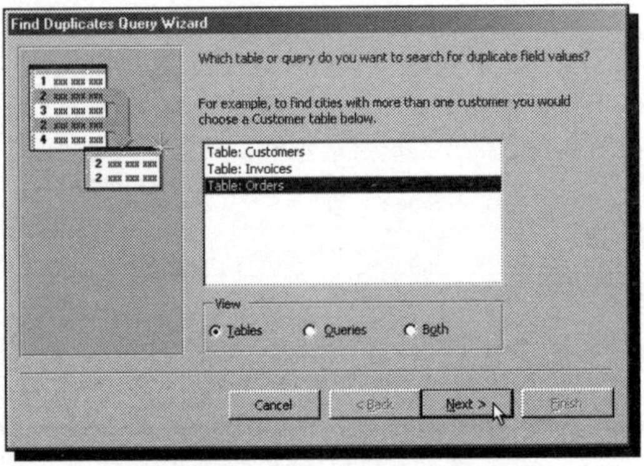

Fig. 14.15 Selecting a Table for the Query.

On the following dialogue box select **CustomerID** as the field you want to check for duplicate values, then press the [>] button, followed by the **Next** button.

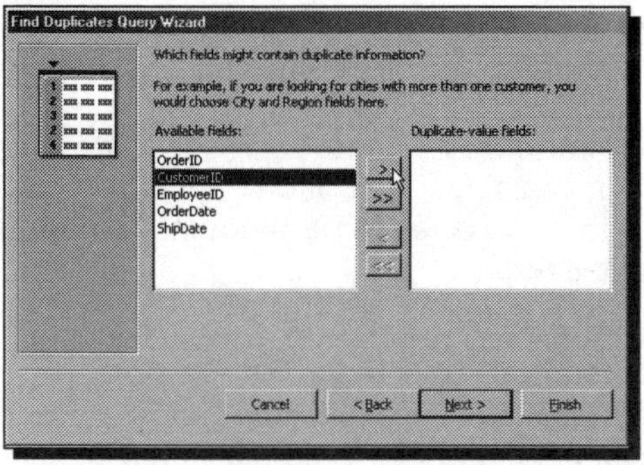

Fig. 14.16 Selecting a Field for the Query.

Finally, select the additional fields you would like to see along with the duplicate values, by selecting those you want from the next dialogue box, either one at a time or, if you decide to select all of them, as shown here, by clicking the [>>] button.

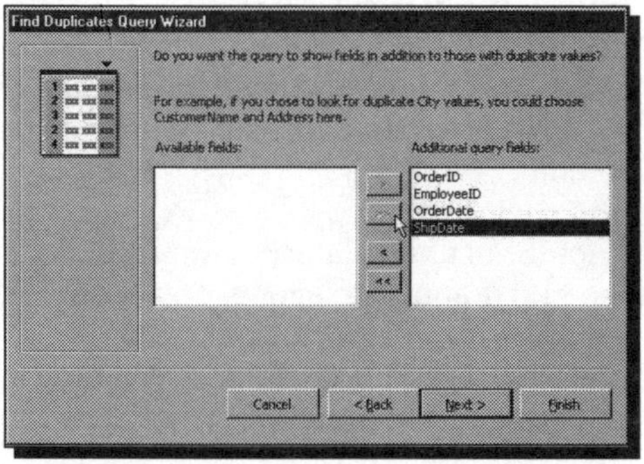

Fig. 14.17 Selecting Additional Fields for Query.

Clicking the **Finish** button displays the Select Query screen shown below.

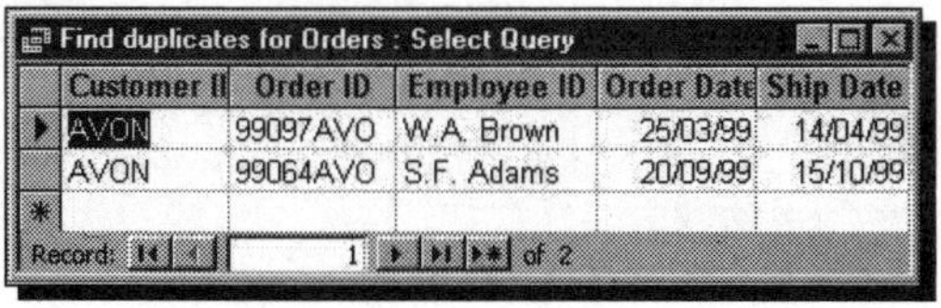
Find duplicates for Orders : Select Query

Customer I	Order ID	Employee ID	Order Date	Ship Date
AVON	99097AVO	W.A. Brown	25/03/99	14/04/99
AVON	99064AVO	S.F. Adams	20/09/99	15/10/99

Record: 1 of 2

Types of Queries

The query we have created so far, is known as a *Select Query*, which is the most common type of query. However, with Access you can also create and use other types of queries, as follows:

- **Crosstab query** - used to present data with row and column headings, just like a spreadsheet. It can be used to summarise large amounts of data in a more readable form.

- **Action query** - used to make changes to many records in one operation. For example, you might like to remove from a given table all records that meet certain criteria, make a new table, or append records to a table. Obviously, this type of query has to be treated with care!

- **Union query** - used to match fields from two or more tables.

- **Pass-through query** - used to pass commands to a SQL (see below) database.

- **Data-definition query** - used to create, change, or delete tables in an Access database using SQL statements.

SQL stands for Structured Query Language, often used to query, update, and manage relational databases. Each query created by Access has an associated SQL statement that defines the action of that query. Thus, if you are familiar with SQL, you can use such statements to view and modify queries, or set form and report properties. However, these actions can be done more easily with the QBE (query-by-example) grid, to be discussed next. If you design union queries, pass-through queries, or data-definition queries, then you must use SQL statements, as these types of queries can not be designed with the QBE grid. Finally, to create a sub-query, you use the QBE grid, but you enter a SQL SELECT statement for criteria, as we shall see in the next QBE grid example.

The Query Window

The Query window is a graphical query-by-example (QBE) tool. Because of Access' graphical features, you can use the mouse to select, drag, and manipulate objects in the query window to define how you would like to see your data.

An example of a ready made Query window can be seen by selecting the Find duplicates for Orders query and clicking the **Design** button on the Database window. This action opens the Select Query dialogue box shown in Fig. 14.18.

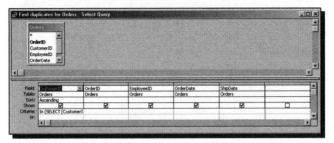

Fig. 14.18 The Select Query Dialogue Box.

You can add a table to the top half of the Query window by dragging the table from the Database window. Similarly, you can add fields to the bottom half of the Query window (the QBE grid) by dragging fields from the tables on the top half of the Query window. Also, the QBE grid is used to select the data sort order, or insert criteria, such as SQL statements.

To see the full SQL SELECT statement written by Access as the criteria selection when we first defined the query, use the **View, SQL View** command.

```
SELECT Orders.CustomerID, Orders.OrderID, Orders.EmployeeID, Orders.OrderDate, Orders.ShipDate
FROM Orders
WHERE (((Orders.CustomerID) In (SELECT [CustomerID] FROM [Orders] As Tmp GROUP BY [CustomerID] HAVING Count(*)>1 )))
ORDER BY Orders.CustomerID;
```

Note the part of the statement which states 'As Tmp GROUP'. Access collects the data you want as a temporary group, called a *dynaset*. This special set of data behaves like a table, but is not a table; it is a dynamic view of the data from one or more tables, selected and sorted by the particular query.

Adding Tables to a Query Window

Below, we show a screen dump created by first clicking the **Queries** button in the **Objects** list, then pressing the **New** button on the Database window. In the displayed New Query dialogue box, select Design View, as shown in Fig. 14.19, and press the **OK** button.

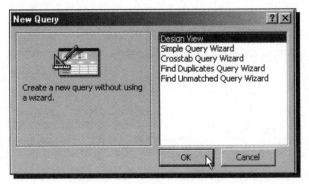

Fig. 14.19 The New Query Dialogue Box.

This opens both the Select Query and the Show Table dialogue boxes shown below. The Invoices and Customers tables were then added to the Select Query window by selecting then in the Show Table dialogue box and pressing the **Add** button, as shown in Fig. 14.20.

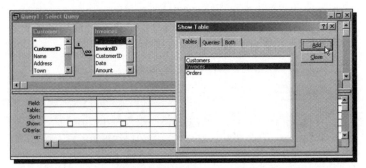

Fig. 14.20 The Select Query and Show Table Dialogue Boxes.

Adding Fields to a Query Window

In Fig. 14.17 we show a screen in which the Paid?, InvoiceID, and Amount fields have been dragged from the Invoices table and added to the Query window. Also, the Name and Contact fields have been dragged from the Customers table and placed on the Query window, while the Phone field from the Customers table is about to be added to the Query window.

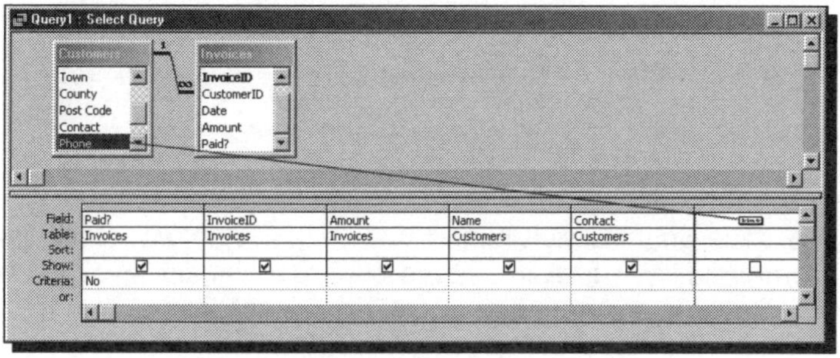

Fig. 14.21 Dragging Fields from Tables to the QBE Grid.

Having dragged all five fields from the two tables onto the QBE grid, we have added the word **No** as the criteria on the Paid? field and selected Ascending as the Sort for the InvoiceID field.

Note that the Invoices and Customers tables are joined by a line that connects the two CustomerID fields. The join line was created when we designed the tables and their relationships in the previous chapter. Even if you have not created these relationships, Access will join the tables in a query automatically when the tables are added to a query, provided each table has a field with the same name and a compatible data type and one of those fields is a primary key. A primary field is displayed in bold in the Query window.

If you have not created relationships between your tables yourself, or Access has not joined your tables automatically, you can still use related data in your query by joining the tables in the Query window.

Clicking the **Run** button on the Toolbar, shown here, instantly displays all the unpaid invoices with the details you have asked for, as follows:

Paid?	Invoice No	Amount	Name	Contact	Phone
▶ No	AD0101	£120.84	VORTEX Co. Ltd	Brian Storm	01776-223344
No	AD0103	£99.32	BARROWS Associates	Mandy Brown	01554-664422
No	AD0104	£55.98	STONEAGE Ltd	Mike Irons	01765-234567
No	AD0105	£180.22	PARKWAY Gravel	James Stone	01534-987654
No	AD0106	£68.52	WESTWOOD Ltd	Mary Slim	01234-667755
No	AD0107	£111.56	GLOWORM Ltd	Peter Summers	01432-746523
No	AD0109	£35.87	WORMGLAZE Ltd	Richard Glazer	01123-654321
No	AD0110	£58.95	EALING Engines Design	Trevor Miles	01336-010107
No	AD0111	£290.00	HIRE Service Equipment	Nicole Webb	01875-558822
No	AD0112	£150.00	EUROBASE Co. Ltd	Sarah Star	01736-098765
No	AD0113	£135.00	AVON Construction	John Waters	01657-113355
No	AD0114	£140.00	WESTWOOD Ltd	Mary Slim	01234-667755

Record: |◀| ◀ | 1 | ▶ |▶|| ▶*| of 12

Fig. 14.22 Unpaid Invoices from the Adept 1 Database.

To save your newly created query, use the **File, Save As** command, and give it a name such as 'Unpaid Invoices' in the Save As dialogue box.

Types of Criteria

Access accepts the following expressions as criteria:

Arithmetic Operators		*Comparison Operators*		*Logical Operators*	
*	Multiply	<	Less than	And	And
/	Divide	<=	Less than or equal	Or	Inclusive or
+	Add	>	Greater than	Xor	Exclusive or
-	Subtract	>=	Greater than or equal	Not	Not equivalent
		=	Equal	Eqv	Equivalent
		<>	Not equal	Imp	Implication
Other operators					
Between	Between 50 And 150	All values between 50 and 150			
In	In ("Bath","Bristol")	All records with Bath and Bristol			
Is	Is Null	All records with no value in that field			
Like	Like "Brian *"	All records with Brian something in field			
&	[Name]&" "&[Surname]	Concatenates strings			

Using Wildcard Characters in Criteria

In a previous example we used the criteria A* to mean any company whose name starts with the letter A. The asterisk in this criteria is known as a wildcard character.

To search for a pattern, you can use the asterisk (*) and the question mark (?) as wildcard characters when specifying criteria in expressions. An asterisk stands for any number of characters, while a question mark stands for any single character in the same position as the question mark.

The following examples show the use of wildcard characters in various types of expressions:

Entered Expression	Meaning	Examples
a?	Any two-letter word beginning with A	am, an, as, at
???d	Any four-letter word ending with d	find, hand, land, yard
Sm?th	Any five-letter word beginning with Sm and ending with th	Smith, Smyth
fie*	Any word starting with the letters fie	field, fiend, fierce, fiery
*ght	Any word ending with ght	alight, eight, fight, light, might, sight
*/5/97	All dates in May '97	1/5/97
a	Any word with the letter a in it	Brian, Mary, star, yard

Combining Criteria

By specifying additional criteria in a Query window you can create powerful queries for viewing your data. In the examples below we have added the field Amount to our Unpaid Invoices query.

The AND Criteria with Different Fields: When you insert criteria in several fields, but in the same row, Access assumes that you are searching for records that meet all of the criteria. For example, the criteria below lists the records shown in Fig. 14.23.

Field:	Paid?	InvoiceID	Amount	Name	Contact
Table:	Invoices	Invoices	Invoices	Customers	Customers
Sort:		Ascending			
Show:	☑	☑	☑	☑	☑
Criteria:	No		Between 50 And 100		Like "M*"
or:					

	Paid?	Invoice No	Amount	Name	Contact	Phone
▶	No	AD0103	£99.32	BARROWS Associates	Mandy Brown	01554-6644:
	No	AD0104	£55.98	STONEAGE Ltd	Mike Irons	01765-2345(
	No	AD0106	£68.52	WESTWOOD Ltd	Mary Slim	01234-6677!

Unpaid Invoices : Select Query

Record: 1 of 3

Fig. 14.23 Illustrating the AND Criteria with Different Fields.

The OR Criteria with the Same Field: If you include multiple criteria in one field only, then Access assumes that you are searching for records that meet any one of the specified criteria. For example, the criteria <50 or >100 in the field Amount, shown in Fig. 14.24, list the required records, only if the No in the Paid? field is inserted in both rows.

Field:	Paid?	InvoiceID	Amount	Name	Contact
Table:	Invoices	Invoices	Invoices	Customers	Customers
Sort:		Ascending			
Show:	☑	☑	☑	☑	☑
Criteria:	No		<50		
or:	No		>100		

	Paid?	Invoice No	Amount	Name	Contact	Phone
▶	No	AD0101	£120.84	VORTEX Co. Ltd	Brian Storm	01776-223344
	No	AD0105	£180.22	PARKWAY Gravel	James Stone	01534-987654
	No	AD0107	£111.56	GLOWORM Ltd	Peter Summers	01432-746523
	No	AD0109	£35.87	WORMGLAZE Ltd	Richard Glazer	01123-654321
	No	AD0111	£290.00	HIRE Service Equipment	Nicole Webb	01875-558822
	No	AD0112	£150.00	EUROBASE Co. Ltd	Sarah Star	01736-098765
	No	AD0113	£135.00	AVON Construction	John Waters	01657-113355
	No	AD0114	£140.00	WESTWOOD Ltd	Mary Slim	01234-667755

Unpaid Invoices : Select Query

Record: 1 of 8

Fig. 14.24 Illustrating the OR Criteria with the Same Field.

The OR Criteria with Different Fields: If you include multiple criteria in different fields, but in different rows, then Access assumes that you are searching for records that meet either one or the other of the specified criteria. For example, the criteria Yes in the Paid? field and the criteria <50 in the Amount field, but in different rows, list the following records.

Field:	Paid?	InvoiceID	Amount	Name
Table:	Invoices	Invoices	Invoices	Customers
Sort:		Ascending		
Show:	☑	☑	☑	☑
Criteria:	Yes			
or:			<50	

	Paid?	Invoice No	Amount	Name	Contact	Phone
▶	Yes	AD0102	£103.52	AVON Construction	John Waters	01657-113355
	Yes	AD0108	£123.45	SILVERSMITH Co	Adam Smith	01336-997755
	No	AD0109	£35.87	WORMGLAZE Ltd	Richard Glazer	01123-654321

Record: 1 ▶ ▶I ▶* of 3

Fig. 14.25 Illustrating The OR Criteria with Different Fields.

The AND and OR Criteria Together: The following choice of criteria will cause Access to retrieve either records that have Yes in the Paid? field and the company's name starts with the letter A, or records that the invoice amount is less than £50.

Field:	Paid?	InvoiceID	Amount	Name
Table:	Invoices	Invoices	Invoices	Customers
Sort:		Ascending		
Show:	☑	☑	☑	☑
Criteria:	Yes			Like "A*"
or:			<50	

	Paid?	Invoice No	Amount	Name	Contact	Phone
▶	Yes	AD0102	£103.52	AVON Construction	John Waters	01657-113355
	No	AD0109	£35.87	WORMGLAZE Ltd	Richard Glazer	01123-654321

Record: 1 ▶ ▶I ▶* of 2

Fig. 14.26 Illustrating the AND and OR Criteria Together.

Calculating Totals in Queries

Access allows you to perform calculations on groups of records. For example, we could find the total value of unpaid invoices grouped by month. To do this, start a new query in Design View, and using the Invoices table, drag the 'Paid?' And 'Amount' fields into the Query window, as shown below. Then enter in the third column (Field row) the formula

```
Month:DatePart("m",(Date))
```

Functions, such as 'sum', are entered in the Total row of a

 query which can be displayed by clicking the **Totals** button, shown to the left, while in Design View. Save this query under the name 'Monthly Invoices', then click the **Run** button on the Toolbar to see the result.

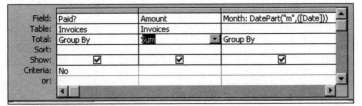

Field:	Paid?	Amount	Month: DatePart("m",([Date]))
Table:	Invoices	Invoices	
Total:	Group By	Sum	Group By
Sort:			
Show:	☑	☑	☑
Criteria:	No		
or:			

Paid?	SumOfAmount	Month
No	£120.84	4
No	£155.30	5
No	£248.74	6
No	£111.56	7
No	£94.82	8
No	£440.00	9
No	£275.00	10

Fig. 14.27. Calculating Totals in Queries.

* * *

We hope we have covered enough features of the program in this book to give you the foundations needed to make you want to explore Access more fully by yourself.

However, if you would prefer to be guided through these and additional topics, in much more detail, then may we suggest you look up the book *Microsoft Access 2002 explained* (BP512), also published by BERNARD BABANI (publishing) Ltd.

15

Sharing Information

You can link or embed all or part of an existing file created either in an Office application or in any other application that supports Object Linking and Embedding (OLE). However, if an application does not support OLE, then you must use the copy/cut and paste commands to copy or move information from one application to another. In general, you copy, move, link, embed, or hyperlink information depending on the imposed situation, as follows:

Imposed Situation	Method to Adopt
Inserted information will not need updating, or Application does not support OLE.	Copy or move
Inserted information needs to be automatically updated in the destination file as changes are made to the data in the source file, or Source file will always be available and you want to minimise the size of the destination file, or Source file is to be shared amongst several users.	Link
Inserted information might need to be updated but source file might not be always accessible, or Destination file needs to be edited without having these changes reflected in the source file.	Embed
To jump to a location in a document or Web page, or to a file that was created in a different program.	Hyperlink

Copying or Moving Information

To copy or move information between programs running under Windows, such as Microsoft applications, is extremely easy. To move information, use the drag and drop facility, while to copy information, use the **Edit, Copy** and **Edit, Paste** commands.

To illustrate the technique, we will copy the **Project 3.xls** file, created in Excel, into Word. We will consider the following two possibilities:

Source File Available without Application

Let us assume that you only have the source file **Project 3.xls** on disc, but not the application that created it (that is you don't have Excel). In such a situation, you can only copy the contents of the whole file to the destination (in our case Word). To achieve this, do the following:

*   Start Word and minimise it on the Taskbar.

*   Use My Computer (or Explorer) to locate the file whose contents you want to copy into Word.

*   Click the filename that you want to copy, hold the mouse button down and point to Word on the Taskbar until the application opens.

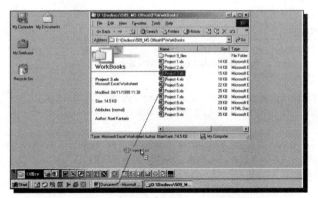

Fig. 15.1 Copying a Data File into an Application.

- While still holding the mouse button down, move the mouse pointer into Word's open document to the exact point where you would like to insert the contents of **Project 3.xls**.

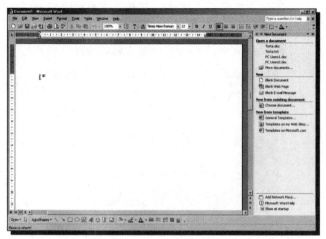

Fig. 15.2 Selecting the Point in an Application in which to Copy Data.

- Release the mouse button to place the contents of **Project 3.xls** into Word at that point.

Project Analysis: Adept Consultants Ltd.				
	Jan	Feb	Mar	1st Quarter
Income	£ 14,000.00	£ 15,000.00	£ 16,000.00	£ 45,000.00
Costs:				
Wages	£ 2,000.00	£ 3,000.00	£ 4,000.00	£ 9,000.00
Travel	£ 400.00	£ 500.00	£ 600.00	£ 1,500.00
Rent	£ 300.00	£ 300.00	£ 300.00	£ 900.00
Heat/Light	£ 150.00	£ 200.00	£ 130.00	£ 480.00
Phone/Fax	£ 250.00	£ 300.00	£ 350.00	£ 900.00
Adverts	£ 1,100.00	£ . 1,200.00	£ 1,300.00	£ 3,600.00
Total Costs	£ 4,200.00	£ 5,500.00	£ 6,680.00	£ 16,380.00
Profit	£ 9,800.00	£ 9,500.00	£ 9,320.00	£ 28,620.00
Cumulative	£ 9,800.00	£ 19,300.00	£ 28,620.00	

Fig. 15.3 The Copied Data within an Application.

Source File and Application Available

Assuming that you have both the file and the application that created it on your computer, you can copy all or part of the contents of the source file to the destination file, as follows:

- Start Excel and open **Project 3.xls**, then highlight the information to copy, change its format from **Currency** to **Custom** so that the £ sign appears just in front of the numbers and click the **Copy** button on the Toolbar.

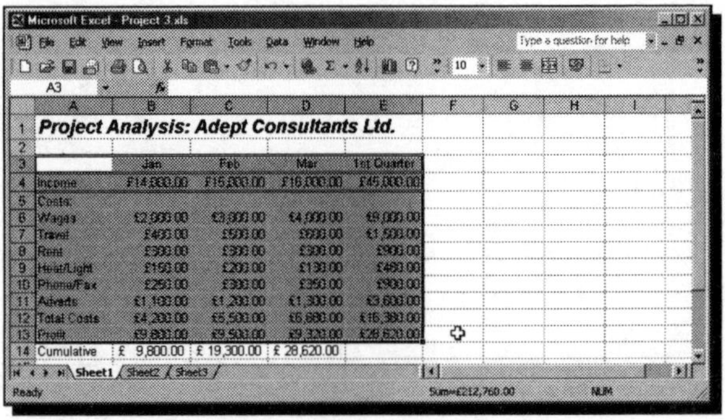

Fig. 15.4 Selecting Data to be Copied to Clipboard.

- Start Word and click the **Paste** button on the Toolbar. Then select the first option from the Smart Tag list.

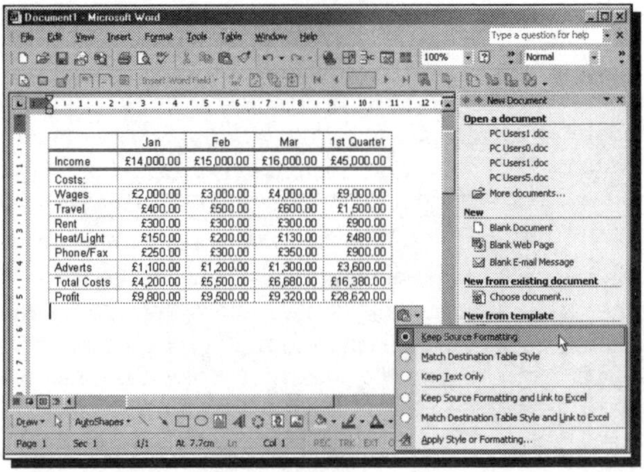

Fig. 15.5 Pasting Data into Application from the Clipboard.

Object Linking and Embedding

Object Linking is copying information from one file (the source file) to another file (the destination file) and maintaining a connection between the two files. When information in the source file is changed, then the information in the destination file is automatically updated. Linked data is stored in the source file, while the file into which you place the data stores only the location of the source and displays a representation of the linked data.

For example, you would use Object Linking if you would want an Excel chart included in, say, a Word document to be updated whenever you changed the information used to create the chart in the first place within Excel. In such a case, the Excel worksheet containing the chart would be referred to as the source file, while the Word document would be referred to as the destination file.

Object Embedding is inserting information created in one file (the source file) into another file (the container file). After such information has been embedded, the object becomes part of the container file. When you double-click an embedded object, it opens in the application in which it was created in the first place. You can then edit it in place, and the original object in the source application remains unchanged.

Thus, the main differences between linking and embedding are where the data is stored and how it is updated after you place it in your file. Linking saves you disc space as only one copy of the linked object is kept on disc. Embedding a logo chosen for your headed paper, saves the logo with every saved letter!

In what follows, we will discuss how you can link or embed either an entire file or selected information from an existing file, and how you can edit an embedded object. Furthermore, we will examine how to mail merge a letter written in Word with a list created either in Access, Excel, Outlook, or even Word itself.

Inserting a Picture

To insert a picture into an application, do the following:

- Open the container file, say Word, and click where you want to embed the new object.

- Use the **Insert, Picture** command, to display the additional drop-down menu, shown in Fig. 15.6.

Fig. 15.6 Using the Insert Picture Menu.

As an example, we selected **From File** (you could select a different option) and chose the **Iceberg.jpg** file, shown here to the right (you could select your own picture). Clicking the **Insert** button on the  Insert Picture dialogue box, embeds the selected picture within Word.

Right-clicking the picture displays a drop-down menu and selecting the **Format Picture** and **Show Picture Toolbar** options, opens up the Format Picture dialogue box and places the Picture Toolbar on the screen. Using these two options you can format and edit your picture to your requirements. Do try it for yourself.

Linking or Embedding an Existing File

To embed an existing file in its entirety into another application, do the following:

* Open the container file, say Word, and click where you want to embed the file.

* Use the **Insert, Object** command, to open the Object dialogue box, shown below, when the **Create from File** tab is clicked.

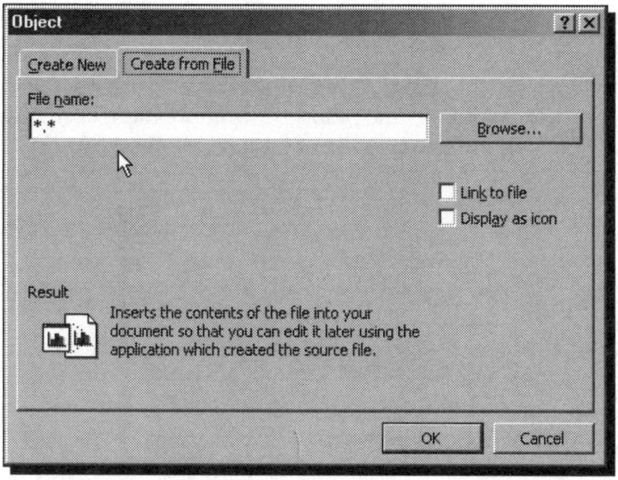

Fig. 15.7 Finding a File to Link or Embed into an Application.

To locate the file you want to link or embed, click **Browse**, and then select the options you want.

* In the **File name** box, type the name of the file you want to link or embed.

* To maintain a link to the original file, check the **Link to file** box.

Note: To insert a graphic from Microsoft Clip Gallery, use the **Create New** tab of the dialogue box in Fig. 15.7 above, and scroll to the Microsoft Clip Gallery entry on the displayed list. You can then first select a Category of clips, then choose the clip you want to insert in your document.

Linking or Embedding Selected Information

To link or embed selected information from an existing file created in one application into another, do the following:

*   Select the information in the source file you want to link or embed.

*   Use the **Edit, Copy** command to copy the selected information to the Clipboard.

*   Switch to the container file or document in which you want to place the information, and then click where you want the information to appear.

*   Use the **Edit, Paste** command to paste the selected information into your document, then click the Smart Tag to display a list of options as shown in Fig. 15.8.

Fig. 15.8 The Smart Tag List of Paste Options.

*   To link the information, click the **Keep Source Formatting and Link to Excel** option, or to embed the information, click the **Keep Source Formatting** option. As you can see, Word (the destination application) sensed that the information we were pasting came from Excel.

Copying information from another word processor, say Lotus Word Pro as in this case, shrinks the Smart Tag list of options as shown to the right, but with sufficient number to complete the job.

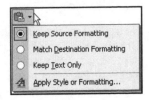

Linking or Embedding into Access

When you link or embed an object in a Microsoft Access form or report, the object is displayed in an object frame. To illustrate this point, start Access, select the Forms tab, and open Customers (created in Chapter 13), and then:

* Switch to Design View, use the **Insert, Object** command, select the source application from the **Object Type** list in the Insert Object dialogue box (we chose the Microsoft Clip Gallery), and press **OK**.

* Select a graphic and click the **Insert Clip** button on the drop-down menu to insert it into an unbound frame which you might have to re-size. To force the graphic to fit into a smaller frame, right-click it, select **Properties** from the drop-down menu, click the down-arrow against the **Size Mode** box, and choose **Zoom**.

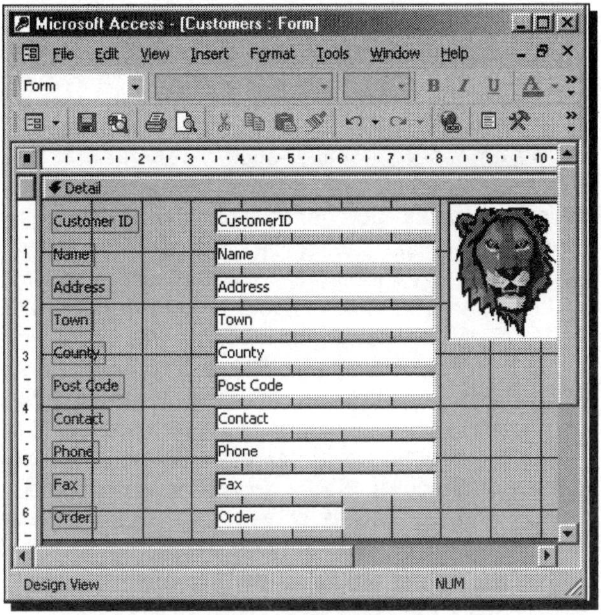

Fig. 15.9 Inserting an Object into Access.

If the object you are embedding is from an Access table, use a bound object frame.

Editing an Embedded Object

If the application in which you created an embedded object is installed on your computer, double-click the object to open it for editing. Some applications start the original application in a separate window and then open the object for editing, while other applications temporarily replace the menus and toolbars in the current application so that you can edit the embedded object in place, without switching to another window.

To edit an embedded object which was inserted into a Microsoft Access form or report, first switch to Design View, then double-click the object to open the application on which it was created.

If the application in which an embedded object was created is not installed on your computer, convert the object to the file format of an application you do have. For example, if your Word document contains an embedded Microsoft Works Spreadsheet object and you do not have Works, you can convert the object to an Excel Workbook format and edit it in Excel.

Some embedded objects, such as sound and video clips, when double-clicked start playing their contents, instead of opening an application for editing. To illustrate this, copy either the **beck.asf** media file from its My Documents\My Music folder in Windows Me, or the **tutor.mpg** media file from its **cdsample, videos** folder in the Windows 98 CD, into

Word using the **Copy, Paste** command (in Windows 98 use **Paste Special** click the **Paste** radio button and the **Display as icon** box on the displayed dialogue box, and click **OK** to paste the required icon). In either case, the appropriate Windows **Media Player** icon is placed in your document, as shown here. Double-clicking such an icon, starts the media player.

To edit one of these objects, select it and use either the **Edit, Package Object** (Windows Me), or the **Edit {Media Clip Object}** (Windows 98) command. What appears within the curly brackets, depends on the selected object.

Hypertext Links

The main applications in Office XP, Word, Access, and Excel, support hyperlinks. A hyperlink causes a jump to another location in the current document or Web page, to a different Word document or Web page, or to a file that was created in a different program. You can, for example, jump from a Word document to an Excel worksheet or to a PowerPoint slide to see more detail.

A hyperlink is represented by a 'hot' image or by display text (which is often blue and underlined) that you click to jump to a different location. To insert a hyperlink into Word,

Access, or Excel files and Web pages, select the display text or image, and either use the **Insert, Hyperlink** command or click the **Insert Hyperlink** button on the Standard Toolbar. Either action opens a dialogue box which allows you to browse for the destination address.

To illustrate the procedure, start Word, open the **PC Users4** memo, and highlight the word 'Explorer' to be found towards the end of it. Next, click the **Hyperlink** button and locate the **explorer.exe** file (in the **Windows** folder) using the **Browse** button, as shown below.

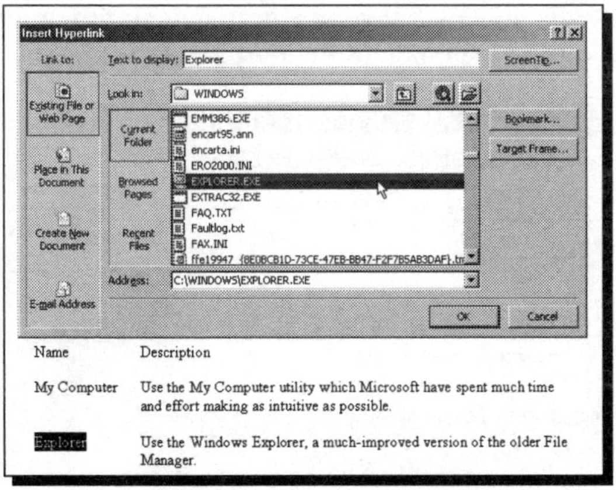

Fig. 15.10 Creating a Hyperlink in a Document.

Pressing the **OK** button, underlines the highlighted text and changes its colour to blue. Pointing to such a hyperlink, while

the <Ctrl> key is depressed, changes the mouse pointer to a hand, as shown here, and left-clicking it, starts the Explorer. When you have finished using the Explorer, click its **Close** button for the program to return you automatically to the hyperlinked Word document.

To remove a hyperlink, place the insertion pointer within the hyperlink word, click the **Insert Hyperlink** button again, and press the **Remove Link** button at the bottom right of the displayed Edit Hyperlink dialogue box.

As a second example, let us add to the **PC Users4** memo the following lines:

Hyperlinks can be used for displaying additional information, such as an Excel sheet, or a PowerPoint slide.

and save the result as **PC Users5**. However, before you can use a range of cells in an Excel Workbook as your hyperlinked object, you must first name such a range. Therefore, start Excel, open the **Project 9** file and highlight the cell range A3:F13 in the Consolidation sheet, then use the **Insert, Name, Define** command and in the **Names in workbook** text box type Year_Summary (named ranges mustn't have spaces between words, hence the underscore). Next, save your changes to **Project 9** and exit Excel.

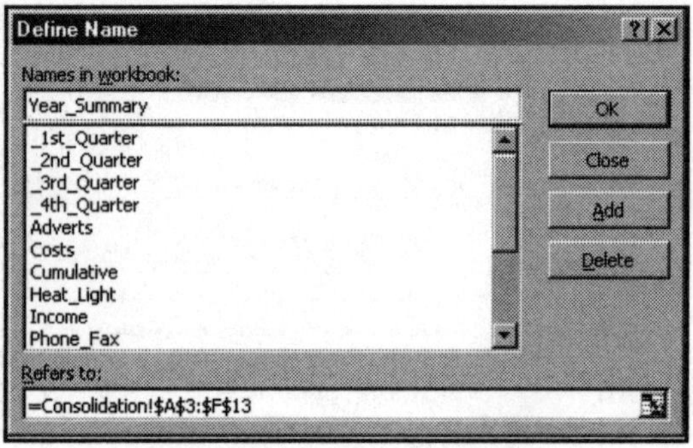

Fig. 15.11 Naming an Excel Range.

Finally, select the word 'sheet' in the Word document to use it as the hyperlink to **Project 9.xls** and browse to the location of the required file, then type after the filename the hash (#) character followed by the name of the required range, as shown below.

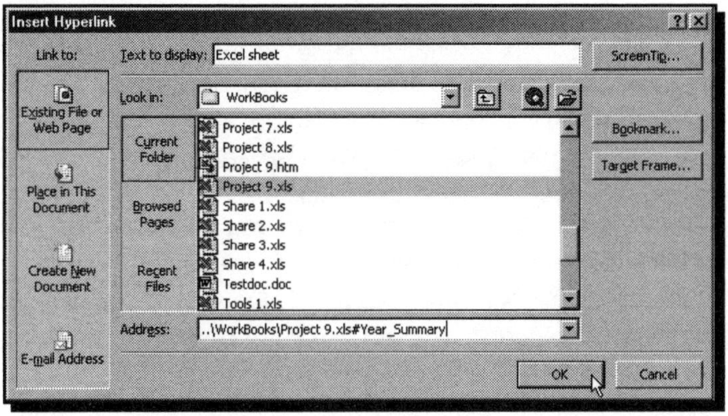

Fig. 15.12 Locating File and Named Range to be Hyperlinked into Word.

Left-clicking the hyperlink in Word will start Excel, open up the **Project 9** file, and display the named 'Year_Summary' range.

For the PowerPoint object, you could select the words 'PowerPoint slide' to use as the hyperlink to **Training 3.ppt**. If you wanted to make the link to a specific slide, then type # followed by the number of the required slide. Below we show the full address of such a hyperlink.

file:///D:\My
Documents\Presentations\Training 3.ppt
CTRL + click to follow link

PowerPoint slide.

Fig. 15.13 The Address of a Hyperlink.

Using Mail Merge

There are times when you may want to send the same basic letter to several different people, or companies. The easiest way to do this is with a Mail Merge operation. Two files are prepared; a 'Data' file with the names and addresses, and a 'Form' file, containing the text and format of the letter. The two files are then merged together to produce a third file containing an individual letter to each party listed in the original data file.

Before creating a list of names and addresses for a mail merge, you need to select the Office application that is most suited to the task. For a mail merge, you can use a list you create in Access, Excel, Outlook, or Microsoft Word.

- For a long list in which you expect to add, change, or delete records, and for which you want a powerful sorting and searching capabilities to your disposal, you should use either Access or Excel, then specify the appropriate data file in the Word Mail Merge.

- To use the list of names and addresses in your Outlook Contact List, you select this list in the Word **Mail Merge** Task Pane.

- For a small to medium size list of names and addresses in which you do not expect to make many changes, you could elect to create a list in the Word **Mail Merge** Task Pane.

We will illustrate the merge procedure by using a memo created in Word (**PC Users1**) and a table which can be created in Word, or already exists either in an electronic book such as Outlook, in Excel or in an Access table such as Customers in **Adept 1**.

No matter which method you choose, first start Word and open the **PC Users1** memo (or your own letter), then provide two empty lines at the very top of the memo/letter by placing the insertion pointer at the beginning of the memo and pressing <Enter> twice. Then select these two empty lines and choose the Normal paragraph style.

Next, select **Tools, Letters and Mailings, Mail Merge Wizard** which displays the Mail Merge Task Pane shown in Fig. 15.14.

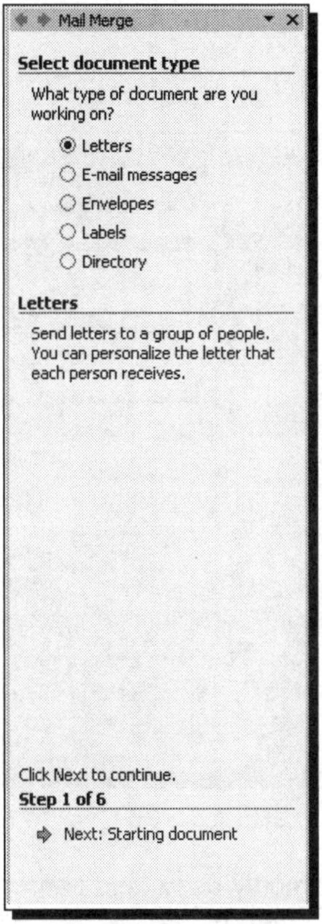

In this Task Pane, you define in six successive steps:

1. The document type to be used.

2. Whether to use the current document.

3. The source of your data - create a new list or use and existing one.

4. Write your letter if not already written, and select type of insert (such as Address block or Greeting line).

5. Preview your letters.

6. Complete merge by printing or editing individual letters.

Fig. 15.14 Mail Merge Task Pane.

In what follows, we will examine each of these steps. You can, of course, skip the Create an Address List in Word section, if you already have an existing data list.

Creating an Address List in Word

On the third **Mail Merge** Task Pane option, click the **Type a new list** radio button, then click the **Create** button. In the displayed New Address List dialogue box, click the **Customize** button to display the Customize Address List dialogue box shown in Fig. 15.15.

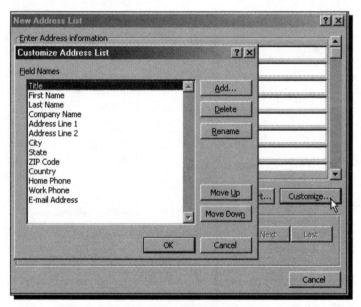

Fig. 15.15 The Customize Address List Dialogue Box.

As you can see, Word provides commonly used field names for your address list. Unwanted field names can be deleted from the list by selecting them and pressing the **Delete** button. To add your own field name, click the **Add** button and supply details in the displayed dialogue box. The **Move** buttons can be used to move a selected field in the list up or down. Finally, an existing field name can be renamed by highlighting it then pressing the **Rename** button and supplying a different name.

Having compiled the required field names for your list, press the **OK** button to display the New Address List dialogue box, shown in Fig. 15.16 in which you can add the names of your contacts.

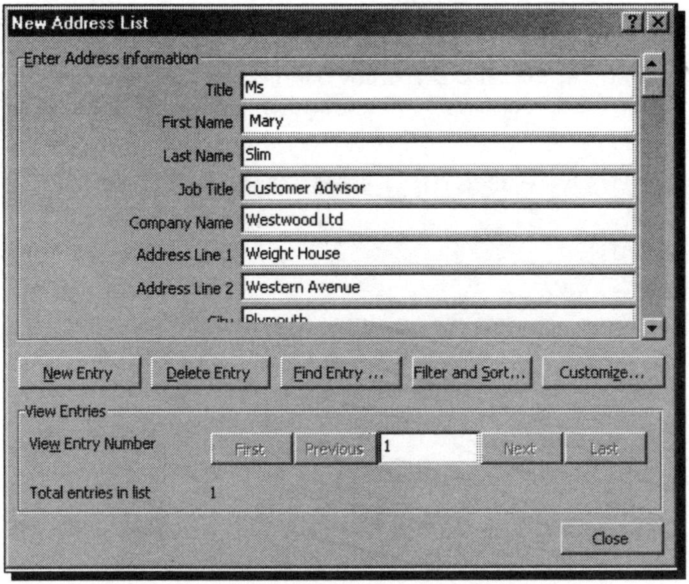

Fig. 15.16 Filling in the New Address List Dialogue Box.

Having completed your list, click the **Close** button which displays a Save Address List dialogue box, shown in Fig. 15.17, for you to name your data list, say **Customers**; Word adds the file extension **.mdb**.

Fig. 15.17 The Save Address List Dialogue Box.

Getting an Address List

On the third **Mail Merge** Task Pane option, you can either use the newly created address list or you can select a different list. You can even edit a list by selecting it and clicking the **Edit recipient list** button which displays the Mail Merge Recipient dialogue box ready for you to edit, as shown in Fig. 15.18.

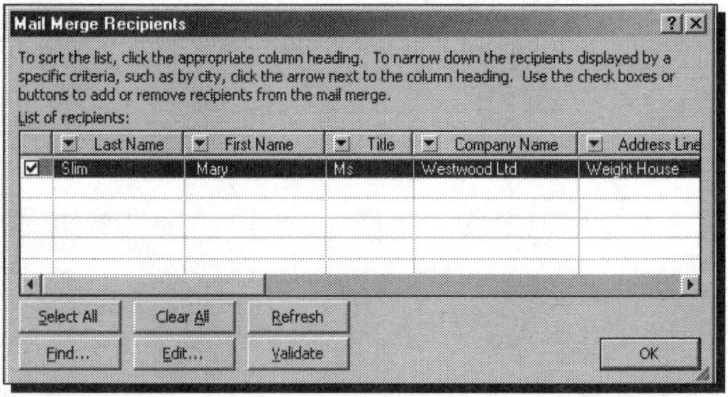

Fig. 15.18 The Mail Merge Recipients Dialogue Box.

Having edited your list, click the **Next** link at the bottom of the

Mail Merge Task Pane to go to the fourth step in which you can click the **Address block** link to display the Insert Address Block box shown in Fig. 15.19. From here you can choose the way the recipient's address will display.

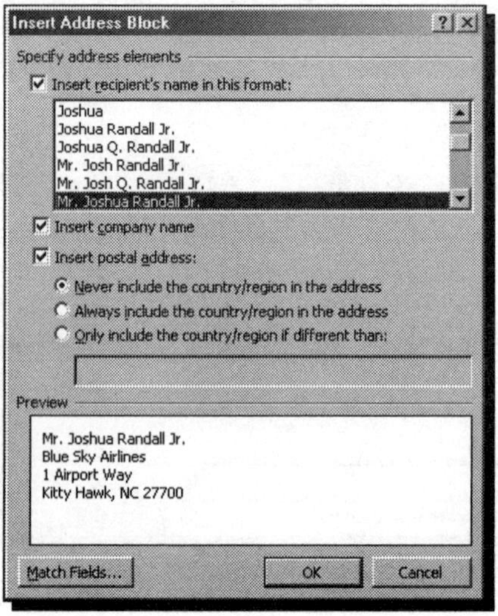

Fig. 15.19 The Insert Address Block Box.

If your have renamed fields or are using an external data file that does not contain the exact default fields displayed in Fig. 15.14, you will need to click the **Match Fields** button on the dialogue box in Fig. 15.19 to open the Match Fields dialogue box shown in Fig. 15.20 below.

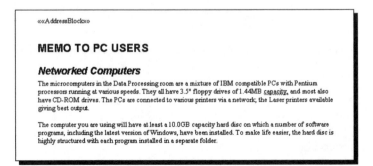

Fig. 15.20 The Match Fields Dialogue Box.

Having matched the fields from your data to the default fields, click **OK** button on each opened dialogue box to obtain:

««AddressBlock»»

MEMO TO PC USERS

Networked Computers

The microcomputers in the Data Processing room are a mixture of IBM compatible PCs with Pentium processors running at various speeds. They all have 3.5" floppy drives of 1.44MB capacity, and most also have CD-ROM drives. The PCs are connected to various printers via a network; the Laser printers available giving best output.

The computer you are using will have at least a 10.0GB capacity hard disc on which a number of software programs, including the latest version of Windows, have been installed. To make life easier, the hard disc is highly structured with each program installed in a separate folder.

Selecting the entry <<<<AddressBlock>>>> at the top of the letter, then right-clicking displays a drop-down menu with options to **Edit Address Block** or **Toggle Field Codes**, to mention but a few. Selecting the latter option reveals the following:

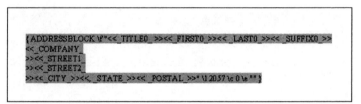

Fig. 15.21 The Field Codes of the Address Block.

By studying these codes of the first four lines you will soon find out how to separate the information on the last line. If you leave these codes as they are, going to the fifth step of the **Mail Merge** Task Pane displays the recipient's address at the top of your letter as shown in Fig. 15.22.

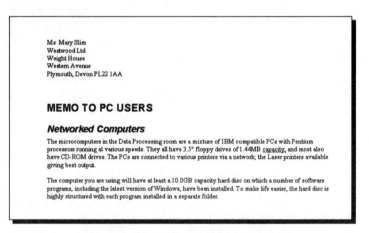

Fig. 15.22 The Preview of a Merged Letter.

The last step in the **Mail Merge** Task Pane allows you to print all your letters or edit individual letters. That's all there is to it. You will possibly find it takes as little time to do, as it did to read about it!

16

Microsoft Publisher 2002

Microsoft Publisher is a desktop publishing program that allows you to quickly and easily create great-looking results that you can print on either your own printer, a commercial printer, or publish on the World Wide Web.

You can use Publisher to either design a publication from scratch with a variety of blank page templates whose margins and folds are already laid out for you, or use one of several Wizards that help you add your own contents to professionally designed templates under different categories. There are Wizards that you can use to create common types of publications, such as Newsletters, Brochures, Postcards, Signs, and Web sites, to mention but a few, with each type of publication offering different designs that you can choose from.

Whichever method you use, the program provides you with ease of use, and advanced desktop publishing features, including the ability to select a variety of colour schemes. In addition, you can put to use all the skills gained in Microsoft Word to create professional looking output.

Starting the Publisher Program

Publisher is started in Windows either by clicking the **Start** button then selecting **Programs** and clicking on the **Microsoft Publisher** icon on the cascade menu, clicking the **Publisher** button, or the **Open Office Document** button on the Office Shortcut Bar, or by double-clicking on a Publisher document file. In the latter case the document will be loaded into Publisher at the same time.

When you start Publisher 2002 the program momentarily displays its opening screen, shown in Fig. 16.1, and then displays a page with available designs for your new publication (more about this shortly).

Fig. 16.1 Publisher's Opening Screen.

Whether you have used a previous version of Publisher or not, the first time you use the program, it might be a good idea to click the **Microsoft Word Help** button, shown here (or if not visible press the **F1** key), and click the **What's new** link in the right pane of the Help screen.

This displays the Help screen shown in Fig. 16.2. Start by looking at the 'Key new features in Microsoft Publisher' option, from which you can find out differences between this version of Publisher and previous versions of the program. As you click each hypertext link, Publisher displays several topics on the subject. After looking at these options, have a look at the other options displayed in the Help screen. We suggest you spend a little time here browsing through the various topics before going on.

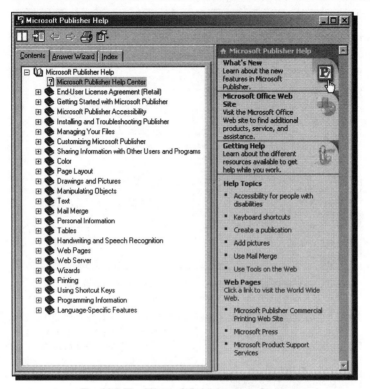

Fig. 16.2 The Microsoft Publisher Help Screen.

For additional Help, click the appropriate Microsoft Publisher Help book shown in the Contents screen above to reveal more topics, then double-click the required topic.

When you start Publisher by either of the first two methods, the program displays a list of New Publications designs in the Task Pane on the left of the screen, with the first item on the list selected and the available designs under that list item displaying on the main panel of the screen, as shown in Fig. 16.3 on the next page.

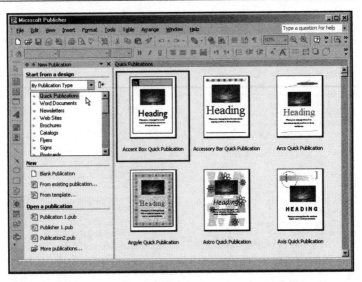

Fig. 16.3 The Available Publisher Designs in the Quick
Publications Category.

Note that clicking the down-arrow to the right of the **By Publication Type** entry at the top of the Task Pane of the Publisher screen, reveals two additional choices, as shown here to the left. You can choose to **Start from a design** 'By Design Sets', or 'By Blank Publications'. Do have a look at all of these options before you start your own design - there are so many options that we are sure you will find one to suit your exact needs.

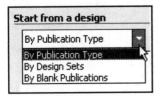

The first time you choose a specific design, left-clicking it starts a Wizard and displays the following screen:

Pressing the **OK** button displays the screen in Fig. 16.4.

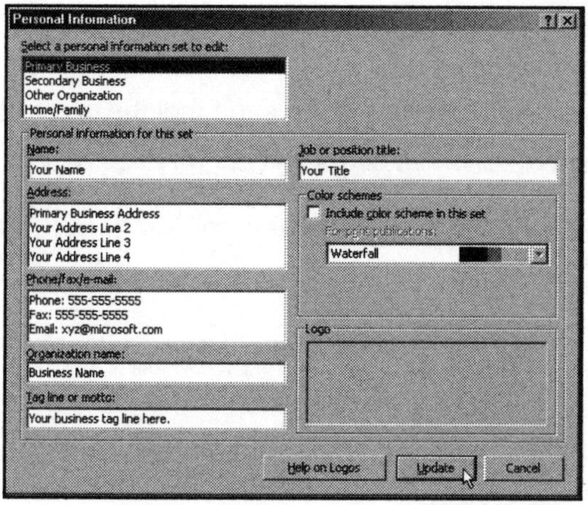

Fig. 16.4 The Personal Information Wizard Screen.

Publisher is asking you to enter personal details, so they can be used to fill in certain types of publications, such as business cards, automatically. Having filled in this dialogue box, press the **Update** button to start the design process.

Creating a Publication

Below we follow step-by-step what would happen had you selected, say, the Arcs Quick Publication Wizard.

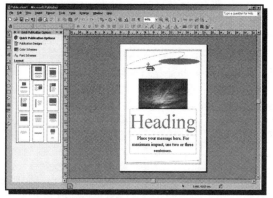

Fig. 16.5 Starting a Publications Wizard.

Note the listed options on the Task Pane. These allow you to select the following:

- The colour schemes of the page (not the graphic).

- The font schemes of the text on the page.

The available choice for these two options is shown in Fig. 16.6 below.

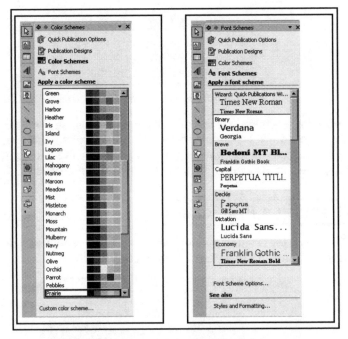

Fig. 16.6 Publisher's Colour and Font Schemes.

Having made a choice for colour and text fonts you will notice that as you place the mouse pointer on various parts of your

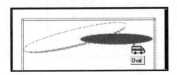

selected design, the pointer changes to a removal van with a flag below it telling you what object on the design you are about to move.

Finally, note the different menus and Toolbars that appear on your screen as you select different parts of your work. For example, selecting a Picture Frame, displays the Picture Bar (see Chapter 12, page 239), and makes unavailable certain tools on the Formatting Bar (see Chapter 4, page 79). When a Text Frame is selected, all the tools on the Formatting Bar become available. The respective effects on the Toolbars for the two selected objects are shown below in Fig. 16.7 and Fig. 16.8.

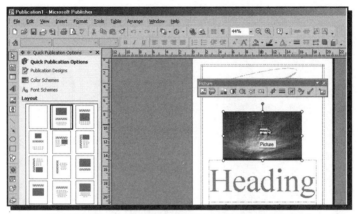

Fig. 16.7 The Toolbars when a Picture Frame is Selected.

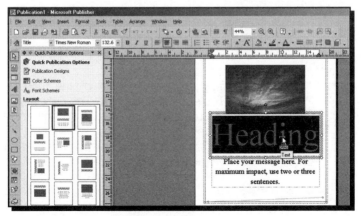

Fig. 16.8 The Toolbars when a Text Frame is Selected.

The Objects Tools

When a Picture or Text Frame is selected, the **Objects Tools** buttons display to the left of your screen. These buttons have the following functions:

Select Objects

Text Box

Insert Table

Insert WordArt

Picture Frame

Clip Organizer Frame

Line

Arrow

Oval

Rectangle

AutoShapes

Hot Spot

Form Control

HTML Code Fragment

Design Gallery Object

The function of most of the Objects Tools are self-evident. They allow you to create various frames and different shapes, including Custom Shapes, as shown here, and a selection of Design Objects. Finally, you can use the Web tools to create a hot spot, form control, or HTML code fragments. For these and other design tools, look up under **Help Topics** on the **Microsoft Publisher Help** screen.

Saving your Work

If you would like to save your Microsoft Publisher work, use the **File, Save**, or **File, Save As** command which displays the following dialogue.

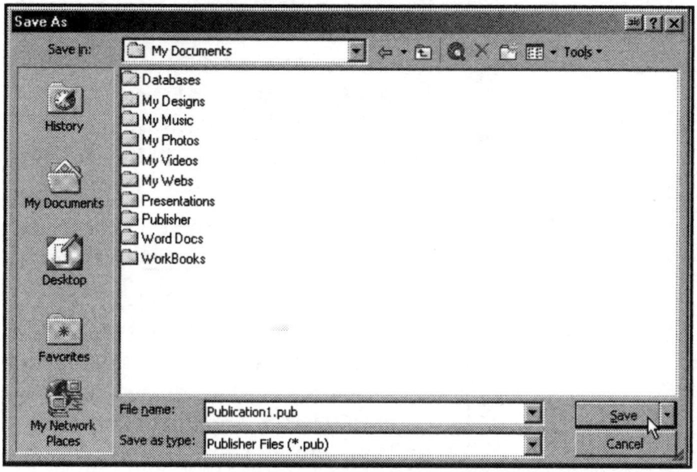

Fig. 16.9 The Save As Dialogue Box.

As usual, we have created a folder within **My Documents** folder to hold our Publisher work. Save your design under the filename **Publisher 1**. The extension **.pub** is automatically added by the program so that Microsoft Publisher can distinguish this file as its own.

Should you try to exit Publisher without saving your work, the program displays the following warning box.

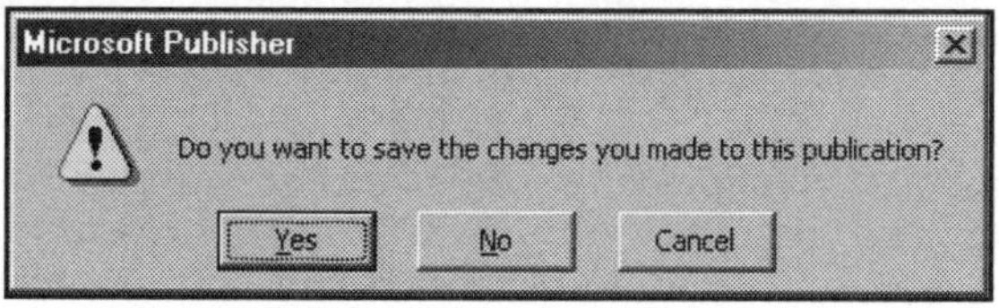

Opening an Existing File

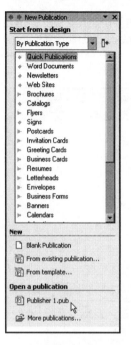

To Open an already saved file when first starting Publisher, click the name of the file which displays automatically under the **Open a publication** option at the bottom of the **New Publications** Task Pane, as shown here to the left. If on the other hand you are already working with Publisher and want to open a different file, then click the **Open** button, shown here, on the Standard Toolbar.

Whichever method you use, Publisher displays its Open dialogue box, as shown in Fig. 16.10.

To open a saved file, navigate to the folder in which you saved your work (ours is the Publisher folder created within the My Documents folder), and either highlight the required file and click the **Open** button, or simply double-click it.

Fig. 16.10 The Open Publication Dialogue Box.

We suggest you open the file **Publisher 1**, which we saved earlier, and practice moving its frames, re-sizing them, adding your own text. Publisher guides you throughout - it couldn't be simpler. Try it.

Creating a Blank Publication

You create a blank publication if you want Publisher to set the dimensions of the publication, but you want to specify your own text and design. To do this, use the **View, Task Pane** command to display the Task Pane, if not visible, then return to **New Publications** and click the down-arrow under the **Start from a design** option and select **By Blank Publications** from the drop-down menu, as shown in Fig. 16.11 below.

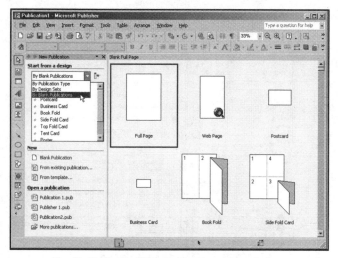

Fig. 16.11 The By Blank Publications Menu Option.

As you can see, there are several page set-ups to choose from, including some that require folding. These type of publications print pages on one sheet of paper that can be folded into a booklet.

To illustrate the process, click on the **Book Fold** publication which causes Publisher to display the box shown on the next page, informing you how many pages are available in the built-in design and asks you whether you would like to add more. In the same warning box, it is also suggested that you press the **F1** function key for help with printing folded booklets.

Doing so, displays the help screen in Fig. 16.12, which we suggest you look at closely if you intend to create and print such publications.

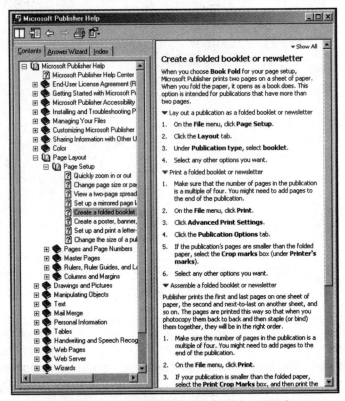

Fig. 16.12 The Create a Folded Booklet Publisher Help Screen.

When you finish creating a blank publication, the Quick Publications Wizard allows you to change its design, colour scheme, and layout, in the same way as when you created a publication using a standard design Wizard.

Multiple Page Publication

If you have more than one page in your publication, Publisher displays page icons at the bottom of the screen, as shown in Fig. 16.13. You can use these icons to navigate through your publication.

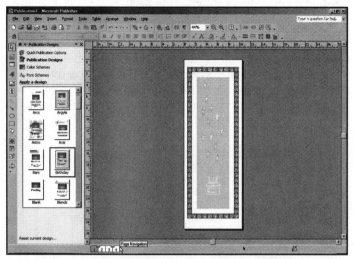

Fig. 16.13 Page Navigation Icons for a Multiple Page Publication.

If you need to add more pages to a publication, use the **Insert, Page** command. Pages can be added before or after the current page using the dialogue box.

Printing your Work

There are three ways to print and reproduce a publication using Publisher. These printing methods depend on the type of reproduction and quality you require.

- Use a desktop printer for a limited number of copies provided the quality of your printer meets your needs.

- Use a copy shop for a large quantity of copies at an economic cost. The quality will be better than most desktop printers.

- Use a commercial printing service when you want the highest quality printing. For large runs, commercial printing costs can be competitive with copy shops. Using a commercial printing service requires you to take your files with you.

Before you print your work on your desktop printer, make sure that you have an adequate supply of the type and size of paper your publication requires. Then use the **File, Page Setup** command to display the dialogue box shown in Fig. 16.14.

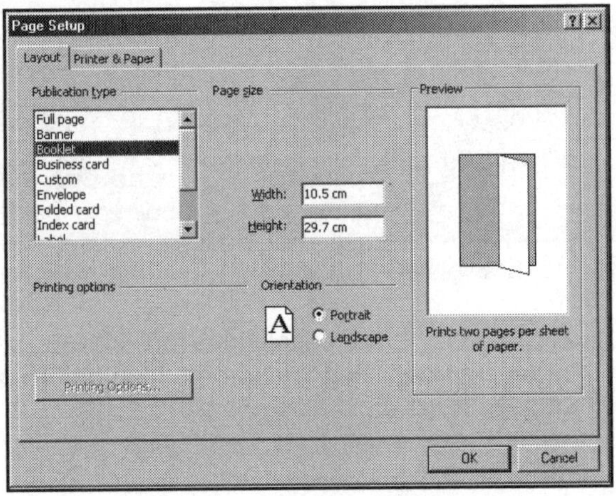

Fig. 16.14 The Page Setup Dialogue Box.

As you can see, depending on the design of your publication, the Page Setup dialogue box reflects the appropriate printing requirements. Make your specific selection and press **OK**, then use the **File, Print** command (or press the **Print** button on the Standard Toolbar), to begin printing. However, before printing your work, don't forget to spell check it, then preview it.

If you intend to have your publication printed at a copy shop or at a commercial printing service, find out their requirements before you start your design. Apart from the available paper size, you need to know the preferred method of delivering your work; take files on disc, send files via the Internet, or deliver a master copy.

Finally, you could use Publisher to design your very own Web site. Have a look at the Web Sites Wizard which helps you put together your requirements. Alternatively, you could design your own publication, then use the **File, Save as Web Page** command, then use the **File, Web Page Preview** to see your creation. We leave this to you to try by yourself, as this is beyond the scope of this book.

* * *

Publisher is obviously capable of a lot more than we have introduced here, but you should now be in a position to explore more of the package's facilities by yourself. Try it and have fun!

* * *

Glossary of Terms

ANSI	American National Standards Institute - responsible for approving standards.
ASCII	American Standard Code for Information Interchange - the default format for plain text.
Attachment	A file that is added to an e-mail because it cannot be embedded within the message.
BCC	Blind Carbon Copy - a way of hiding all the recipients' addresses in an e-mail.
CC	Carbon Copy - sending an exact copy of a message to several recipients.
Client	Any computer that requires information from a server.
Clipboard	A temporary storage area of memory, where text and graphics are stored with the cut and copy actions.
Configuration	A term referring to the way you have your computer set up.
Dial-up connection	A popular form of Internet connection for the home user, over standard telephone lines.
Default	The command, device or option automatically chosen by the system.
Domain	A group of devices, servers and computers on a network.
Encryption	A method of making data or e-mail messages private by converting them

	into a secure form which then needs a special key to unlock or decrypt it.
Exchange server	Microsoft's messaging and collaboration server, used primarily for e-mail, but can also be used to share calendar, tasks and contact information.
FTP	File Transfer Protocol - the procedure for connecting to a remote computer and transferring files.
Host	A computer acting as an information or communications server.
Hyperlink	A segment of text, or an online image, that refers to another document on the Web.
Hypermedia	Hypertext extended to include linked multimedia.
Hypertext	A system that allows documents to be cross-linked so that the reader can explore related links, or documents, by clicking on a highlighted word or symbol.
Intranet	A private network inside an organisation.
LAN	Local Area Network; PCs, workstations, or minis, sharing files and peripherals within the same site.
POP3	Post Office Protocol - a method of storing and returning e-mail.
RTF	Rich Text Format - an enhanced form of text with some formatting that can be used for e-mail messages.
SMTP	Simple mail transfer protocol; used with POP3, but for sending mail.

Index